16550

Cambridge Studies in Social Anthropology

General Editors

M. FORTES, J. R. GOODY, E. R. LEACH, S. J. TAMBIAH

10

WOMEN AND PROPERTY IN MOROCCO

OTHER TITLES IN THE SERIES

WOMEN AND PROPERTY
IN MOROCCO

Their changing relation to the process
of social stratification in the
Middle Atlas

VANESSA MAHER

CAMBRIDGE UNIVERSITY PRESS

Published by the Syndics of the Cambridge University Press
Bentley House, 200 Euston Road, London NW1 2DB
American Branch: 32 East 57th Street, New York, N.Y.10022

© Cambridge University Press 1974

Library of Congress Catalogue Card Number: 74-80351

ISBN: 0 521 20548 4

First published 1974

Printed in Great Britain
at the University Printing House, Cambridge
(Brooke Crutchley, University Printer)

Contents

Tables, Figures & Map

TABLES

vii

FIGURES

MAP

Preface

This study was carried out in three phases: a first year during which I studied Berber and classical Arabic, and acquired a grounding in North African and Islamic sociology and history; I then spent nearly eleven months in the field interrupted by a long period of illness; and finally two years on research and writing a Ph.D. thesis (if the period of illness is included). This book is based largely on the thesis, with quite radical reproportioning, so that the emphasis should fall on women rather than 'social stratification'. I am indebted to the British Department of Education and Science for a three-year Hayter Studentship, to the Wenner–Gren Foundation for Anthropological Research for a generous field-work grant, to the Faculty of Archaeology and Anthropology, Cambridge, for awarding me the Anthony Wilkin Studentship in 1970–1, and to Girton College, Cambridge, for the J. E. Cairnes Research Scholarship which was generously awarded to me in 1969, 1970 and 1971.

My intellectual debts are many and their value more difficult to measure. I have to thank Dr James Bynon of the School of Oriental and African Studies for a patient and expert introduction to the subtleties of Berber language and culture, and Dr Robin Bidwell of Cambridge who generously opened his entire bibliography to me, commented with humour on some of the preliminary chapters and even acted as my supervisor at one stage. I am grateful too to Commandant Malekot and the staff of the Centre de Hautes Etudes sur l'Afrique et l'Asie Modernes in Paris for making available to me the memoirs written by French administrators of the Protectorate, and to Colonel Guy Boula de Mareuil for giving me the benefit of his immense experience of Morocco. I am indebted to Dr Debbasch of the Centre d'Etudes et des Recherches sur les Sociétés Mediterranéennes in Aix-en-Provence for allowing me to make use of the Centre's excellent library and for his kind hospitality. I have derived many insights from discussions in the Research seminars at Cambridge, the 'Sociology of Islam' seminar at the London School of Economics and particularly in the 'Anthropology of Women' group

ix

established in London early in 1972. While the stimulus and analytical perceptions of many friends and fellow-anthropologists have been invaluable, I would like to thank especially Dr Audrey Richards for her 'training', Dr Esther Goody for her encouragement and Anne Whitehead, who read the thesis in draft, for her astute and valued criticism.

My parents heroically visited me in the field, surrounding me with an aura of respectability, and undertaking major haulages of field-equipment. Their comments on how Akhdari society looked to them, and my father's insights into the agronomic aspect of things were as valuable as their moral support. But there would have been no play without the 'actors'. My debt in general and in particular to the inhabitants of Akhdar is inestimable, and I will always wonder at the way in which my friends and adopted families took me into their midst with such tolerance and sympathy and 'told me things'. I have the greatest admiration for the intelligence, imagination and humour with which they live their hard lives.

Finally, I wish to acknowledge a debt of gargantuan proportions to my supervisor, Dr Jack Goody, whose interest, careful criticism and friendship have been a constant source of inspiration, and to thank Mrs Edna Pilmer and Mrs Varney for their painstaking work in typing the various drafts.

V.A.M.

NOTE ON ORTHOGRAPHY

I have used the French transcription for proper names, as is done in Morocco; I have attempted to avoid the orthographic confusion over Berber and Arabic transliteration by keeping as close as possible to the phonetic transcription. I have used the roman capital letter H for the voiced ح and the capital letter T for ط.

Most of the place-names and personal names are fictitious. However, I have not changed the names referring to cities (e.g. Meknes, Rabat) or tribes.

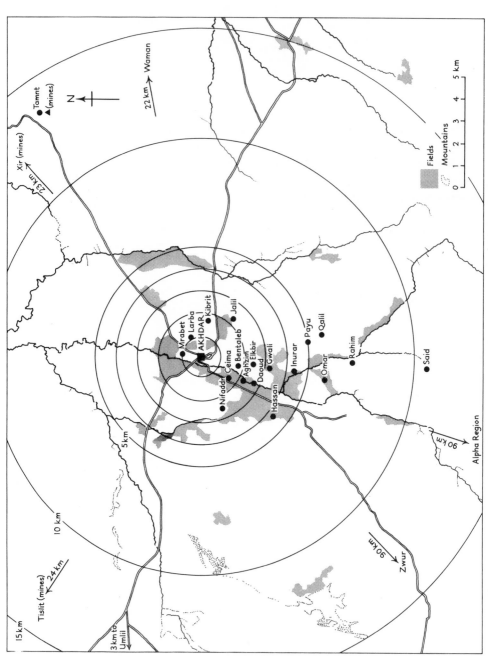

Map of the Akhdar region

xii

Introduction

In a country in which the majority of the population cannot be assured of long-term employment, it may be expected that the market will not serve as the only vehicle of exchange and distribution. In the Middle Atlas of Morocco where this study was carried out, conditions of high unemployment obtain. Further, women do not work for wages because their participation in the 'public sphere' is considered immoral. Thus, some members of the population can sell their labour in the market; to the majority, this option is not available (see Table 2).

These two sets of circumstances give rise to two different modes of social relationship. The one is characterised by some of the traits which Weber associated with the rise of Western capitalism, and indeed, has become more widespread with the intensification of economic and cultural exchanges with Western Europe (particularly France) since the beginning of the twentieth century, and with the United States since the war.[1] The belief in the legitimacy of working for gain, and of accumulation, the belief that the individual is his own best patron, and a diminished dependence on ascriptively recruited groups for economic and political support – such traits are typical of this outlook.

The other mode of relationship, on the contrary, provides for the exchange and distribution of goods and services, and for the definition of social and political roles, .outside the framework of the market. These processes take place, rather, through membership of ascriptively recruited groups and patron–client relationships. Vertical links of interdependence, those of kinship and simulated kinship, are of paramount importance in determining an individual's lifechances.

In the semi-urban environment with which I shall mainly be dealing, there are not two discrete 'systems'; it is necessary to insist on the phrase 'modes of relationship', for to a single individual both may be significant. The consumer goods which belong to the cash nexus are desired by those who cannot acquire cash by selling their labour in

---

[1] This is not to disregard the history of capitalism in an Islamic context (see for example M. Rodinson, *Islam et Capitalisme*, 1967).

1

the market. On the other hand, goods obtained in the market are channelled through 'kinship' networks and patron–client relationships to non-earners, who themselves supply services in the name of 'kinship'. More important is the fact that even participants in market relationships work through regional and patron–client networks in order to acquire wives, and the statuses and esteem which the community awards for command of numerous dependants, proper celebration of *rites de passage*, and proper and generous response to the claims of kin, whether true or classificatory.

The task I have set for myself in this book is the exhaustive analysis of the roles of women in lending intensity to the status-based mode of relationship. They increase the significance of the systems of social stratification to which it gives rise, a system of segmentary tribal groups, and a system of hierarchically arranged 'estates'. These systems continue to have economic and political importance, partly because it is only through them that the majority of people can derive benefits from the market and from government, via patron–client relationships. I shall also study the social mechanisms, both political and ideological, by which women are confined to these roles.

It is this second concern which has led me to concentrate on the perspectives and activities of women, and, flying in the face of convention, to treat those of men in a more cursory manner. This emphasis follows naturally from the nature of my field-experience which afforded me more reliable insight into the world of women than into that of men. In a similar way I knew more of social life in the semi-urban context than I knew of either town or country, and I was less acquainted with the élite in the towns and the *haratn* in the countryside than I was with other categories of the population. This bias was not accidental, nor inevitable as in the case of my having better information on women; it enabled me to concentrate my attention on the area of 'contact', where the market principle and the prerogatives of kinship and status relations struggle for hegemony.

Perhaps the chief locus of this conflict is marriage. The world of women is structured much more consistently in terms of kinship obligations (which are extended to patron–client relationships) than the world of men, which is not wholly geared to the market either. To a wife in the *ksar*, kinship is a much more reliable source of economic and social support than the husband and his connections. This state of affairs is at once the cause and the result of acute marital instability. On the other hand, where a husband has a successful relation to the market as in the case of a well-to-do trader or a government employee,

2

he is able to check the corrosive effect of his wife's social world by secluding her, and controlling her contacts with kin so that she becomes more or less integrated into his own kin group, and begins to identify her interests with his. Although the strains may be acute, the outcome is not inevitably separation, and the divorce rate is lower. Secluded wives resort to subterfuge more often than to confrontation. As in the *ksar* marriage, children act as cement to a union, but their presence does not necessarily reduce the antagonism of interests between husband and wife. Finally, where both husband and wife are educated and working (a situation which is rarely found in the Akhdar region) or where the kin interests of husband and wife are identical as when élite marriages are arranged to cement a business alliance, the divorce rate seems to be lower still. The wife's dependence on her kin is reduced by her control of a dowry, and her husband's ability to provide for her handsomely. Marriage here serves to promote capital accumulation. In the course of this study I point out that marriage has a different social significance in each of these three social settings: the proletarian, the petty bourgeois, and the accumulative elite. The relation of the conjugal household to the market is crucial in determining the importance it attaches to relationships based on ascriptive statuses, which will increase as access to the market becomes more uncertain. This lays a premium on the roles of women and on relationships between them which are generally regulated according to the ascriptive principle.

However, although women's relationships have most structural significance in the semi-urban and rural context, the social situations of women in all milieus are similar enough as to impose severe limits on the operation of the market economy.

Sources

The study is based on field research carried out in the Akhdar region between September 1969 and June 1971. I spent three weeks in a quarter of the town of Akhdar, where I made several lasting contacts, before moving to the *ksar* of Aghzim, where I lived for about ten months in all. During this time I travelled three times to the Alpha area to visit the kin and region of origin of Aghzim residents, and made three visits to northern towns with the same object, but most of my material was collected in the *ksour* situated not more than 10 kilometres from Akhdar.

In the assessment and interpretation of my material I have drawn on various written sources, notably the reports written on the area by French administrators during the first half of the century, and kept as unpublished memoirs in the Centre de Hautes Etudes sur l'Afrique et l'Asie Modernes in Paris.

This study was not intended to take the form of a comprehensive ethnography, but to focus on some aspects of the society rather than others, notably the way in which social structure, and social stratification in particular, is affected by the roles and relationships of women.

Chapter 1 is a brief historical introduction to the Akhdar region, in which I attempt to assess the main changes which took place in the pre-Protectorate political and economic organisation, as a result of French penetration. My picture of the Akhdar region at the turn of the century is built up from documentary sources, from travellers' accounts of visits to the Middle Atlas, from informants' narration of their own experience, and more detailed histories of an anecdotal kind which they had received from their parents. These I have attempted to check against each other, and have supplemented by my own observation of remote rural communities.

In the next two chapters I map out the systems of stratification based on ascribed statuses and analyse the ways in which they are interlaced today with that generated by the market economy. I go on to describe the ways in which different categories of the population are related through the processes of production, distribution and exchange within and outside the money economy. I discuss the system of land tenure and its relation to community organisation, pointing out the importance of patron–client relationships (especially among women) in compensating for the inadequacies of community support, and for the failure of the market as a mechanism of distribution.

Chapter 4 presents a detailed description of the economic organisation of a semi-urban *ksar*, and discusses the way in which the intrusion of *Makhzen* institutions has affected inter-*ksar* and interpersonal relations, separating the economic destinies of men but making women more interdependent. Following a study of a town quarter, I present a comparison of economic and social conditions in town and *ksar*.

The next two chapters show the cultural mechanisms which operate to exclude the majority of Akhdaris from mobility via the market. Education, by its content and its distribution has this effect. Further, different but overlapping systems of religious belief provide the rationales for 'capitalist' and 'status-bound' behaviour respectively. Special attention is paid to the religious justifications of women's

4

non-participation in the 'public sphere' and to the idea of women as dangerous to men.

I go on to describe (Chapters 7 and 8) the division of labour which allocates the public sphere to men and the domestic sphere to women, noting the areas of overlap. I point out that because of the segregation of men's and women's roles there is intense interaction among women, which is regulated by a clearly defined authority structure. Women have a visible system of social organisation of their own. Moreover the bonds between matrilaterally-related women have such structural importance that they resist severe strains. This fact helps us to understand the social significance of the institution of fostering (Chapter 9) which links matrilineal kin, and the prohibition on adoption which would upset these structural arrangements among women. I discuss fostering as an extension of patron–client relations, emphasising that the transfer of children can have many different meanings.

The next three chapters deal with the structural adjustments entailed in different forms of marriage, how they are affected by the marketability or non-marketability of patrimony, and how they are symbolised in different kinds of marriage payment. I pay special attention to the extent to which marriage disrupts a wife's relations with her kin, preventing her from realising certain values which she often continues to hold. Since the wife's world-view and social links are of necessity different from those of her husband, the marriage becomes a struggle in which the single-minded victory of the wife may mean the re-establishment of her pre-marital relationship with her kin, and therefore divorce. Only the birth of several children can impede this outcome.

In the last chapter I discuss divorce in *ksar* and town, suggesting that in the Middle Atlas marital stability, and the truncation of women's social networks, are necessary conditions for the 'achievement orientation' of the husband, the dominance of the mode of relationship governed by the market and consequently for capital accumulation.

1
The background

In this brief account of the geographical and historical background of Akhdar and its region, I wish to stress the pre-Protectorate opposition between the impersonal and centralised authority of the *Makhzen*, and the 'egalitarian', segmentary organisation of the tribes 'outside the law', which was modified by alliance strategies and by the chance economic disequilibrium, ground for petty tyrannies to germinate.

The town immediately before the Protectorate in a more thorough-going sense than today was the site of market relations and the state machine; the social structure of the rural Middle Atlas was barely affected by these institutions. Here, social life was organised according to the principle of ascribed status. French penetration extended the economic and political sway of the central authority over the country-side. It did little to abolish the structural antagonism between them. This factor goes some way towards accounting for the importance of status-based social relations in the Middle Atlas today.

Climate

The study was carried out in the anticline which separates the southern slopes of the Middle Atlas from the northern ones of the Central High Atlas.

Although it is high, at 1700 metres (5000 feet) Akhdar is reputed to escape the rigours of winter experienced by the mountains to the north and south, and the waterless barrenness of summer reported from the Tafilalet region to the south. However, in winter, the snow falls to a depth of two or three feet, and winds rage; during the day, and especially the night, temperatures often fall far below freezing point. The mountain villages are a memory left over from summer and Akhdar itself is frequently cut off from the north by snow between December and February. With the milder spring weather and rain, the mountain snows melt, and the rivers turn into raging torrents which break their banks, often causing disastrous floods and carrying away crops, animals and houses. I witnessed this in two consecutive springs in the Akhdar region. From April onwards the temperature rises to its peak between mid-June and mid-September. In June there are fierce hail storms which ruin ripening grain. This is the period of long siestas and school holidays but also includes the two main harvests of the year: wheat in June and maize towards the end of September.

Ecology

The settlement pattern of this region plays on the theme which runs through the Middle and Central High Atlas, varying slightly according to topology and proximity to a town offering agricultural employment.

The hamlets, comprising from ten to thirty households, are usually built on the slope of a river valley or on a rising which overlooks it. The fields of a hamlet, *ksar* (pl. *ksour*), are cultivated in strips perpendicular to the upper banks of the stream, like the teeth of a comb. Above the fields, linked to the stream by irrigation channels, and by paths which the women use to fetch water, are the clusters of daub houses. Today most hamlets are linked to the nearest market and to the main road by a rough track.

The lower bank of the river, generally flooded in spring, provides daub for building houses and clay for making pottery. Most households keep a few animals – sheep and perhaps a cow or mule – which are taken to browse in the mountain pastures. For these families, lucerne and hay for winter fodder figure importantly in the list of crops grown, mainly cereals, barley, wheat and maize, pulses and root vegetables. Some peasants also plant cereals in small well watered mountain fields.

The surrounding plains offer little in the way of vegetation to the eye of the stranger: camel thorn and clinging xerophytic plants, grey clumps of tough grass on which the sheep graze, shading reluctantly to green towards the bases of the mountains, which clutch scrubby oakwoods in their crevices. But these plants also count in the Berber peasants' economy. Reeds for making carpets and brooms, wild rosemary and thyme, used for a wide range of medicinal purposes, wild lettuce and berries, the wild acorns and small animals found in the woods. Bees are caught and kept in rectangular mud hives and pigeons may provide an occasional meat-rich meal. Scrubby bushes (*ifssiyn*) and the stunted oaks and species of pine in the mountains provide fuel for the fires or stoves which people cook on throughout the year and huddle around in winter.

7

In the flat region immediately surrounding Akhdar the *ksour* are generally built on ridges and rocky outcrops, in strong positions overlooking the river valleys where their fields are planted. Some sites have been occupied for three and even four centuries, though the buildings are rarely more than 150 years old. The older ones are protected by a high mud wall, broken only by two narrow entrances north and south. At the corners rise the powerful towers (*borj*) characteristic of the Tafilalet, the arid region to the south of Akhdar.

Transhumance

At the turn of the century, the Akhdar plain was overrun, season by season, by transhumants from the less favoured regions of the Tafilalet and the north-eastern plains, bringing their flocks of sheep and, more rarely, goats. Usually they set up tents, but occasionally a transhumant group would build a village in land ceded to them by the host tribe, but this was rare, occurring as a result of a national disaster or tribal war.

Tribal wars took place in a context of fierce competition for pastureland between transhumant groups. The situation was particularly acute for the smaller tribes. Ruet, writing as an *Officier des Affaires Indigènes* in 1952, describes the pre-Protectorate winter transhumance in the Akhdar region thus: 'Lorsqu'une tribu du Moyen Atlas était suffisament forte pour choisir sa zone d'habitation elle s'installait sur une bande de terrain grossièrement orientée N–S. Son territoire comprenait alors des pâturages d'été et des terrains en plaine où pâturaient les troupes pendant l'hiver....Pour de telles tribus, la transhumance d'hiver restait une transhumance intérieure.'[1]

For the rest the annual transhumance was often preceded by a battle, but the receiving tribe was usually able to gauge when it would be useless to fight. In such a case the receiving tribe had to move north, pushing yet other tribes out of their territory. The weakest and most desperate tribes might be forced to move into the despised pastures vacated by richer ones.

If the adjacent tribes were at peace their *jema'aiya* (councils of elders) would meet to decide on the movement of sheep. Ruet cites the agreement of 31 January 1921 between the Ait Mguild and the Ait Guerrouane: 'La transhumance correspond à une nécessité de la vie pastorale, elle est consacrée par un long usage. Ce droit a été légué aux gens du présent par leurs ancêtres et exercé, de tout temps, sans

[1] C. Ruet (1953).

8

qu'aucune redevance n'ait été aquittée en retour. Le jema'a des Ait Mguild demanda toutefois qu'il leur soit donné acte qu'il ne s'agit que d'un droit d'usage qui ne crée aucun droit sur le bien fonds. C'est seulement une servitude qui grève leur droit de propriétaire.'[1]

However, according to the relative strength of the tribes the treaty might favour one or the other. Between tribes of equal power it was common that a proportion of the lambs born during the period in question should be divided among the receiving tribe. It was a grievance which the Ait Hadiddou nourished against the Ait Morghad that the latter never gave them anything in exchange for pasturing concessions.

All this points to a history of sharp struggle over land, water and stock, both among the autochthonous *ksour* and against less favoured groups from the south fleeing from drought, floods and intertribal wars. 'It was just like Texas then,' I was told. No stranger ever left his village to travel to another one unless he had intimate friends in the other village who would act as protectors and guarantors. People constantly risked assassination. They made no windows unless they were very high up and at night kept them always shuttered for fear that an enemy, seeing a shadow pass across the candle-light would fire. Some people made windows by fitting the sieve part of the *kskas* (double pot for steaming *couscous*) in a hole made in the wall and filling the holes with *couscous* (semolina), so that outsiders could not see in, but the inmates still had light and safety.

'Makhzen' and 'siba'

Before the Protectorate the Moroccan tribes were said to be in a state of *siba*, which has been translated as 'anarchy' but corresponded more closely to the segmentary organisation of the so-called 'stateless society'. They acknowledged the spiritual overlordship of the Sultan but not the secular authority of his government, the *Makhzen*. The term *Makhzen* signifies also the regions and tribes under its aegis.

The relationship of *bled-es-siba*, the country of dissidence, to the *Makhzen*, or centralised political organisation, has been aptly described by Gellner: 'Siba was a political condition and a condition of which people were explicitly aware: local tribesmen themselves employ this concept...Such tribesmen know the possibility, indeed the most ambivalently regarded obligation of being incorporated in a more centralised state, sanctioned by their own religion; indeed they

[1] Ibid.

may have deliberately rejected and violently resisted this alternative.' And again '...the inconveniences of submission make it attractive to withdraw from political authority and the balance of power, the nature of mountainous or desert terrain, make it feasible'.[1]

This attitude of the Berber tribes to external authority seems to have been evident from the time of the first Arab incursions (and the Romans met with it even earlier). Religious heresy was an important corollary, and expression of political dissidence. Ibn Khaldun remarks that after the invasion of Morocco by Uthman's governor in A.D. 647, the Berbers 'continued to rebel and apostatised time after time. The Muslims massacred many of them. After the Muslim religion had been established among them, they went on revolting and seceding, and they adopted dissident (Kharijite) religious opinions many times.'[2]

The authority exercised by the central government on the Akhdar region is best described as concessionary or contingent. It depended most of all on the personality and power of the Sultan's emissary, the *caid*, to whom were allocated the duties of tax-collecting and other forms of profitable mediation between the Sultan and his people. The *caid* was sometimes a stranger to the region. The limits of his powers were set by the tribesmen themselves but because of their factionalism they put up with a great deal of petty tyranny. The pretext for an uprising was often that the *caid*, the Sultan's emissary, had made an assault on the moral and social order of the tribes. It was expressed in these terms, however bitter might be the grievances on grounds of economic exploitation and political oppression, for the tribes acknowledged only a mystical relationship with the Sultan. The following legend is a typical instance: In the reign of Hassan I (1875–90) a certain *caid*, who had abused the Ait Izdeg for too long, finally ignited their fury by demanding to see the face of a woman in one of the houses he visited. Unfortunately for him, she was a *sherifa*, so that his demand constituted a sacrilege. The tribes armed against him, defeated his forces, killed him and carried off his head with which they played football in the villages. A village woman had the head stolen and sent to the king, who marched on the Ait Izdeg with an army of 10,000 cavalry to avenge his emissary. He was met by a delegation of *shurfa*, sent by the Ait Izdeg, to persuade him to listen to their grievances and redress their wrongs rather than punish them for bringing a tyrant to justice. The Sultan, being a descendant of the Prophet himself, recognised the validity of the pleas.[3]

---

[1] E. Gellner (1969), 1–2.   [2] Ibn Khaldun, trans. F. Rosenthal (1958), 332.
[3] Account given by Ali of Ceima, with corrections and comments by Haddou of Ceima.

The background

The story presents a good picture of the tribes' relationship with the *Makhzen*. We see not only that the *Makhzen* was interested in the *bled-es-siba*, but that the tribal recognition (under duress) of its legitimacy was made in such a way that the *Makhzen* was forced to accept as equally legitimate the fact that tribes managed their own affairs and *Makhzen* hegemony was therefore limited.

Vengeance and the law of talion

The result of the scarcity of resources combined with the ineffectiveness of central authority was that the law of talion prevailed. It operated patrilineally. A murdered man's family could kill one man of the offender's family, himself, his father, son, brother or brother's sons – then, any male of his village, if he had none of these relatives. No maternal relatives could be killed. Sometimes the family would accept *dia*, bloodwealth, on the intervention of a *sherif*. This amounted to about 1000 old francs, a considerable sum at that time.[1]

Each Berber was bound to his ten nearest male agnates, the *Ait Ashr'a*, by his liability for their offences and vice versa. They should avenge his death and shared with him rights over brides and property. Each by the rules of agnatic solidarity was obliged to swear, before the *imgharn* (elected elders) of the lineages of offender and offended, to his agnates' innocence if the latter committed a crime. If only a few testified or refused to testify, the minority was forced to meet all the costs of defeat in the oath.[2] Thus agnatic betrayal was punishable but all too possible. I shall return to the unreliability of agnates in the discussion of lineage organisation below.

The original murder which led to the development of a feud often occurred during the course of a raid on the cattle and mules of an enemy village or as a result of an affront to a female relative of the assassin. Accounts return repeatedly to the themes of the solidarity of agnates, the weakness and treachery of women and the conflict between affines, but these seem to represent foci of anxiety rather than ascertainable facts. These themes reoccur in the history of tribal wars.

[1] 2 francs were given as a token marriage payment. One would buy 100 grams of tea, a costly commodity. The value of a franc was roughly 20–30 p today.
[2] E. Gellner (1969), 113.

11

Lineage organisation in pre-Protectorate Morocco

Reliable material on lineage organisation immediately before the Protectorate is hard to come by. The tribe (*taqbilt*) appears to have been a territorial unit, composed of clans of varied regional origin. A genealogical fiction justified its cohesion in war. The smaller group or clan which exercised pasture rights and migrated together might be spread over several villages or occupy only part of one. Within a village might be found several lineages of different origin, each comprising a man and his children and the descendants of his male descendants, a group of thirty to fifty people. This group included female agnates, but only residually their descendants. Women had second-rate status. The bloodwealth paid for them was half that paid for a man and was shared among half as many agnates.[1]

In spite of this neat pyramidal presentation, it should be borne in mind that the definition of the segments and sub-segments of the lineage system was largely contextual, and their boundaries blurred, particularly since the common genealogical origin of their members was a fiction, an analogy which served to indicate the unconditional nature of their mutual bond. Thus it is that the concepts other than *taqbilt* which indicate a social group, e.g. *nikwa*, may refer to a segment at any level of segmentation; and that the prefix *Ait* meaning 'brothers', 'people of', can be used to refer to any named group, to a nuclear family (e.g. Ait Addi ou Hussein) or to a confederation of tribes (Ait Yafelman), to people occupying a specific territory or merely vaguely to indicate the inhabitants of a region, whatever the relationship among them.

Indeed the need for each segment to be represented by an *amghar* for the regulation not only of internal affairs, but of relations with other segments, suggests that the segmentary system did not work automatically along well-oiled lines of agnatic solidarity, but that it was unstable enough to need constant supervision. Even agnates could not be relied on to co-operate in war and transhumance without being subordinated to some authority. This is also apparent in the 'minority rule' in the oath, designed to bring wayward agnates to heel. The preference for endogamy can be regarded as another measure intended to reinforce a weak agnatic structure.

One of the reasons for the weakness of the agnatic structure was that agnatic rights were conceded to women. A women married virilocally and her children belonged to her husband's lineage. Her

---

[1] D. Jacques-Meunié (1964), 76.

property rights, which according to Koranic law amounted to half the share of her brothers, also passed under her husband's control for the duration of the marriage, and if transferred to her definitively would be inherited by their children, members of his lineage. Berbers tried to get round this threat to lineage interest by endogamy, the preferred match being between the children of brothers, and by evading the law of female inheritance in practice while allowing it in theory. The contradiction between the solidarity of the agnatic group and its survival was a recurring one, implying a conflict of principles at the structural level, and of loyalty at the individual level.

Estates

Agnatic solidarity was further threatened by the integration of Berber families into a hierarchy of social groups, who lived together in the villages of the Atlas. These groups – *shurfa* (descendants of the Prophet), *haratn* (descendants of slaves), Berbers, and Jews, I call 'estates', since it was not so much genes which separated them as social status, and to a lesser extent wealth and cultural characteristics.

The estates were ideally endogamous, but in fact exercised assymmetrical marriage rights, those groups with higher ritual status marrying women from lower groups but not vice versa. Thus each village household was individualised by its extralineage relationships which included control of *haratn*, patronage of Jews, spiritual favour acquired through contact with *shurfa*, and the relations of affinity it had acquired among these groups and in Berber lineages other than its own. All these links gave rise to and reflected divergent interests within the agnatic lineage and occasioned conflicts of loyalty.

In the myth of origin of a group in the village where I lived this problem is resolved hopefully in favour of agnatic solidarity. All the members of a given village are descended, it suggests, from a single ancestor, one Lhadj Mimoun. He married in turn a *sherifa*, a Berber (from whom my informants claimed descendance) a *hartaniya* and a Jewish woman. He had a penchant for partridges which he kept as pets, and which have assumed the significance of totemic animals for his descendants who are not allowed to kill or eat one to this day. In Aghzim, a small boy who trapped one was struck dumb, it is said, for three days, and still today has a speech defect.

At the top of this hierarchy of 'estates' were the *shurfa*, held to be the descendants of the Prophet, therefore kin to the Sultan and exempt from taxation.

Shurfa were called by special saintly titles; all men's names are preceded by 'Moulay', or 'Sidi' if the name is Mohammed. Women are called 'Lalla...'. Even as children, *Shurfa* are deferentially treated. Traditionally, in the countryside, they lived in a *zawia*, slightly apart from the main village to which they were attached. They were served by *haratn*, black slaves who would often cultivate their fields. Even today most *zawias* have *haratn* attached to them as labourers who are paid in kind. The villages near which *shurfa* lived obtained grace by offering them gifts or sustaining the scholars who lived in the *zawia*. *Shurfa* acted in a spiritual capacity, bringing *baraka* (blessing or increase) by their presence, which was therefore sought at all rites of passage and celebrations. They acted as mediators in disputes and as go-betweens in marriage arrangements.

They played a necessarily ambiguous role. On the one hand, they were described in the Akhdar region as 'the family of the Sultan', on the other their local allegiance was clear. On the one hand a *sherif* was a sacred and privileged person (exempt from taxes), on the other the *shurfa* were used as pawns in the power struggle with the *Makhzen*. They were on the one hand honorary members of the community, whose safety and status were first to be at risk in times of crisis; on the other they were indispensable in obtaining safety and status for their community and its constituent members, because of their interstitial position – mediating between rival transhumant tribes,[1] murderers and avengers, tribesmen and *Makhzen*, a role of which the French took full advantage.

The status of *shurfa*, and that of saints who were liable to be assimilated to *shurfa*, bore some analogy to that of Jews (in fact many saints had Jewish names; see Voinot: 1948, 150). The crucial difference was that Jews, being outside the *umma* (Muslim community) had a negative charisma. Their mediation was in functional areas such as trade between strangers; for they could not administer justice whose main sanction was religious (on the contrary the enforcement of Jewish law was in the hands of Muslim authorities), nor mediate in a political relation whose rationale was religion.

The Jewish minority in Morocco was generally without land and therefore marginal in relation to the local community, as well as being subjected to severe limitations on their political rights (they should not bear arms in their capacity as *mwali*, dependants or protected persons; they should wear special clothes, build only one-storey houses, etc.).

[1] E. Gellner (1969).

The background

Relations between Berbers and Jews

At this time and indeed right up until 1956 many villages, Ceima, Daoud and Elkbir in particular, contained important settlements of Jews. Their pre-Protectorate monopoly of trade suggests that the market-place, too, was marginal to the economy at that time. They enjoyed a certain protection under the French but few of those who were petty traders in the time of Moulay Hassan I rose to higher status later, although a few Andalusian Jews occupied professional posts and established large stores, selling sophisticated products, based on their literacy and organisational skills. Apart from the latter category, they left, to a man, with the advent of Independence and the intensification of Arab–Israeli hostilities. Until the French came there was an important *suq* on the hill behind Ceima, where most of the traders were Jews. (This is why the Jewish cemetery is behind the hill towards Nifaddn, and the synagogue is on the ridge between Ceima and Aghzim.) Their position in the village was insecure and they would choose Berber protectors, good strong families, before whose house they would sacrifice a sheep placing an *ar* (conditional curse) on the household, obliging them to accept the role.

In the last analysis a Berber afforded protection to a Jew as a concession made to an individual which barely affected his own political situation except to mark him as a man of honour. But his participation in the segmentary organisation was the condition of his political existence and he would readily sacrifice the Jewish connection to the latter.

Haratn

It is probable that the forebears of *haratn* were slaves brought from Mauritania and Senegal from the eighth century onwards. However, from what I could discover of their situation among the southern Berber tribes in the nineteenth century, it appears that their relationship to full tribal members was closer to one of clientship. Generally they did not own land so that they were not assimilated (e.g. by a fiction of agnatic kinship) to the land-holding community to which they were attached. This placed them in a situation of grave political weakness, since they could not always command the loyalty of a segmentary group in times of danger. Yet, unlike Jews, they belonged to the *umma*, which guaranteed them a minimum of protection. According to Mareuil, some *haratn* among the Ait Morghad cultivated

15

land, paying for the tenancy in kind, but this classical *khammes* status is everywhere defined as far inferior to that of a land-owner.

'*Haratn* should marry each other and white people should marry each other', say Berber migrants from these areas, who lay particular stress on their superiority to *haratn*. However, Berbers occasionally married *haratn* women.

I have insisted above on the existence of a hierarchy of groups: *shurfa*, Berbers, *haratn* and Jews, distinguished by different degrees of wealth and social status. Indeed, it is difficult to see where the much-cited 'little Berber republics' whose 'democracy' so attracted French observers fitted into such a social structure, which is nevertheless well documented. It can only be assumed that the French observers did not consider the existence of slavery, pariah groups and ritual differentiation alien to 'democracy', which was to be defined rather by the existence of periodically elected officials (*imgharn*) and village assemblies (*jema'aiya*) which appeared to be promising embryos of Presidents and parliaments respectively.

To complete the social landscape we should add Arabs, who were the inhabitants of the towns and purveyors of Arab-dominated *Makhzen* culture. Pre-Protectorate Morocco resembled many a Muslim state in that the autochthonous tribes were considered to have a different status within the *umma* or religious community from those descended from or assimilated to the invading Arabs.

The Arabs, living in cities, orthodox Sunnis, literate, became identical with that part of the Moroccan population under *Makhzen* rule. To be in full possession of Arab culture a man had to live in a town, and therefore to follow an urban occupation related to the market economy or centralised power. Only through such an occupation could he obtain the means to fulfil the cultural requirements of full Muslim citizenship (e.g. life-style and the payment of bride-wealth). Since the towns were continuously refurbished by Berbers, it would be rash to regard Berbers and Arabs as different 'ethnic groups'. Berber and Arab are cultural distinctions, with some political and economic connotations.

The household

I do not think we can leave the social organisation of the immediate pre-Protectorate period without giving a thought to the household, in spite of the paucity of data. The aspects of lineage organisation mentioned above – that women adhered to the agnatic group, and that the interests of agnates did not always coincide – had to be reflected in the household. According to all accounts, most households were comprised of a man and his wife and children. However two social units corresponding to different stages in the family's developmental cycle were probably represented in the village. Given the reports of early adolescent marriage, we may surmise that new conjugal households were at least temporarily lodged patrilocally, giving rise to extended households. I use the term 'extended household' to mean a household containing a man and his married sons, over whom he exerts absolute authority as well as retaining sole control over any property accruing to the household. A situation which was probably more common and enduring, given the diversity of agnatic interests, was that in which a man and his married children were established in separate households and constituted separate social personae. Although socially distinct, their common patrimony remained in some respects undivided and they maintained links of social and economic co-operation at least until the death of the father, and in rare cases after it. I call this group an 'extended family'. Probably most men had belonged to one or both of these social units before setting up a separate nuclear household. A household of many years' standing would certainly contain female agnates who had returned home on widowhood or divorce, for marriage was extremely unstable. In a village where I lived the divorce rate appeared to have been as high among people born between 1895 and 1915 as in later generations (49% of all marriages).

The impact of French penetration

'Pacification' spelt disaster for the tribes and their way of life. Transhumance was repressed in three ways.

1. Pacification, to be successful, depended on the tribes being rendered immobile, their powers of combination and communication controlled. Transhumance was severely discouraged and receiving tribes prevented from moving on to find pasture for themselves.

2. The division of the country into administrative units and the restriction of the mobility of their populations made it impossible for the less populated regions to receive 'guests'.

3. The distribution of pasture-lands to local administrators and settlers and the encouragement given to nomadic and transhumant tribes to become sedentary rapidly reduced the area available to the southern shepherds. Bidwell writes '...At the time of pacification the

Beni Mtir owned about 250,000 ha. but by 1947 this had shrunk to 138,000, much of it poor land in the mountains.'

In 1939 there was a meeting at Meknes of the *Commission Régionale de Transhumance* which came to the conclusion that transhumance must be wiped out. By 1952 four tribes at least faced impoverishment.[1] The Ait Messaoud for example had had to reduce their stock from 43,000 head to 1500 for 662 households, half the tribe becoming completely sedentary in land hardly suitable for cultivation.[2]

The flocks were reduced for many transhumants to the point of non-viability. This resulted in the hoped-for transfer of labour to the newly opened French mines and *colons'* farms, but it also meant destitution for whole tribes.

Markets and French penetration

The Akhdar region was at once a filter for the trans-Saharan trade routes and a cross-roads for internal exchanges. Important for this region was the triangular flow of goods between Fez, Rissani and Marrakech. Imported European goods – tea, sugar, fabrics – travelled southwards from Fez towards Rissani, against a northwards flow of wool and wool manufactures, wheat, hides for the leather craftsmen of Fez, dates and *henna*. Lying at the base of the mountains, Akhdar and its region was the natural venue for the diverse tribes who converged on the plains in either summer or winter to pasture their flocks.

One of the tactics of French penetration was the control of markets. Lyautey's explicit policy was to establish a *poste*, administrative centre and military stronghold in places where he found a market, which he regarded as the node of a region's life, economic and political, and the nerve-centre of its communications network. Combined with a war of attrition waged against dissident transhumants, the market may well have assumed an importance under the French out of all proportion to its pre-Protectorate functions. 'Mes postes doivent être le noyau de futurs cantons de colonisation. C'est pour assurer aux colons, après la clientèle militaire, une nombreuse clientèle indigène, que j'ai établi mes postes dans le voisinage des grands marchés marocains. Ces marchés se trouvent naturellement au carrefour des grandes voies de pénétra-

---

[1] During the course of the war against the French, the flocks of dissident tribes were decimated, because they were unable to get at pasture during the winter: 'The Ait Oumnasef of the Beni Mguild fled up to the summits and in a single winter their flocks were reduced from an average of 300 or more sheep for each tent to 10.' R. Bidwell (1970), 38.

[2] C. Ruet (1952). See also R. Bidwell (1970), 486–502.

tion, aux points stratégiques du commerce. Loin de chercher à dissoudre ces marchés, je m'efforcerai de les développer...La considération économique s'accorde avec la considération militaire. Tant que je tiendrai les marchés au bout de mes canons je commanderai le pays, car je puis à ma volonté faire l'abondance ou la famine.'[1]

Akhdar as a 'poste'

The pre-Protectorate market at Ceima was held on a narrow ridge above the *ksar* which itself seems precariously situated. Akhdar with its gentler slopes may have seemed to the French to offer greater prospects for urban expansion. In 1917 a military garrison and *bureau*, or administrative office, were set up in Akhdar and the inhabitants of the surrounding *ksour* 'encouraged' to move there. Trading in Ceima was forbidden and the traders moved to the white arcades of the new market opposite the barracks of the *mokhazni*, or special soldiers of the administration. One *ksar*, Kibrit, was burnt down and its inhabitants moved to a new site where houses were built for them. Although this move was intended to swell the 'urban' population, Kibrit has retained the appearance and many of the essential features of a *ksar*, being surrounded by orchards and fields, its inhabitants speaking Berber and marrying with other *ksour* rather than with the Arabic-speaking townspeople. For a long time the social impact of the *poste* was negligible. 'They proved often little more than a spur to further xenophobia and a source of arms.'[2]

Functions of the 'poste'

The *poste* in dissident territory was primarily a military garrison. Its administrative functions were the responsibility of the *caid*, perhaps a local notable, in areas traditionally under the control of the *Makhzen*, or he might be a 'foreigner' from one of the big cities or from the royal dynasty. The *caid* co-operated with the local French officer for *Affaires Indigènes*, who was ostensibly there in an advisory capacity. However, since the *postes* were integrated into a bureaucratic system, using French and Arabic, and many of the *caids* could not read or write in either, the A.I. officer was in virtual control.

The charges of both officials reveal that 'administrative functions' were really mediating economic control.

[1] Kuntz (1913) quoted in R. Bidwell (1970), 40.   [2] R. Bidwell (1970).

The market became an administrative concern and though for a time the traditional market dues were abolished, their collection today is an affair of the *bureau*. The *caids* and their aides, the *khalifas* were responsible for collecting taxes, and were allowed to keep 6% and 4% of the total respectively. Their traditional prerogative to call on members of a community to work on community projects without pay was widely abused, both to their own profit (for they would put peasants to harvest their crops at a time when the peasants could not spare a day from their own fields), and to that of the French administration who frequently made use of unpaid labour in order to build the magnificent network of roads of which Lyautey was so proud. The *bureau* thus served to recruit labour, both for public purposes and for private ones, e.g. for the foreign companies who exploited the Xir and Tamnt lead mines, or won contracts for large projects, such as the construction of a hospital and a school in Akhdar. The state machine served, and does still, to expand the sphere of influence of 'the market'. The administrative centre became the vehicle for the operation of government organisations, such as the *Travaux Publics* – a self-explanatory title – and *Eaux et Forêts*. The latter was mainly concerned with reducing the flocks of transhumants and attempting to settle them in villages. They were considered to be causing soil erosion through over-grazing the land and pressing on the scarce forests. This situation became acute as French protégés took over common land and pastures, disregarding traditional tribal arrangements. The orientation of *Eaux et Forêts* today is rather towards re-afforestation. Its efforts in the direction of soil conservation are supported by *Centres de Travaux*, operating an agricultural extension service.

Justice

The pressure on the land which resulted from the encroachments of *colons* and *caids* meant that land disputes became more frequent, for groups who had hitherto kept a 'no-man's land' between them, or whose land had diminished, were now forced to be close neighbours and quarrel over boundaries and pastures. These were settled by the *caid* and *khalifa*, as well as by the A.I. officer as he toured the village on horseback. He often settled private cases on his rounds, if they could not be resolved by the 'customary courts' or *jema'aiya* reconstituted by the notorious 'Berber *dahir*' of 1930.

The Berber *dahir* became the focus of vehement nationalist opposi-

20

tion. It was the clearest pointer to the ultimate consequence of the French 'Berber policy'; the development of two distinct cultural and political blocks in Morocco, based on a supposed Berber–Arab, tribesman–*citadin* opposition. The Berber bloc, drawn into alliance with French interests, would be used by them to contain the urban Arab-speaking political groups from whom came the most articulate and organised threat to French supremacy. To place the two 'sectors' of the population under different judicial systems was to deny their identical relation to the Moroccan nation, and to deny the political unity of Morocco which the ongoing process of Arabisation, tending to follow the expansion of towns and the improvement of communications, was likely to fix in the awareness of Moroccans.

After independence, the re-establishment and development of Muslim law as a factor in the unification and de-colonisation of the country, enhanced the importance of the *mahakma*, or law courts, in Berber regions such as Akhdar. Here, disputes were settled according to *Shari'a* or Koranic law; here also marriages, births and deaths began to be registered more or less regularly.

The enforcement of 'law and order' today is effected through the *mokhazniya* on an informal level, both as mediators for the settlement of internal quarrels in the *ksour*, and as aides for the police force proper which operates in conjunction with the *commissariat* where offenders are held before trial and which runs the local prison. The *bureau* co-ordinates these institutions.

Effects of 'pacification' on tribal organisation

With 'pacification', the subordination of the tribes to the central government, and the end of transhumance, many of the functions of the larger segmentary groups lapsed. The tribe (*taqbilt*) became a theoretical, administrative entity. In the new sedentary context, smaller groups than had been necessary for the protection of transhumants now became viable. This meant that the village assumed greater significance at the expense of the clan. This tendency was reinforced by the government which regarded the hamlet (*ksar*) and the group of hamlets (*commune*) as the primary administrative units, and appointed local officials accordingly. Thus the elders (*imgharn*) previously elected annually by the lineages, became permanent officers of the central government. Since they no longer represented the balance of power among the lineages, but French authority, it was easy for them to establish themselves as petty tyrants with the connivance of the colonial authorities who saw in them an effective instrument of control.

Migration: the dispersal of male lineage members

Although mobility between *cantons* had been restricted under the French, they themselves promoted migration by recruiting North Africans in great numbers, Berbers among them, to fight in the French forces in the two World Wars and in Indochina. The number of Moroccans alone who fought in French wars was nearly 200,000. This kind of migration from which many never returned was only part of the story. The migration to the cities which was to assume such nightmarish proportions after Independence was well under way by 1945, for the agricultural resources of the tribes had diminished to a point where peasant households were no longer self-sufficient. They were forced to buy consumer goods and to earn money to pay for them. During this period tens of thousands of North Africans, particularly Algerians, were shipped to France to work in French factories, especially during the wars.[1]

The growth of wage labour and mass migration to the cities, where, however, unemployment was rampant, had two implications for social organisation at the domestic level. The first was that sons no longer followed in their father's footsteps. In fact, the prospects for the extended family were improved if adult sons left home even before they were married. Of the urban sample in the national census of 1960, 65% of migrant household heads had left home between the ages of ten and twenty-nine.

The second consequence was that women were left, more than ever, to fend for themselves and their families. In times of *siba*, when the men were often away fighting or visiting distant markets, the women at least had land and animals, productive resources with which to sustain their families. Now, since the taboo on their entering the public sphere prevented them working for wages, they were forced to fall back on or to create kinship-based networks of mutual help and clientship outside the market economy. Indeed, in the face of widespread dispossession and unemployment, both men and women tended to depend on kin or on patron–client relationships, so that for them the forms of association created by the operation of market forces, for

[1] Between 1934 and 1945 20% of Muslim landholders in Algeria lost their land. By 1954 30% of the male population was unemployed. The situation in Morocco was not so horrifying but serious enough.

example occupational groups or those based on common class, became redundant or secondary. In the next chapter I will discuss the alternative forms of association in the post-Independence situation and the pressures making 'traditional' ones more attractive to certain sections of the population, particularly to women, than those typical of the market.

2

Estates, tribal groups and the market today

Three organising principles

Social stratification in the Akhdar region today is compounded of a 'traditional' system in which membership of social groups is by ascription; and a system of social relations organised by the market, in which birth status has little relevance, and social mobility is feasible. The extent to which market forces affect different sectors of the population and pervade different areas of social life tends to determine whether the ascriptive or market principle of social alignment predominates. The fact that women, and their sphere of activity, are only marginally related to the market has important implications for this thesis.

To attempt to describe stratification in the region in terms of a single series of hierarchically arranged strata would be a gross misrepresentation. I treat stratification as having several dimensions corresponding to different principles of social organisation. Here I discuss those which operate in the absence of a market economy and to which individuals are aligned by ascription. I will consider what changes have been brought about, since pre-Protectorate times, in the system of estates of *shurfa*, Berbers, Arabs, and *haratn*; and the tribal system of segmentary groups, strictly speaking vertical sections, within which peasants exercise economic rights by virtue of their membership of a (putative) agnatic community.

Finally, I will attempt to assess how French penetration and modern developments have affected the relative importance of estate, segmentary and market principles of social organisation.

The estate system today

Shurfa. They are the putative descendants of the Prophet. There are two distinct lines which have significance for the inhabitants of the Middle Atlas: those descended from Moulay Ali of Rissani in the Tafilalet, and those in the line of Moulay Idriss, the founder of Fez. Most *shurfa* of the Akhdar region are descended from Moulay Ali, who was also the ancestor of the Moroccan ruling dynasty.

Estates, tribal groups and the market

Shurfa are ideally endogamous, and empirically the majority marry within their estate. *Shurfa* women, especially, should not marry men who are not of their rank, since Moroccan children inherit estate membership from their father. They enjoy great esteem in the community, especially among women, but there are many poor *shurfa* and those in the *ksour* do not enjoy noticeably better life-chances than most Berbers, although the *shurfa* in the town fall among the richer half of the population. They tend to avoid public places, and *shurfa* women are more strictly secluded than others of their community.

Haratn. Colour is a defining attribute of *haratn* – there are no light-skinned ones – in a way in which it is not of Berbers or Arabs, whose status as people claiming rights in a political community is counted more significant than their skin shade. Within a single family there may be dark- to very pale-skinned children. Nevertheless Moroccans, especially women, are chronically colour-conscious. Paleness is highly valued on the marriage-market. The prejudice of women can be traced in the play-ditties which girls sing, and in the fears which small children express about black bogey-men.

Strictly speaking, there is no segregation of *haratn* from other social groups; they are often close friends and confidants of Berbers and Arabs. But, especially in rural communities, there is an elaborate protocol which defines them as political inferiors. They tend to serve wherever they happen to be.[1] On ritual occasions, when they are nominally guests like anyone else, they tend to take undignified roles – servant, musician, fool. They frequently send their girl-children to be 'fostered' in richer households, where they are in fact maids-of-all-work. People make jokes about their appearance which they are expected to take in good part.

A gamut of beliefs attributes to them mystical powers. The *jnun*, or spirits, are often represented as negroes. All the spice and potion-dealers, the *tabub* or healers, the men and women sorcerers whom I came across were *haratn*. (The milk from a *hartaniya*'s breast is supposed to have curative properties, especially for eye diseases which are lamentably common.) In the religious sphere, the number of *haratn* (men and women) who took a prominent part in the Sufic ecstatic dances of *hedra* was out of all proportion to their numbers in the population at large.

In the towns *haratn* tend to be poorer than other groups, having

---

[1] Cf. Niebuhr, I, 623: 'It is probable that the population in servitude were still *as a whole* at the disposal of the patricians.' Quoted from K. Marx (1969), 102, my italics.

negligible property in the forms valued in the society – no carpets or gold, no land or houses. Their social connections are mainly with other *haratn*, but with the accession of younger *haratn* to new occupations the relegation of the entire 'caste' is becoming a thing of the past. Another factor in this improvement is that *haratn* women are more ready than those of other estates to undertake paid work as domestic servants or as carpet weavers. Yet many *haratn* are still the bound henchmen of *shurfa* or Berber land-owners.

Berbers and Arabs. Intermediate between the categories of *shurfa* and *haratn* (lit. ploughmen, or cultivators) lies the rest of the population variously identified as Berbers, who are assumed to be rural, and Arabs, a name which may refer either to nomadic tribesmen (*bedawiyin*) from the East or the *gish* tribes, or more usually to the inhabitants of towns.

The distinction which members of these groups draw between themselves and *haratn* is that they are 'white' and *haratn* are 'black'. Taken in a literal sense, these labels do not have much descriptive value today, whatever their original accuracy. Their meaning is metaphorical and political. Pressed further, Berbers and Arabs describe *haratn* as *khadam* (labourers) or even *'abid* (slaves), which was their pre-Protectorate status. There is a sense in which *haratn* are still at the command of Berbers and Arabs, a relationship which helps to define the free status of these groups: 'Arab' and 'Berber' are not ethnic categories. They imply different life-styles and a different orientation towards the market and towards ascribed statuses. The majority of 'Arabs' in Akhdar are of rural Berber origin. Here I often refer to the semi-urban *ksour* in the same breath as the rural *ksour*, for culturally they have much more in common with them (in terms of language, dress, religious activity, economic activity, style of life) than they do with the town. The semi-urban *ksour* I refer to are all within four kilometres of the town. On a clear day they are within earshot of the *muezzin* calling from the town mosque. Yet the cultural break between the town and *ksour* is startlingly abrupt.

'Arabs' in Akhdar speak Arabic, attend the town mosque, and abhor heretical Sufi practices, such as those current in the *ksour*. They dress distinctively, the men in Western-type clothes, perhaps with a *tarboush* (little felt hat or beret) or a *djellaba* and fine leather slippers. Arab men seclude their women, who, if they venture out at all (to the *hammam* or public baths for example), wear the long hooded *djellaba*. Older women who have children, and whose allegiance to the conjugal unit is thereby guaranteed, may go out more often to visit kin and friends. The richer and more westernised women may go unveiled but always with a scarf tied French-peasant style.

The term 'Berber' is used by all Moroccans in the town to refer to the Berber-speaking people living in the mountains and the *ksour* surrounding Akhdar town. Self-identified Berbers emphasise their discreteness from Arabs. For example, the transhumant Ait Morghad, who use the same pastures in the same season as the Eastern *bedawi*, told me that they never so much as speak to them. Similarly *ksour* Berbers will explain the behaviour of a townsman by saying, 'He's an Arab.' On the other hand, some townsmen will say, 'Berbers, Arabs – it's all the same. Everyone has a Berber grandfather; we just speak different languages.' Others, particularly from the traditional urban bourgeoisie of Fez or Rabat, show contempt for the 'lazy', 'gossiping', 'dirty' Berbers, who 'share everything – they have everything in common' (educated Fassi lady). The standards of judgment are reminiscent of 'the Protestant ethic'. Berber men wear the woollen hooded *djellaba*, turban, and rough leather sandals; women a long brilliant *tshamir* (simple dress) with a flimsy glittering *tfina* (a dress with two separate panels at the front) and bead necklaces. When they are in their own *ksar*, walking to the fields or to the stream to wash, they are generally unveiled (except *shurfa*), but if they leave it they inevitably wear a white drape *izar* over their clothes, and sometimes a veil. Only the wives of men aspiring to Arab status are secluded, but women with town connections (if for example a woman has been married to a townsman) like to wear a *djellaba*.

Language. Out of a sample of seventy-four household heads in Akhdar, 71·9% are bilingual, speaking both *Tamazight*, the Berber dialect of the Middle Atlas, and Moroccan Arabic, *darija*. None speak Berber only. It is not the instrumental language in Akhdar. Of their wives, 58% are bilingual, but 40% speak only Arabic, compared with 28·1% of the men. Only one woman speaks only Berber, this after living in the town for eight years. From my experience, and the fact that the first language of many infants is Berber (soon abandoned for Arabic however), it seems that husbands and wives who are bilingual may often speak only Berber at home. The language and cultural idiom of the wife predominates.

Although the majority of Berber women learn Arabic there seems to be little pressure on Arabic-speaking women to learn Berber. In towns all over Morocco, and Akhdar is no exception, Arabic is the language of higher status, used in commercial and legal transactions, for administration and education. Arabic-speaking women are usually Arabic-speaking because they have always lived in a town. Since women in towns are much more secluded than those in rural areas, they are not likely to make many contacts outside the home when they come to Akhdar and even less likely to seek out Berber-speaking country-people for whom they feel some disdain, in general.

On the other hand, I have met several Berber women living in Akhdar who speak only defective Arabic. I will argue below that this is not only because they too must conform to the urban pattern of seclusion, but because they attach great importance to relationships formed within traditional reference groups, in which Berber is at a premium.

Men, having a wider and more heterogeneous acquaintance, formed as a function of their public life rather than their domestic one, tend to be bi-lingual. Their approach to relationships is more open-ended. Although Arabic, the language of government and the élites, is at a premium, traders and craftsmen find that to know Berber is an asset, for the population from which they draw their clientèle is largely Berber.

Relation of estate to economic status

It is common for Arabs and Berbers to intermarry, men tending to marry Berber women. It is rare for people of both groups to marry *haratn*, who marry among themselves. Only occasionally does a man from either group marry a *sherifa*, even if the case of a Berber or Arab woman marrying a *sherif* occurs more frequently.

The fact of intermarriage suggests that Arab or Berber identity is not seen as an ascribed status. No elaboration of beliefs concerning pollution or the transmission of sacred powers surrounds the contact between Arab and Berber. There are many concerning the contact of Arab and Berber with either of the other estates. The cultural status of Arab and Berber is largely based on economic distinctions and therefore achieved. An Arab is an individual who operates largely within the market, and whose relation to property is as to a commodity. A Berber does not possess saleable property, but land which he regards as non-convertible, since his property interest defines his membership of a particular community.

Yet this is to simplify the situation today. A person may retain his membership of a rural community, while possessing moveable capital. However this often means that he has to some extent become 'Arabised', engages in trade or in wage-labour, and is influenced by urban models of behaviour. To be a Berber is no longer a definitive description of political and economic status, as it may have been under *siba*. Nevertheless both Berbers and Arabs continue to behave as if these labels described innate identity. This is especially true of women, for whom the prospect of social mobility is remote, given their estrangement from the market.

Tribe, lineage and community among the Northern Ait Izdeg

The tribe of Akhdar *cercle* (administrative district) is the Northern Ait Izdeg, whose southern counterpart is to be found in the Central High Atlas, where many of the inhabitants of Akhdar and its satellite *ksour* originated. *Ksour* children of immigrant Berber parents will describe themselves as Ait Izdeg, whatever the origin of their parents. The *ksour* nevertheless include members of other tribes of the region, the Ait Tislit of the mountain slopes, the Beni Mguil of the rich wool- and wheat-producing Bardia region; this as a result of the area's history of exchanges with transhumants, the dispossession of these tribes by powerful landlords especially during the protectorate, and Akhdar's growing significance as an economic and administrative centre.

There are also many migrants from the inhospitable Ait Morghad and Ait Hadiddou homelands in the Central High Atlas and its south-western slopes. They have been driven north by the periodic drought and floods (every year travellers bring the same tragic story of devastation of fields and houses, death of animals and often of the friends and kin of their listeners). In the past they fled from tribal wars and the impracticability of their transhumant life, harried by the government as they were, and skimped of pastures by the encroachments on tribal lands which I have described above.

The *ksar*, hamlet or village, is therefore a complex social unit whose inhabitants are linked more by their expectation of a common future than by their having shared a common past. Nevertheless it is with this community of neighbours that the individual feels himself closely identified, and he calls his fellow-villagers *imlahlin*, father's brother's sons, or even 'brothers'. In the rural areas a *ksar* comprises between ten and fifty households, but it verges on a hundred in the immediate neighbourhood of Akhdar town.

It is often internally divided into named lineages, as in the case of Aghzim which I will discuss in more detail below. These tend to form interest groups; and like their pre-Protectorate prototypes, they are based on agnatic descent from a common ancestor three or four generations back and include women as well as men. The members of a lineage may not co-operate day by day or in harvesting, and the association is a loose one, particularly since lineages in the same *ksar* are often linked by intermarriages. Generally lineage affiliation is submerged in the more significant community life of the *ksar*. In *ksar* Aghzim, only three-quarters of the families belonged to the lineages of which the *ksar* was said to be composed. Nevertheless, group-membership is of paramount value, and the individual is nothing. This presents a striking contrast with the town situation where the individual is socially mobile, and the entrepreneur is king.

The concept of outsider, or *brrani*, is central to the everyday organisation of life of a *ksar*; it carries values not only of exclusion but of hostility and some contempt. Its definition varies according to the context of the activity in question.

Although the community of a *ksar* is based on neighbourhood, the ideal is that neighbours should be members of the same kinship group, 'cousins', and the qualifications for cousin status are rigid and explicit. The more complete a man's qualifications, the higher his status within the *ksar*. A resident who belongs to a founder family fulfils all of them.

It is necessary to have been born in the *ksar* of parents who live there to continue living there oneself, and to be buried in its ancestral cemetery. (Each *ksar* has its own cemetery.) A stranger who has married a *ksar*-girl and lives uxorilocally remains an outsider as far as other members of the *ksar* are concerned. But a woman who marries a *ksar*-man is no longer an outsider once she has borne a child to him. If a man's mother belongs to a *ksar* he is conditionally welcome, treated as not altogether an outsider, and may make visits to his mother's village. Rights to *ksar* property held by both men and women seem an important aspect of insider status. One man who came from Zwur and married the daughter of an Aghzim man is no longer regarded as an outsider – this was emphatically stated – because he has built a small house which he rents to his brother-in-law, and has bought fields which he rents to his mother-in-law. The fact that he is a soldier, and lives permanently away from Aghzim, staying there only for short periods during the summer, does not affect his status.

Membership of a *ksar* by filiation or marriage confers on women 'ownership' of *hedra*, the ecstatic Sufi dances, and only women of that *ksar* are likely to get up and dance. To go to the *hedra* assumes a whole gamut of distinctly Berber cultural commitments: heterodoxy, and maraboutic religion whose special feature is the veneration of saints.

Property, the market and social structure in the Akhdar region

In order to understand how the populations of the *ksour* and the town are related to land and to saleable property, and to gauge the nature of their internal stratification, I will first indicate the place of these populations in the national schema. Here, I outline the national distribution of land, and quote various sources on the property relations of Moroccan cities and the shape of urban stratification.

French penetration, to recapitulate the arguments of Chapter 1, disrupted the traditional segmentary organisation of the local tribes. It brought the imposition of strong and pervasive state control, and the creation of a labour market.

The disruption of the segmentary system took place through the appropriation and redistribution of tribal pastoral land. As tribesmen became impoverished, they were impelled by the market for land and labour to treat as commodities what had been regarded hitherto as aspects of social life. The strong state, backed by the French arsenal, extended the domination of the *Makhzen*, imposing new taxes and controls (such as the introduction of pass laws and the suppression of transhumance). Recruitment to the French army was no longer the prerogative of a few *gish* tribes as it was under the *Makhzen*. It provided a new channel of mobility, by-passing the process of Arabisation. Expertise in French not Arabic cultural skills was demanded similarly in education and administration.

French influence and the spread of the market economy were endorsed by the increasing supplies of foreign consumer goods and the generalisation of money transactions. The demand for labour in the new mines and farms of the *colons* drew impoverished transhumants from the south into the market economy. Yet a large proportion of migrants could not be employed. All these changes as I will stress below (the end to raiding, the recruitment to the army's administration, wage-labour, education, migration) affected men more severely and directly than women, whose relationship to the market and to the control of property barely changed. Their world now is still structured largely according to the traditional criteria of status and segmentary alignments.

31

Women and property in Morocco

Social and economic relationships after Independence

To understand the current situation in the Akhdar region, it is necessary to outline economic and political trends after Independence. The similarities with Protectorate times are striking. The strength of the state has been maintained, and its influence possibly extended through taxation, the introduction of the *Shari'a* to Berber areas, the expansion of primary education, and attempts to provide new facilities in rural areas – markets, schools, ovens, mills, baths. Besides this are the programmes of public works – dams and the massive rehousing projects which must accompany them, and finally the responsibility of the government for the distribution of American A.I.D., on which many rural villages have become dependent.

In spite of the nationalist emphasis on the importance of Arabisation in education and the law, the main channels of social mobility remain the army, the government bureaucracy, educational and administrative service, and finally, to a much lesser degree, industry, for all of which the essential qualification is a Western education. Indeed the majority of all secondary school teachers are still French so it is difficult to see how Arabisation can proceed. Since educational facilities grow worse and more inappropriate with every step down the social ladder, and reach their nadir in the rural areas, a change in the structural relations between groups relegated by the market to higher and lower social, economic and political positions cannot be expected. This theme will be elaborated in Chapter 5.

The currency of French culture in the towns is one element which helps to explain the demand for new manufactured consumer goods. Their availability creates a spiral. Peasants become increasingly familiar with the mechanisms of the market, aware of the low profitability and high risk of unmechanised agriculture; they migrate from the land thus reducing the labour input, and ensuring its low productivity. More frequently now the sequence ends in sale of fields, because migrants remain unemployed, and in the accumulation of lands by townsmen waiting to invest their profits. Such townsmen are often able to introduce machinery or employ wage-labourers and thus to derive greater benefits from the land than their former owners. However as I have remarked above there is as yet little irrigated land being sold in the region. The association of moveable or convertible capital with the town, and landed property with country and people whose point of reference is a *ksar* (which includes many town migrants), is still 75% valid.

32

Estates, tribal groups and the market

Stock, on the other hand, is commonly bought and sold, particularly in the weeks preceding the *Aid-l-Kbir* (the feast of Ishmael when every Muslim family must kill a ram). In the *ksour* animals are scarce because there is little pasture-land and they must be fodder-fed. Each family restricts its stock to the amount of land it is prepared to put aside for the production of fodder crops, hay and lucerne, so that, of those families owning under 5 hectares, none keeps more than a couple of sheep. Two or three of the more prosperous families may own a couple of cows or mules and others may share rights in such an animal. When someone is in severe financial straits, the first thing he does is to sell his animals, which may also serve to finance a 'rite of passage' celebrated in the household.

Land tenure in Morocco: the small farmer[1]

About 1·4 million hectares are worked in Morocco by relatively modern methods of cultivation: of this area about 300,000 hectares are managed by the state and about 450,000 hectares are cultivated by foreigners (as in 1971).

Under traditional methods of agriculture there are 3,902,000 hectares of which 3,429,000 hectares or 87·9% are privately owned lands (*melk*). Some of this land carries more than one crop in the year so that a total of 3,725,000 hectares is planted in this category.

The holdings which are in the category known as *melk* – the privately owned areas – bear the relationships as shown in Table 1. The average area planted per household, overall, is 3·3 hectares or an average of 2·7 hectares for the three classes with less than 20 hectares. Indeed a million households cultivate less than 4 hectares and 500,000 less than 1 hectare.

It is considered that the condition of the considerable number of holdings on which less than 2 hectares are cultivated approaches that of the rural households without land under cultivation (80,000).

In Morocco 71% of the active population is engaged on agricultural pursuits (Villeneuve, p. 96) and produces only 30% of the total production. This is a proportion similar to that occupied in agriculture in Britain during the Middle Ages or in other countries which are not yet developed industrially. 65·5% of the rural households are engaged solely in agriculture and only 19·3% have two activities, one

[1] Based on Villeneuve, 1971. I am indebted to my father, Colin Maher, for many helpful discussions and professional observations on Moroccan agriculture, as well as for the assessment of Villeneuve on which this account is based.

Women and property in Morocco

Table 1. *Distribution of land in Morocco*

Area sown per household	% of households	% of the area planted
Less than 2 ha per household	48·2	11·8
Between 2 and 8 ha per household	24·3	30·9
Between 8 and 20 ha	5·0	18·3
More than 20 ha	1·1	11·5
The remaining area (generally less than 10 ha planted per household) is made up by areas held collectively, especially areas without agricultural value, and areas granted collectively to old soldiers, etc.	10·6	10·1
Other areas planted	10·8	17·4
Total	100·0	100·0

Villeneuve, 1971: 70

of which being of a non-agricultural nature. 10·2 % of the households are engaged exclusively in non-agricultural pursuits and 5·0 % have no activity.[1]

Several households may associate in order to raise adequate resources of capital and labour for efficient production. In Morocco as a whole, out of a total of six million cultivated plots, more than half were cultivated by one household alone...Nearly a million were cultivated by two households together. Half of these associations took place between two households from different villages, a further quarter between a village and a town household, the remainder between households from the same village.[2] 1·3 million plots were cultivated by three or more households acting together. None of these more complex associations involved only households in the same *ksar*. The census of 1960 gave the following figures regarding the farming population:

11 % are employers;
47 % work on their own account;
20·4 % are salaried;
21·5 % live with their family whom they aid with their labour.

[1] In the so-called *région agronomique No. 3, montagnes pastorales* (Enquête, 1964), which includes the area under study, 144,673 households were surveyed, of which 50 % combine agriculture with stock raising and cultivation of fruit trees; 41 % combine agriculture with stock raising only; less than 4 % are 'pure pastoralists'; less than 1 % are 'pure peasants'.
[2] Tableau XV, Répartition, 'Résultats de l'Enquête' (1964), 189.

34

Living on his own land or associated in some way with some cultivation, for example with a share-cropping landlord, the average farmer may be considered as independent; but he sells little, buys little, and is only good for limited credit. It is stated by Villeneuve, however, that there is practically no agricultural proletariat in Morocco; but this does not obviate the presence of great poverty and the existence of many of the rural population on a level of bare survival.

Nevertheless, Villeneuve points out, the cultivators are far from anxious to take advantage of technical aid and to embark on a course of action whose outcome is not clear to them, and whose success depends anyway on more general economic conditions. The type of small-scale agricultural enterprise does not lend itself to rapid improvement being too weakly based while supporting a heavy human burden. The possibilities of land reform are reduced by the fact that the agricultural sector cannot yet pass on to other sectors that part of the population for which it provides insufficient employment.

Economic insecurity and title to property

In the property relations of contemporary Akhdar and its dependent *ksour* we discover the significance of land registration as an instrument of domination and, in the French case, of colonisation. Although it may have been intended to provide universal security of ownership there are few signs that it was adapted to Moroccan forms of land-holding, but many that it resulted in a situation where vast tracts of land, being collective pastures, remained unregistered and could be regarded as unowned, and therefore fit to be appropriated for colonisation; or where several people claimed the same piece of land hoping to sell it later on.

Tribes who lost some of the land in which they had exercised common rights were inevitably left with the least fertile parts. The colonial depredations were not as ruinous as in Algeria and Tunisia, especially in the case of the *habous* or religious trusts whose value actually increased under the Protectorate, and the funds were devoted to Moroccan interests. Yet they were serious enough to stimulate the growth of a debt-ridden and poverty-stricken proletariat where once there had been 'a proud tribe of independent shepherds'.[1]

Today *ksar* property is no more 'secure' than before. Only the properties in the immediate vicinity of Akhdar have been officially registered. They include very few small plots of cultivated land,

[1] R. Bidwell (1970), 208.

35

consisting rather of houses, shops and sites for building. Their owners have security of tenure, backed up by government authority. The only available plan of *propriétés immatriculées* dates from 1941, but by 1971 the *titres* office of the *Mahakma* in Akhdar had records of 19,000 registered properties. Each of them has been surveyed and a *titre foncier* drawn up, with a map, description of the property and of the owner. When the property is sold, the *titre foncier* is brought to the law office and transmitted, before witnesses, to the new owner.

Conversely, property outside Akhdar, which is generally in the form of land and houses, has not been surveyed or registered. Only if a piece of land has been sold (thus moving into the category of convertible capital) do the current owner and the buyer draw up an *acte* with the notaries, and they have the field measured in square metres. But fields are not often sold. In the normal course of events, a man's fields are transmitted to his heirs and the boundaries observed because they are known to other field-owners and members of the *ksar* community.

One indication that fields are rarely sold is that the prices quoted per hectare are very variable. However, this apparent uncertainty about the market value of land appears less significant when the mode of assessment is taken into account. Fields are not sold by the hectare but simply as cultivable units, often identified by a name, over whose advantages and disadvantages (in terms of the site, state of soil, accessibility to main irrigation ditches etc.) buyer and seller may argue until they agree on an appropriate price. A field should be sold with a crop already grown. Irrigated fields were valued by the notary in charge of the *titres fonciers* at roughly 500 *drahem* (£50) per hectare. He described unirrigated land outside the town as 'worthless', but conceded that it might fetch 200 dirham per hectare for building. The absence of official titles outside the town means that *ksar*-people feel their ownership threatened. The objective causes of their fear are not far to find – the increasing tendency of townsmen to invest in land (especially the recently swollen numbers of salaried civil servants, often of peasant origin) and their vulnerability to those of their own community, who through serving the government have become 'notables' and are not averse to extending their imperium (by claiming lineage land as their own, or buying it at a low price for example, and having it registered). However, *ksar* smallholders were particularly afraid that the government itself would take away their land, either in the interests of private individuals – this was their experience under the French – or in order to put up government buildings. These might be schools, shops, or houses for soldiers, but they represented an incursion of foreigners into the established and mutually loyal community.

There is a large category of smallholders whose migration to the town does not mean that they have sold their land, but that they want to supplement the income they derive from it, in order to meet their more sophisticated wants without selling land. This phenomenon, the reluctance to give up one's landed status and all it implies in terms of community support, has been attested by Couleau of Soussi agriculturalists, but inhabitants of the semi-urban *ksour* surrounding Akhdar behave in the same way. By migrating to a town, a peasant does not necessarily secure immediate control of goods derived from the market economy, for he will probably be unemployed (like 20% of all urban males aged between twenty and sixty, see Table 2). However, he will make use of kinship links in order to acquire patrons among those who do have such control.

The articulation of estate, segmentary and market principles of social organisation

There is a tendency for the market to be rendered imperfect by the trammels of ascriptive status-allocation in the following ways.

Firstly, because people with access to scarce resources such as education, jobs, economic opportunities, tend to share them with those to whom they are related or who become their clients, the principles of segmentary solidarity or of patronage are brought into operation. In Akhdar this is especially visible in the way migrants from the same area help each other, and keep such close identity of interest that they can be said to form informal associations.

Secondly, people tend to operate with the prejudices derived from the estate system. Thus a *sherif* would find a clerical or a high status job more readily than a *hartani*. More important is the fact that political activities perpetrated by *shurfa* are legitimated by the ritual status of the agent. Thus a high proportion of civil servants are *shurfa*. Moreover those traders who are *shurfa* have more 'good-will' because contact with them is associated with 'increase' and blessing. The most prosperous traders in Akhdar were *shurfa*. Many of them therefore retain their roles as patrons. On the other hand low status and poorly rewarded jobs were often held by *haratn* who are often clients and rarely patrons. At the top and bottom of the hierarchy then, market and estate principles of social organisation tend to reinforce each other. Ossowski's generalisation is appropriate: 'As the society that is

Table 2. *Muslims in the labour market, by age-groups*

| | Urban Morocco as a whole | | | |
| | Male population | | Female population | |
Age	Working	Unemployed	Working	Unemployed
Less than 15 years	1·7	0·1	2·3	—
15–19	28·3	14·7	10·8	0·3
20–24	64·2	21·4	9·0	0·5
25–29	73·7	20·9	8·6	0·5
30–34	74·8	20·8	10·6	0·5
35–39	75·0	19·8	12·3	0·6
40–44	73·9	19·8	14·6	0·7
45–49	73·0	20·1	14·7	0·7
50–54	68·5	22·0	14·1	0·7
55–59	63·9	23·8	12·0	0·9
60–64	53·3	26·4	10·7	0·5
65–69	46·9	3·7	8·3	0·2
70–74	8·8	2·8	6·5	0·1
75 and over	25·4	2·5	4·1	0·1
Age not declared	32·0	7·7	7·5	0·3
All ages	*37·2*	*11·1*	*7·2*	*0·3*

This table has been compounded from several in *Résultats du recensement de 1960*, vol. II, Population Active, Service Central des Statistiques (Rabat, 1965), pp. 177–80.

Rural: province of Alpha (to which Akhdar belongs)

| | Male population | | Female population | |
Age	Working	Unemployed	Working	Unemployed
Less than 15 years	3·2	—	0·7	
15–24	72·4	12·0	3·1	
25–44	86·7	10·6	2·8	
45–64	84·7	7·5	3·0	
65–74	68·1	3·2	1·7	
75 and over	47·0	0·8	0·6	
Age not declared	27·9	6·6	—	
All ages	*46·3*	*5·3*	*1·9*	

Unemployed refers to those people who stated that they were seeking work with no success, which leaves a surprising proportion who do not expect to sell their labour. To these figures should be added the provisos that they do not show the high level of seasonal unemployment for men, and that women's outside activities are often continuous with their domestic work (e.g. care of stock and processing of dairy products and wool) so that they would not describe themselves either as 'working' or as 'unemployed'.

emancipated from estate restrictions approximates more closely to the ideal type of capitalist society, the nature of the wealth possessed ceases to be significant for the determining of an individual's position. An owner of moveable capital may become a land-owner and vice versa. Apart from market fluctuations, the main things that hinder such changes are psychological factors such as traditions, habits, personal inclinations, life aspirations or professional qualifications."[1]

[1] S. Ossowski (1963), 62.

3

Patron–client relations

The discussion of property-holding reveals that the majority of the population owns very little. Their plots of land are too small to provide them with subsistence, let alone with a surplus to sell for cash, which they need to pay taxes and to buy consumer goods, such as sugar, tea, clothes and paraffin. It is difficult to find a way of supplementing this meagre income within the market economy for jobs are scarce, and a minimum of capital is needed to trade. Those categories of the population such as small-holders, southern migrants, and women who cannot get a living within the market economy, must fall back on extra-market relationships.

These are of two kinds, those entailing obligations of mutual help, and those predicting a political relationship of subordination and dependence. The first is specific to members of a 'tribal' or 'lineage' community, who must have rights in lineage property to qualify as such. The fact that support is available from this source goes some way towards explaining why there is such resistance to selling land. The second type of extra-market relationship is the patron–client relationship which provides for the patron's dispensation of goods and protection in exchange for the client's performance of various services; although the distributing of wealth and the command of services is no longer so closely associated with the estate system, the latter is clearly still relevant.

The category of 'patron–client relations' is often treated as if it constituted a single and homogeneous institution; yet closer scrutiny reveals various modes of association, each of which operates within a different structural framework. Common to all of them is a special relationship of economic dependence in which the patron dispenses material help in exchange for the services of the client. That is all. The various modes differ as to permanence, the degree of control exercised by the patron over the client, the degree of respect apparent in the client's behaviour, the type and range of the services offered by the client to the patron, and the benefits he receives; and the specificity of the relationship: is it extended to the client's family or to the patron's family? does it continue in perpetuity?

40

Patron–client relations

In my analysis of patron–client relationships in the Middle Atlas I distinguish three types. The first is a permanent relationship between political equals (e.g. members of the same lineage); the second temporary between people of different political status (a government official and a migrant); the third permanent between people of different political status (people of different estates). This last is a form of bondage approximating to slavery, except that it is theoretically possible for the client to transfer his allegiance.

It seems that any individual may enter into a variety of relationships. Further networks of friendship may link several patrons with several clients in type (i), and may exist among patrons and among clients as separate groups in type (iii), but type (ii) is characterised by competition among patrons for political power and among clients for favours.

People without the opportunity to produce must consume nevertheless, sometimes out of all proportion to their means. In order to do so, and to share in the life-style of a more privileged class, migrants and people from the *ksour*, especially women, become involved in relations of clientage with richer *ksar*-dwellers or with town patrons. The patron or patroness may be selected by a fiction of kinship; or, as in the case of a *sherif*, the estate membership of patron and client may come to the fore. In the latter case the client acquires grace by the contact. Otherwise he performs services and swells the entourage of his patron, who provides hospitality, uses his power on his client's behalf (e.g. to get his son into school, or his wife into hospital, or to find him a job) or lends him money. The more distant the segmentary relationship between patron and client, the greater the subordination of the latter, and the stress on estate differences. (For example, the uncouthness of a distant Berber cousin will be stressed by an Arabised patron.) The belief in innate ritual differences between estates, which have authority according to the degree of their sanctity, is symbolically expressed in a hundred daily gestures.

The idiom of estate-clientship affects particularly all voluntary clientship entered into by *haratn*, even today when the estate hierarchy is being corroded by market relationships. Because *haratn* are often taken into servitude as children, many relationships between foster-child (*hartani* or not) and foster-parent have the flavour of patron–client relationships as I shall discuss below.

41

New forms and functions of segmentary organisation

Migrants present the type case of involvement in patron–client relationships. They are generally poor, having left home in search of a living; they are generally rural in origin, and in the town their income is unpredictable. They indicate a tribal segment when asked where they come from (Ait...). In Akhdar the majority of migrants have a strong cultural community with the Ait Izdeg, which is anyway composed of former migrants from the same area. They generally retain land rights in their home area, and by forming casual associations based on friendship and obligations of mutual help, they remain socially distinct in their host-community.

The patron–client relationships which inevitably develop within such an association, between poorer and richer members, and between those longest established and those recently come, are especially pronounced among women, and are characterised by elements of companionship and equality and not by emphasis on difference of status.

Women as agents of lineage cohesion

I have pointed out that not only do migrants have reason to depend on kin, because they have no reliable source of sustenance, but the property focus of lineage cohesion survives their migration. What are the mechanisms by which the contacts among kin and the ideology of kinship are maintained?

Marriage is perhaps the most important and it is women who arrange marriages; in fact, women take the most active part in all proceedings involving the reiteration and utilisation of kinship bonds. They return to their *bled* to have their children, to visit their mothers, to find brides, attend funerals. In the summer women scatter to all corners of Morocco to spend a few weeks with their sisters, daughters or mothers and if they cannot manage the trip they send their children, who may also visit the kin of their father. Women take charge of family rituals, the celebration of weddings, naming ceremonies and circumcisions. Further, they present the extreme case of dependence on kin; for they are excluded from the labour market, marriage is never a safe bet, and they retain an economic claim on the kinship group all their lives because they do not receive their inheritance. Women maintain contact above all with female uterine kin. The links among them provide a safety net for divorcées, widows and the

42

children of broken marriages. But they also have a concrete economic utility, for they constitute channels for the exchange of goods and services outside the market economy and safeguard their families from its vicissitudes – unemployment, failure of crops, inflation. Thus poorer women wash the floors, run messages and help at the feasts of richer women, who call them 'sister', lend them money, invite their families to meals and make them gifts.

In sum the dispersal of lineage members and the invasion of the market economy, signifying chronic economic and social inequalities, have increased the social importance of uterine kinship and supportive relationships among women.

The case of Baha, a woman living in Bentaleb, features many of the tendencies discussed above. Baha came to Bentaleb in 1965, with her husband, aged sixty and twenty years older than herself, after floods had devastated their fields in the husband's village in southern Ait Izdeg territory. They had at first gone with their three sons aged fourteen, seven and four, and one daughter aged eleven, to stay with Baha's brother who lived in another valley about 50 kilometres away, that of Bassou in fact. Baha had sold her fields to her brother, maintaining possession of some fruit and nut trees, and a patron of his had helped to get a menial government job for Baha in the Akhdar area where she had kin, such as the son of her half-sister. She at first lived in Mrabet, then found a job in Bentaleb where the family rented a house from one of the founding families of the *ksar* whom Baha called her father's brother's son.

Besides her job which brought in 400 *drahem* (£40) a year, Baha relied on the benefits from a number of clientship, kinship and friendship relations based on common regional origin. In Bksar, she became maid of all work to a government official, whose wife she liked. She cared for the children of the wife, who could speak only Berber, and the children came to call her 'Mum', and would often stay the night in her bare home. In exchange for these services, she would be given occasional gifts such as money to buy shoes, cast-off clothing, dates and figs from the wife's home, for Baha to take as presents to her other patron-friends.

She performed similar services – washing and sweeping for the wife of one of the big landowners of Aghzim, receiving milk, fruit and the use of the oven, until the more class-conscious husband ordered his wife not to let her use the oven, because she was a 'parasite'. Finally, an important administrative official and opulent landowner, whose patronage she sought because his father had known hers (he had been a *shirkh*) also called on her services from time to time, and employed her husband to work in his orchard for a while. She often complained that although he was her father's brother, he didn't want to know her, because she was poor.

Her other sources of help were a woman, *Aqshou*, whose husband had a steady job in Akhdar, and whose family she had known in her husband's *bled*. This woman called on Baha's services frequently and arranged for her to act as cook at the celebrations of friends from their *bled*. However, their relationship was rather a close friendship than a minion–mistress type of rapport, and Baha would often stay with her when she felt tired of the *ksar* environment where she found her servant status humiliating and inhibiting of her other social contacts.

She borrowed money from Aqshou, came there to partake of the gentle life, and often invited the family to take meals with her. Baha's son later became apprenticed in the same garage where Aqshou's sons were working. Her husband's brother had a café where Baha could always count on a free meal. Aqshou and Baha had almost the same network of regional friends, among them the wives of three brothers, two of whom made a good living as electricians, and counted among the wealthier of the network. Baha had acted as wetnurse to one of the wives and was always invited to their celebrations, where she would meet with more friends from her adopted (i.e. her husband's) *bled*. Among them were the young cousins of the family, two girls and a teacher.

People from Baha's husband's *bled* came to see her, often in passing, or to go to the hospital; some of them even came to see her when they were pasturing their herds in the nearby pastures surrounding Youmi town, and then Baha would often take them to visit these two sets of families, especially if her guests were women. The families were always delighted to see her, as she had a forceful and amusing personality. Her entertainment value appeared to be an important 'professional' asset, in that her patronesses were wooed by it.

Migrants, marriage and clientship

The presence of many migrants in the Akhdar region places a premium on relationships among women, especially on their wife-seeking function, thus creating an important category of women clients whose chief claim to a special relationship with a patron is based on their role in arranging marriages.

Comparison of the town population with the *ksar* population reveals

44

Table 3. *Family heads and their wives born within 50 km of Akhdar*

Sample	Family heads %	Wives %
Town		
Household survey	14	34
Primary school parents	10	55
Ksar and town		
Secondary school parents	28	36
Ksar		
Household survey	53	21
Primary school parents	75	70

Sample	Composition of sample Family heads	Wives
Household survey of town quarter	8	19
	n = 59	56
Parents of final year in girls primary school, Akhdar*	3	11
	n = 30	20
Parents of second year in mixed secondary school, Akhdar†	7	9
	n = 25	25
Household survey of Aghzim and six households of Bentaleb	17	6
	n = 32	28
Two classes in the penultimate year of primary school serving Aghzim and neighbouring *ksour*‡	24	24
	n = 32	34

* 15 fathers are government employees, 8 are traders.
† This school serves the entire Akhdar district, so the parents are not strictly a town population: 6 live in Akhdar, 13 within 15 km, 6 in more remote *ksour*.
‡ 7 fathers are *fellahin*, 6 are 'masons', 5 labourers, 5 miners, 4 small traders, and 7 government employees.

that the overwhelming majority of men in the towns are first generation migrants (since Akhdar has only been a 'town' since 1917) and
most of them refer to a *town* of origin rather than to a rural area.
However they have intermarried with local *ksar*-women to the degree
indicated by the higher percentage of autochthonous women living in
the town. This trend is reversed in the semi-urban *ksour* where
community of interest and virilocal marriage dominate the scene.

Women and property in Morocco

Migrants and 'ksar' marriage

Migrants, especially those who intend to settle permanently in Akhdar town or in the *ksour* round about may use marriage as a way of acquiring a helpful local network. Where a migrant already belongs to a network of fellow migrants from his region (e.g. the Alpha network to which Baha belongs) he is more likely to be found a wife by one of his real or putative kinswomen, from among themselves or through communication with the home region. If he has no such connections, he will marry a *ksar*-girl from the Akhdar region.

The advantages of marriage into the *ksour* are the low brideprice, common cultural background and the ability of the bride to adapt to the precarious conditions in which the migrant often lives during the first few years in Akhdar. Moreover she will fulfil the traditional role of a spouse humbly, unlike the town girl whose more sophisticated domestic skills are matched by an appetite for clothes and furnishings whetted by her exposure to the urban model of consumption. Town wives are notoriously apt to seek status in the eyes of other women through their possessions and gold jewellery.

The role of women in marriage-arranging

Two circumstances favour the trend of intra-neighbourhood marriage on the one hand and the flow of *ksar* wives to the town on the other. The first is the necessity for women to play the major part in marriage-arranging, not only in choosing the spouse but in introducing their sons into families where they might meet marriageable girls in a quasi-kinship capacity (or such girls might visit a man's mother or sister). The second factor is the stricter seclusion of townswomen, which means (1) that women are more likely than men to know eligible girls; (2) since women should not know strangers, the girls they know are likely to be from families with whom they already have some connection, i.e. from their region; (3) *ksar*-girls are more 'visible' than town girls, and command a lower brideprice.

Estate and segmentary systems at 'rites de passage'

Apart from visiting, and casual meetings in the *hammam* (a favourite occasion for assessing the points of a young acquaintance), women meet for life-crisis rituals. The tendency is for such meetings to have a regional basis, on the one hand, and on the other for the gathering to

46

be predominantly of the estate (*shurfa*, Arabs, Berbers, *haratn*) to which the hosts belong, outsiders playing a functionally specific or peripheral role.

At these celebrations the relationship between the different estates is defined in exaggerated, ritualised activities. Thus the *shurfa* are called upon to bless the dancing, and are themselves withdrawn and silent – unworldly. At a wedding they are given the task of displaying the items of the *henna* and calling out the names of other donors. The *hartaniyin* joke and play with abandon, and they are called upon to perform ridiculous and humiliating dances of sensual import. Self-identified Berber and Arab women are distinguishable by their dress, the readiness of the former and reluctance of the latter to sing and dance, etc. Potential brides are thus assessed within a context where estate membership manifestly influences behaviour and consciousness.

In the semi-urban *ksour*, such gatherings usually consisted only of the women in the *ksar* of the host. Women in the *ksar* were in fact excessively shy of townswomen towards whom they have a strong feeling of inferiority. The more affluent *ksar*-women usually invite a sprinkling of outsiders. I once held a naming ceremony, and the first reaction of my *ksar* friends was that they couldn't come if there were going to be townswomen there. 'We are just poor women from the ksar', they said. This attitude is understandable when one takes into account the fierce competitiveness in terms of finery and gold which characterises townswomen's gatherings.

The heterogeneity of a town is such that a person's neighbours and acquaintances are likely to be of many different regions, but hosts always attempted to have as many of their kin at their celebrations as possible. Especially where the regional community was strong, as among migrants, the composition of the gathering was as exclusive as that of the *ksour*, even if the base of recruitment was different and extended over several villages in the home area. Not infrequently *ksar*-women attended these celebrations in the role of compatriot, client or – because of a friendship begun at the house – of a common acquaintance. The tendency was for the daughters of *ksar*-women to be assessed by their urban counterparts more frequently than the other way round. They would be more often asked to dance and to fetch and carry, since in that context they were of lower status. This would favour the formation of marriages between townsmen and *ksar*-women.

Intermediaries

What of the migrants who have no kinswomen to look out for wives for them? The disadvantages of their situation are discernible in the awkwardness of men who tour *ksour* in pairs asking if there are any brides to be had.

This is a situation which indigent and/or elderly divorcées and widows are glad to exploit, by acting as intermediaries between wife-seekers and wife-givers. However, intermediaries need several qualifications. An effective intermediary should have many and far-flung family connections to act as her informants, and she needs to be able to move about freely and talk to male wife-seekers, without the interference of her male guardian. Generally only women past the menopause qualify. Such a woman must be a generally welcome figure, whose judgment is widely respected.

Men sometimes act as intermediaries, but do not become 'specialists' who are sought out, for they suffer from several handicaps. The chief handicap is that it is not considered proper for a man to enter other people's houses, unless the owners belong to his close kin or he is invited by a male occupant. Nor should he have frequent dealings with women, and that is a grave disadvantage for an intermediary since it is women who know the marriage market and the characters of the girls in question.

The intermediary acts with an eye to her own interests, arranging marriages between parties she thinks worth cultivating. She is generously rewarded, invited to all celebrations of both families, and, more important, she can call on their man- and child-power when she is short of labour resources. She may ask for help with heavy farming or transactions with the bureaucracy, and in fact becomes an honorary kinswoman. Moroccans are more mobile than they have ever been, and the role of intermediary has acquired proportional importance, for the days are gone when people could choose a mate from among the children with whom they grew up. Yet the intermediary was probably indispensable even at the turn of the century, for by no means all marriages could be made within the *ksar*. The anthropological models which present only 'wife-givers' and 'wife-takers' as marriage-agents and ignore the intermediary do not reflect accurately the interests which go to make up the marriage patterns of any society in North Africa.

Patron–client relations

Association among women and clientship

Women are often in a position to need help in the performance of their domestic tasks. This is true not only under special circumstances such as pregnancy, illness and childbirth, and in preparations for feasts at life-crises but for the completion of routine domestic tasks, given the low technological level. Women co-operate in washing clothes, sorting grain, caring for children, and are always on the borrow for a pinch of salt or a sieve from a neighbour or kinswoman. The dependence of women on other women is all the more necessary given the segregation of men's and women's roles. And the expression of this segregation is at its most intense, taking the form of a mystically sanctioned taboo on a husband's presence, precisely when his wife is least able to help herself, namely in late pregnancy and child-birth.

Links of co-operation between women are to a large degree independent of, or are not necessarily mirrored by, those formed by their male kin and affines.

The women who help each other to perform domestic tasks tend to associate in a more or less consistent way, visit each other, take part in each other's feasts and act more freely with men of their generation, related to the women of the group, than they would with strangers. At the core of these associations is 'the kindred of co-operation' generally comprising members of the same nuclear family, who interact continuously. Peripheral members who may or may not be kin join them from time to time. Peripheral members are those who have no property or kinship rights in the household where ego, the kindred of co-operation, is resident. They share in the goods of the household on a clearly temporary basis, as a reward for service. However, it is the visitors' estate and degree of material dependence which determine whether they assume subordinate roles or not. Often they are described in kinship terms by ego.

I will take grain-sorting as an example of the kind of co-operative activity in which extra hands are needed other than household members in order to clarify the role which peripheral 'members' play.

Many of the helpers in this case are widows and *hartaniyin*, the latter in a capacity which closely resembles that of clients to the wife of the grain-owner, the former performing any little task which will provide them with a meal and company, and is within their physical range. The situation of the helpers is rendered ambiguous by the presence of friends of the grain-owner, who have come mainly to

Table 4. *Sorting grain: an example of co-operation
and patronage among women*

Grain of household	Working members of household	Living in	Status of helpers	Living in
1	Wife	Akhdar	Husband's sister	Akhdar
	2 daughters	Akhdar	Married neighbour	Akhdar
			2 widows	Akhdar
2	Wife	Akhdar	Wife's widowed	Staying for
	1 daughter	Akhdar	mother	a while
3	Wife	Akhdar	Husband's father's brother's wife	Waman
			Married *hartaniya* neighbour	Akhdar
4	Wife (of notable)	Bentaleb	Husband's sister	Bentaleb
			Wife of notable	Bentaleb
			Wife of migrant *hartaniya* widow	Bentaleb
5*	Wife	Bentaleb	2 *hartiniya* widows	Bentaleb
	1 daughter	Bentaleb		
6	Wife	Bentaleb	Wife's widowed	Staying for
	1 daughter	Bentaleb	mother	a while
7	Wife (of *sherif*)	Bentaleb	Wife of notable	Bentaleb
	1 daughter	Bentaleb		

* This family live next door to the household of the husband's brother, whose wife and daughter do not help with co-operative tasks.

gossip and socialise, but lend a hand with a joke such as, 'if you want to eat you should work'.

Often a group has a fairly consistent membership, so that the peripheral members become to some extent identified with the 'kindred of co-operation' and can plausibly be called clients. The composition of the group over time is best conveyed by considering a series of action sets mobilised to deal with exceptional circumstances, in which the interests crucial to the women of the patron families are at stake.

The family of Moulay Ahmed

Moulay Ahmed is a prosperous merchant living in Akhdar. He started from humble beginnings and married a Berber woman, to the horror of his *shurfa* family, although this kind of marriage is not uncommon. His contacts with his sister are few and lacking in warmth. For reasons which I failed to establish, his wife is also estranged from her sister, who when she comes to Akhdar will only visit Moulay Ahmed's eldest daughter Lalla Batoul. (Moulay Ahmed's marriage is neolocal, neither of the couple having kin in the region.)

Lalla Batoul married a non-*sherif* merchant from another town, also without kin in the Akhdar area. Since their house is only a few yards from Lalla Batoul's parents, and her husband's shop is furnished by his father-in-law, the latter experiences all the constraints of uxorilocal marriage. They have six children.

Moulay Ahmed had three sons and three daughters, of whom only Lalla Batoul is married. His eldest son recently died. Moulay Ahmed employs the married son of Ba'adi in his shop. The second son of Ba'adi is engaged to the daughter of Ahmed. The third son of Ba'adi (who is a rich peasant) has worked since childhood in Ahmed's shop and lives with Ahmed's family who say 'he is like a brother', returning to his own home for lunch. The daughter of Ba'adi frequently visits the daughters of Ahmed, and helps them with their everyday chores.

Action-sets

1. At the ceremony held at Ahmed's house to end the forty days' mourning for his eldest son, there were present:
   Ahmed's wife
   Ahmed's eldest daughter, Lalla Batoul
   Ahmed's third daughter who cooked
   Ba'adi's daughter who served and washed
   Malika, a young divorcée who washed and served.
   As this was a family occasion, the other members of the family were also there, i.e. Ahmed and his other two sons, and his employee, the third son of Ba'adi.
2. When Lalla Batoul had a baby, she was helped at childbirth and the receiving of guests on the third day by:
   her mother – Ahmed's wife
   Ahmed's third daughter
   Ba'adi's daughter
   Malika, the same divorcée.
3. When Ahmed moved into the new house he had built, the women cleaned and prepared it. They were the same five mentioned above and Ahmed's second daughter who had returned from another town. Ahmed's wife did very little work, but helped to cook.
4. When Lalla Batoul's husband had a mental breakdown, at first her sisters looked after the children in her father's house. Then Lalla

Batoul herself moved in. Finally she decided to go back and the second daughter went to sleep in her house. Ba'adi's daughter came to help at this time. Lalla Batoul's sister, when she had an opportunity to leave the house, came to see Ba'adi's wife and daughter who commiserated with her.

5. When the eldest daughter of Ba'adi had a baby, her mother went to help with the birth, and Ba'adi's daughter and Ahmed's two daughters went to help prepare the *sebueh*, the naming feast.

6. When Ba'adi's son's wife had a baby, Ba'adi's wife and daughter helped with the birth. Ahmed's second daughter came to stay, and later his third daughter to help with the *sebueh*, assisted by a *hartaniya* friend.

7. At *Aid-l-Sgher*, the feast which marks the end of Ramadan, Ahmed's entire family visited Ba'adi's family. At *Aid-l-Kbir*, mutual feasting went on.

The women's group, with Moulay Ahmed's family at its core, consists of the following people: Moulay Ahmed's wife, three daughters, and Ba'adi's daughter, peripheral members being Ba'adi's wife and daughter-in-law, his married daughter, and Malika, the divorcée. The quasi-group, with Ba'adi's family at its core, consists of Ba'adi's wife, daughter-in-law and daughters, with Moulay Ahmed's daughters slightly removed. Peripheral members are Moulay Ahmed's wife, his married daughter, Ba'adi's brother's wife and daughter who are neighbours, the daughter of an old *ksar* family whom Ba'adi's daughter meets at the stream, and two *hartaniyin*. All these people would be at the centre of a household feast and carry out domestic tasks, serving the guests of the family.

4

How it looks on the ground

Following the general account of the relation of the population to property and to the market, I present more detailed material on the economic organisation of two *ksour*, Aghzim and Bentaleb, noting that there are marked social and economic inequalities among *ksar* residents. Relations between the *ksour* have been affected by the intrusion of the *Makhzen*, and with it of institutions related to the market economy – shops, schools. Nevertheless certain areas of social life, such as marriage, are still governed by regional and estate interests.

I go on to discuss the economic organisation and occupational structure of a quarter in Akhdar town, and to contrast the economic and social conditions prevailing in town and *ksar* respectively.

The valley and the 'ksour'

The stream which sustains the *ksour* runs northwards from the mountains. In the spring, it collects the melting snow, often flooding its banks and ruining riverside fields. It is harnessed to run water-mills – several operate in each riverside *ksar*. In the summer it is channelled off to irrigate lucerne fields, and in the autumn the wheatfields before the ploughing begins.

Aghzim and Bentaleb, my host *ksour*, are built on a rocky hill which drops steeply on three sides, leaving the fourth one to slope more gradually towards the north. Bentaleb on the east side of the hill commands the river running at its base. Aghzim on the western side, built only 200 metres from Bentaleb, faces a *ksar* called Daoud, 1 kilometre away over the valley to the west. This *ksar* is served by a canal, since it has no access to the river. Confronting the two *ksour*, 1 kilometre away across the southern valley, rise the battlements of Elkbir; then beyond the mound of the local saint or *mrabt*, towards the mountains, the *ksour* edge the river at intervals of about 2 kilometres.

The northern end of the Aghzim hill is the site of Kasbah, the home of a community of Franciscan nuns. They run a workshop of weaving and embroidery, employing local women, and a school for teaching

53

Table 5. *Summary of landholding in Aghzim*

Ksar-dwellers	
With over 5 ha of land	6
With under 5 ha	16
With land elsewhere	5
Without land	7
Others	3
Total	37

Table 6. *Householders' occupation or market status*

Fellahin – full-time	5
Masons – casual	8
Government employees	7
Petty traders and servicers	5
Labourers and *khammes* (sporadic employment)	4
Miner and unemployed miner	2
Widows and divorcées	6
Total	37

homecrafts to *ksar*-girls. Some work at the hospital in Akhdar and run a small dispensary for the nearby *ksour*. They are also responsible for distributing American A.I.D. food supplies among the *ksour*.

Finally at the snout of a ridge which rises just beyond Aghzim's northern end is *ksar* Ceima, 1 kilometre away; and turning east across the river lies the town of Akhdar, which completes the social universe of Aghzim. Each *ksar* is fringed by its orchards, in which are planted apple, plum, peach and nut trees – the pride of its more prosperous members.

Paths link all these *ksour* to each other, and vein the valley, running between fields. The field pattern is complex since each field-owner has several patches, each in a different part of the valley. Informants told me that this was in order to share agricultural advantages equally, so that each cultivator has well-watered and dry land, land suited to the different crops, flat and sloping fields, and so forth. The distribution is stated in terms of an agreement among the members of the community. If such an agreement was made, it was at the founding of the *ksar*, and today it cannot be put into force, because individuals may alienate or buy land at their own option, thus disrupting the equitable distribution. However, land has remained largely in the hands of the founding families, partly because they have preemptive rights if one of their members wishes to sell land. The belief concerning the fair sharing of fertility still corresponds to actual holdings, although no redistribution on this principle takes place. Later settlers acquired worse land on the stony slopes far from the river; they are never in an economic position to challenge the prestige and power of the founding families within the *ksar*.

The fields of the different *ksour* are mixed. Bentaleb shares the valley to its north with Ceima, and a couple of landowners of Fssa town; and Kibrit *ksar* shares that to its east and south with Elkbir. The majority of Aghzim's fields are in the long southern valley, which is cultivated also by Elkbir and Daoud. Daoud also shares with Aghzim the valley between them to Aghzim's west.

Irrigation

The agricultural system of the *ksour* depends on a supply of water for irrigation during summer and autumn. This puts the *ksour* built nearest the river in a strong political position vis-à-vis their waterless neighbours. The riverside *ksour* are, in fact, the oldest established – Gwali, Ait Elkbir, Bentaleb and Ceima.

These *ksour* have yet another economic advantage and means of control – that of being able to run water-mills. There are seven at Ceima, five at Gwali, four at Elkbir; descendants of four Ait Black brothers from Aghzim own a mill in Gwali. Since the canal has been built to supply it with water Daoud has set up its own water-mill, an important sign of independence. It is not clear why Bentaleb has never built a mill. The explanation may be that its section of riverside is too frequently flooded, or that the distance between the *ksar* and the river is too great. The mill with its grain stores would be exposed to attack and theft. In the other *ksour* the mill is surrounded by houses.

Ceima, Daoud, Aghzim and Bentaleb share an 'irrigation system': that is, they co-operate in the distribution of water among their fields – its spatial and temporal organisation. There is a record of hostility between Elkbir, Gwali and the other *ksour*, endorsed by differences of custom. These two *ksour* have their own arrangements for irrigation.

The main irrigation channels are dug and maintained by the owners of the fields which border them. They are under strong pressure to co-operate because of the time they spend together harvesting, sowing and ploughing in neighbouring fields; and their wives in cutting hay and lucerne together endorse these relationships – which may be among members of different *ksour*. In addition each field-owner will dig a ditch to serve his own field.

When it is time to begin irrigating, the *amghar-n-waman*[1] (senior man in charge of irrigation) from Ceima organises the distribution so that each *ksar* in turn has four days supply of water. This ruling, still obtaining today, is antique. The assumption is that the needs of the *ksour* are equivalent. This was the case when the size of a ksar's population was limited by the area of land available for cultivation. In homogeneous peasant communities, such as inhabit rural areas in Zwur, the size of a single *ksar* rarely exceeds thirty households. But the *ksour* in the surrounding area must be regarded as 'semi-urban fringe' and their size reflects this fact. Today Ceima comprises 130 households, Bentaleb 75, and Aghzim 40 households.

That they should continue to share irrigation water in equal parts would be absurd if the proportion of land held by each *ksar* had not also remained constant, and roughly related to the size of its original agricultural population. This suggests that recent immigrants did not succeed in obtaining land, or at any rate, that they now derive a livelihood from some other source. The changes in population do not reflect changes in land ownership, or an extension of the area owned by larger *ksour* at the expense of smaller ones. This seems to be the consequence of rare land sales and a social norm which obliges a man, constrained by circumstances to sell a field, to offer it first to primary then lineage kinsmen, then to friends within the *ksar*, and finally to *ksar* membership in general before he can offer it on the open market. Since the price of the field rises with the social distance between buyer and seller, the fact that so little land has come into the open market reflects the strength of community ties within the *ksar*.

In sum, this tendency to the 'conservation of patrimony' by pre-emptive right of *ksar* members, seems to have slowed up the transfer of land between *ksour*, in spite of the changes in their relative size over the last fifty years. However, in the larger *ksour* where occupations are more various, agriculture, previously the central pre-occupation of the community, no longer commands the same attention. One indication of this is the looser organisation of irrigation. Once, each *ksar's amghar* (a senior man who was elected to his office for a year) would see that the water was shared equally among the field-owners in the *ksar*.

---

[1] An *amghar* was an office-holder elected by the *jema'a*, or village assembly, to take charge of certain areas of community life (e.g. war or irrigation) for a short time, usually a year. Government office-holders in the villages are sometimes called *imgharn* – but the word is more often used to mean 'respected old man', 'elder'.

How it looks on the ground

When a man's turn came, he opened his ditch and used as much water as his field needed, during the time allocated to him. But today, there is a tendency for the strongest to win out. Widows and divorced women, in particular, are anxious about their fields, calling on their male kin to ensure that they are watered. One complained, 'There is no *amghar* nowadays – it's each man for himself.'

Water is a focus of hostility and competition... 'No water for our fields...it's those sods at Daoud guzzling it all again' has been the sentiment expressed in my hearing on more than one occasion. Behind this recognition that the identity of interest between *ksour* is only temporary and circumstantial, lies the strongly exclusive ideology of the *ksar* – the community of 'cousins', as its members often call themselves.[1]

Bentaleb

Bentaleb is a large *ksar*, of some seventy-five households. Its population is more heterogeneous in origin and occupation than Aghzim. For this reason many of its members are hazy about its history, but its beginnings can be placed conjecturally at the start of the nineteenth century. Ba'adi, the seventy year old head of one family, told me that his grandfather migrated here from Rahim, about 16 kilometres away towards the mountains. At that time, mid-nineteenth-century Bentaleb was still a small *ksar*. This family, Ait Ba'adi, claims to be the longest established in the *ksar*, a pretension supported by its control of considerable fertile, well-irrigated land. This prosperity is characteristic of the other old families. The ancestors of three of these also came from Rahim, and two of them flourished under the Protectorate as administrative appointees. All these families and several others, more recently arrived and claiming a 'father's brother' relationship to the heads of the most influential families, describe themselves as Ait Bb, a fraction of the Ait Izdeg of the Alpha area, some 80 kilometres to the south. They say they came to the Akhdar area originally because it was a valley with fertile land and good water.

Five of these large land-owners have built palatial houses for

---

[1] The sharing of water is a crucial symbolic expression of this relationship. Water imagery and symbolism appears repeatedly in stories and songs and a procession to the river is a feature of most *rites de passage* involving adoption into the local community. The high point in the circumcision rites is a noisy procession to the river, drumming and dancing, carrying the small boy who has just been circumcised. The practice of carrying a new in-marrying bride to the river so that she can 'fetch water', *ad-ttagm waman* (Berber), has lapsed among 'town-Berbers' and even in Aghzim, but it is considered proper by Ait Izdeg and still takes place in rural *ksour*.

themselves. Most of the rooms are empty, a precaution against the future. If the sons marry and then quarrel, they can move to opposite ends of the house, but the unity of the kinship group will be saved – so informants told me. The *ksar* is built of tamped mud, with high towers at the corners and narrow slits for windows. The oldest part is the inner section. Here the houses are closely pressed together like cells in a honeycomb, and open on to dark roofed passages like tunnels. All the houses are double-storeyed, and most have access to a rooftop terrace, where clothes are dried, *henna* sorted, and maize sunned, beaten and winnowed. The ground-floor is usually used as a stable and a store for fodder, but since these houses generally belong to the poorest members of the community, their stables rarely contain more than a few chickens.

Aghzim

Aghzim was built just before the French came – in about 1914. One of the founders is still alive and several of the older inhabitants were children at the time. The first settlers were refugees from the *ksar*-cluster of Zwur, in the Central High Atlas. Living in this and neighbouring *ksour* were both Ait Hadiddou and Ait Morghad tribesmen. In fact the arrangement of the valley is described as an alternation of Ait Morghad and Ait Hadiddou settlement, sometimes in the same village, sometimes not. The quarrel which originally broke out was between two individuals of different tribes and eventually aligned the entire valley into warring camps, on the basis of tribal membership. The two men were said to be 'brothers-in-law'. It is not clear whether they were real affines or whether this is a figurative way of representing the relationship between the two tribes who tended to intermarry.

Some of the Ait Hadiddou fled north to seek asylum with the Ait Izdeg. Again political alignments are conceived of in kinship terms. The ancestor of the fraction that fled was supposed to be the brother of the ancestor of the fraction that stayed.

The refugees did not all seek asylum in the same place. Some went to Tislit, one to Umlil about 80 kilometres west of Akhdar (Ait Hadiddou territory), one to live with Beni Mgil people. Their whereabouts are still known and visits are periodically made. It is remarkable that after more than fifty years people in Aghzim still retain rights to fields in Zwur. They stress that they have many contacts with the village. They even visit the children of cousins, who cultivate the land of their absentee kin, and send them a token share of the harvest or cash from the sale of the crop.[1]

Aghzim is a smaller and more compact *ksar*, built on the north–south axis of its main street. Two other streets, of the old tunnel-like kind, meet at the corner of the main street in a V.

The houses in the inner part of the *ksar* are built in the traditional style. On the ground floor are two or three rooms for keeping animals and fodder. Upstairs is a big reception room, where carpets are spread when guests arrive and on feast-days. There is also a kitchen, with a wood-stove in the centre which provides warmth and is used for cooking. This room is the most lived-in, especially during the winter when more time is spent indoors, but it serves as the 'women's room' throughout the year. Visiting kinsmen may come and sit there, and women guests chat to the women of the house as they go about their work. There may be two or three other rooms for sleeping and storage. There is no lack of space, for daub houses are cheap to build.

Near the north entrance of the *ksar* is an old mosque. It is no longer used except as a refuge for beggars, and for the non-orthodox *hedra* gatherings of ecstatic dancing which takes place at religious festivals.

Relations between 'ksour'

The constraints of neighbourhood and the necessity for economic co-operation lower the barriers between *ksour* from time to time. The oldest families of both *ksour* own threshing grounds (*inurar*) inherited from their forebears, in the area between the *ksour* which has a hard rocky surface. They are, of course, the most significant land-holders. Smaller land-holders, generally members of the same lineage, may borrow their threshing grounds (I have not heard of any case where payment was exacted), thus incurring obligations to the 'founding families' which enhance the latter's status. The threshing grounds of Aghzim are closest to the houses called *brra* (outside), but some are farther away interspersed with Bentaleb sites. Men on neighbouring sites shout to each other and sing together, help each other to manage the teams of mules which thresh the wheat. Similarly the owners of neighbouring fields, often from different *ksour*, co-operate in the maintenance of irrigation ditches. The teams of men who thresh maize in the autumn often include people from different *ksour*, and helpers may be paid in maize or cash for their services. So the occasions for

[1] Accounts of Bedda of Aghzim and her mother (aged 80+). Interviews with Aoman (aged 60+), born in Kibrit but living in Aghzim since he was seven.

interaction between people from different *ksour* are many; but the occasions on which a *ksar* is distinguished, when the exclusivity of the community of 'cousins' is stressed, are more significant. At the family events, life-crisis rituals (the birth of a child, its naming ceremony, circumcision, marriage, death), the *Ait taddart* (people of the house) will invite only the members of their own *ksar*. Concessions are sometimes made to uxorilateral relationship, or for the inclusion of workmates if the father or groom works in the town, but these are pointed out as exceptional.

Women and the older members of the *ksar*, who have little opportunity to make outside contacts through work (or gathering in cafés to play cards as men do) tend to stress the 'cousin'/outsider distinction. Children, however, who play together at school, deplore the 'prejudices' of their parents. Children are the category whose interaction is perhaps affected more strongly than that of any other category by the new communal buildings.

Aghzim and Bentaleb are the central *ksour* of a *commune*, the administrative unit which also includes Ceima and Daoud. An area of several hectares formerly served as a no-man's land separating Aghzim from Bentaleb. This area has now been appropriated by the government for the construction of 'communal' facilities. The buildings are concrete, their sharp whitewashed contours presenting a stark contrast with the mud walls of the *ksour*.

There is a primary school accommodating nearly 350 children from the four *ksour*. Beside it is a spacious house for the headmaster, and a series of small ones for teachers and other government employees. In a central position is a block of small shops, two butchers' and a grocer's and nearby is a big white-towered mosque. Opposite the mosque is a public tap (few of the houses in Bentaleb and none in Aghzim have running water). A public oven and *hammam* (Turkish bath) have also been built, and rented to an entrepreneur.

These amenities in common have clearly had a drastic effect on the traditional relationship among the four *ksour*, particularly that of Aghzim and Bentaleb. The school has brought children from several *ksour* together – Aghzim, Bentaleb, Ceima, Daoud, Fssa and Gwali. They do not feel the same opposition of interests as their parents, since the economic constraints which govern the lives of adults affect the children only indirectly. So friendships among children do not follow the same pattern as that of children of the previous generation, although the closest friendship networks are still those formed within the *ksar*.

How it looks on the ground

The long-term 'occupation' of the *ksour* by 'foreign' teachers and soldiers also has far-reaching implications. It represents the incursion of urban petty bourgeois models, with such features as the use of Arabic, and ostentatious seclusion of women. Although the newcomers are the targets of considerable hostility, they bring contacts with urban ideas and commodities which have a better reception.

The shops and the mosque have to some extent become a meeting-place for *imgharn* – the 'elders' who used to form ad-hoc assemblies to settle disputes and discuss problems facing the *ksar* as a whole. Their political and judicial roles have been largely whittled away as the control of the central authorities has tightened. They sit and gossip. The central mosque has stolen the show from the small *ksar* mosques. But women in particular, who do not go to the mosque, consider that the *fqih* 'from town' knows nothing about cures and protective amulets, for which they will go to one of the 'unemployed' *fuqaha* in Bentaleb, or in another village.

On the other hand, women are brought together around the oven, the *hammam* and the public tap. They still invite only members of their own *ksar* to their houses, but their acquaintance, even their friendship network, may include women from others. These chance meetings in the 'inter-*ksar* sphere' provide an ideal opportunity for older women, on the look-out for good wives for their sons, to form gradually an idea of the character, industry and personal charms of the younger ones. This kind of minute observation was previously possible only within their own community of cousins.

Marriage

The extent to which cross-*ksar* acquaintance promotes marriage is uncertain. It is worth noting that not a single woman who has married into Aghzim comes from a Bentaleb family. However the pattern of established marriages in Aghzim shows a strong tendency for men (the role of their female kin, especially mother and older sisters, in finding a suitable girl should not be forgotten) to choose spouses from nearby *ksour*, and/or from their villages from which their forefathers came. It is common, too, for a wife's ancestors to be from the same region as her husband's and her family think of his as remote kin, *Ait nukwni* (people of us).

The tendency in Aghzim seems still to be to marry first within traditional reference groups with a putative genealogical base and shared social status. The next option is to take a wife from a nearby

61

friendly *ksar* such as Hassan, Jalil or Kibrit. The absence of spouses from the hostile Elkbir and Bentaleb is striking; Daoud also, where one Aghzim lineage has kin, is not favoured. This may be because many of Daoud's inhabitants occupy individually an inferior status to people in Aghzim, being employed as hired labourers, and Aghzim people say that all the people in Daoud are *haratn*.

Yet to marry near at hand means to activate brother-in-law ties and the wife's rights to patrimony in land. If a wife has such rights and moves away, she cannot make claims to help from her family, and they cannot use their affinal connection or avail themselves of her services.

The economic argument seems to be corroborated by the fact that the landless strangers and *haratn* take spouses from farther afield. This is a function of their greater mobility. If they are not landowners, alliances with friendly *ksour* are not so valuable to them; nor do their women have rights in land, which would predispose them to marry nearby.

Town quarter: Akhdar

The survey was carried out in one of the oldest quarters of Akhdar comprising two parallel streets running in a north–south direction.

Mosque. At the corner of the spinal street of the quarter is the main mosque of Akhdar. It is in the care of an *Imam*, who leads the prayers and directs the religious community of the town, and a *muezzin* who calls the faithful to their prayers five times a day. Other *fuqaha* (religious scholars) may perform special offices, such as reciting the Koran on the night of *fdela* (grace), three days before the end of Ramadan.

The mosque was built perhaps a century ago for a smaller congregation than that of modern Akhdar. At the Friday noon prayer it bulges at the seams and there is usually a line of people kneeling on the pavement outside. It is clear nevertheless that only a small fraction of the male inhabitants of Akhdar ever go inside the mosque, except on special holy days. Women never do. The explanation usually put forward is that they would distract the men from their pious duty. Country women and the majority of those in the town say that they don't know how to pray. Women who do know how to pray say that they might go into a mosque in a big town like Meknes where they are unknown, but in a little town like Akhdar 'evil tongues' would wag. 'She must have gone to meet a lover.'

Nevertheless, in spite of the meagre attendance, the mosque plays an important part in the regulation of community and domestic life. People tell the time by the calls to prayer, refer to the *fuqaha* in illness and for important family rituals, and accord them a great respect. During Ramadan the *muezzin* calls people from their long fast at sunset, and a drummer wakes them for the morning meal, rumbling through the streets at dawn.

Madrassa. Near the mosque is the local Koranic school, where three *fuqaha*, certificated teachers of the Koran and the elements of Arabic orthography and arithmetic, see to the education of about 150 children between the ages of four and seven. Since Independence, attendance at a Koranic school has become, theoretically, a precondition of acceptance at primary school. According to the general tendency such schools are confined to urban centres, so that the ruling on pre-primary attendance can hardly be strictly applied. In rural areas the *fqih* in the *ksar* mosque still teaches a few boys, but relies on the parents' gifts to make it worth his while.

Parents who send their children to the Koranic school pay a small weekly fee, which is enough to serve as a deterrent to many Akhdar people, since it is difficult to view the fee as alms. Combined with the law on sending one's children to school it seems rather to be extortion. Many parents do not send their children, and the number of girls is negligible. Some parents, such as the more educated soldiers, are dissatisfied with rote-learning of Koranic texts as nursery education, and discussed eagerly with me the rumours of a kindergarten being set up. 'That will teach children worthwhile things, how to play,' said one soldier.

The Mill. An important feature of the quarter is the diesel-run wheat mill which is owned by a Frenchman. Local families prefer to have their own grain milled rather than buy flour. Although the *ksar*-women say they prefer their own water-mill because it does not leave the taste of diesel in the flour, many of them bring their grain to the town, as the diesel mill works more rapidly, and does a roaring trade.

Sloping uphill from south-east to north-east is the spinal street of the quarter. This street is lined with shops and small craft enterprises. There is a bellows-maker, a bicycle repairer who also mends motor-cycles, and a radio repairer. Two of the largest grocery stores patronised by the bourgeoisie are here, besides the most popular *hammam*. Bearing westwards, the street leads into the Friday market.

63

The Friday market. In spite of its name, this market is a permanency, merely bursting into more purposeful activity on Fridays and Sundays when crowds flock in from the hinterland to buy and sell. The market, as an architectural entity, takes the form of a large arcaded square. Carpet merchants and auctioneers rent the stalls under the arcades – spice and potion sellers, straw merchants, and butchers. These traders normally operate from their small shops under the arcades but on Fridays and Sundays they move into the central space to display their wares to greater advantage. The square is also invaded by merchants who travel from *suq* to *suq*, selling dates or donkey panniers...

The *suq* can be entered from three sides. At the top of the slope is the main road, at the bottom a street of vegetable and grocery stalls (leading from the main street), butchers, sellers of domestic hardware, clockmenders. Outside the north wall of the *suq* is a street of vegetable stalls, and in the part of it nearest the main road are clothes shops and a couple of cafés.

Behind the street below the market are the barracks of the *mokhazni*. They are no longer elegant, their age suggesting that the first idea of the French administration was to survey the market, and keep it under military control. The *mokhazni*, as recipients of a regular wage and agents of the administration, enjoy high status among the local population. Many of them are *shurfa*. In this way their traditional mediating role corroborates their modern disciplinary one.

It is clear that the quarter is closely connected in space with several of Akhdar's central institutions – the mosque, the market, the *mokhazni*. It is near one of the main commercial streets and the *hammam*. These relationships are reflected in the predominantly commercial–professional composition of its population, strongly petty bourgeois, with a large component of government employees and soldiers. Many inhabitants are employed in commercial and modern-type craft occupations which serve the town, besides a small group supplying specifically rural needs, whose standard of living is indistinguishable from that of the urban or rural proletariat.

The degree of occupational specialisation is very low. Many so-called skilled workers have run through a series of occupations – cook, shopkeeper, mechanic, to take one example – attempting only to stave off unemployment, or having to take low-status jobs, such as labourer or sweeper.

Table 7. *Occupational structure of men in the town quarter*

Category	Details	No.	Percentage of total
Government employee	Teachers		
	1 primary		
	3 secondary	4	
	Clerks	3	
	Agricultural technicians	3	
	Nurse	1	
	Policeman	1	
	Soldiers	16	
		28	39
Workers with traditional skills	Mule-saddle maker	1	
	Blacksmith	2	
	Fqih	1	
	Peasant	1	
		5	7
Workers with modern skills	Mining prospector	1	
	Carpenters	4	
	Mechanics	3	
	Drivers	4	
	Cinema technicians	2	
	Tailors	2	
		16	22
Services	Grocers	2	
	Vegetable retailer	1	
	Vegetable wholesaler	1	
	Baker	1	
	Waiter	1	
	Café owner	1	
		7	10
Unskilled workers	Dustbin emptier	1	
	Labourer	2	
Unemployed		3	
Too old to work		8	
Temporarily in Algeria		2	
		16	22
Totals		72	100

Women and property in Morocco

Life-style

The category of educated salaried employees and soldiers is an élite in Akhdar. They pay high rents, not only because they are able to, but because they are largely foreign to the area. They do not evoke charitable feelings in the heart of the proprietor, and have no local support to increase their bargaining power in situations of housing shortage. The rents of 28% of the houses are over 50 *drahem* per month, – half the wage of a manual worker. Only 41% of the houses are owned, compared with 88% in Aghzim. They are entirely in the hands of migrants from the South or people of local origin

The quarter has a prosperous air, seventy-four of the houses being built of cement or cement plastered, with cement floors. Some inhabitants have boasted that their houses are at least a hundred years old. Most of the houses, however, are more recently constructed, and many of the older ones have been renovated to conform with new urban standards. Now their woodwork is painted, their floors tiled in bright designs. Most of them have a central courtyard, and none are more than one floor – in contrast to the *ksar* where the roof is for social gatherings, at least among women, and the ground floor for animals.

In spite of this cheerful appearance, 26% of the houses are built of tamped mud, 33% have no domestic water supply, and a number of people live in very insecure and wretched circumstances. Since twenty-nine of the houses in the quarter have no domestic supply of water, the river is important. There is a public tap for drinking water, but for such large-scale operations as washing the clothes of the entire family most women tend to go to the river.

Regional Origins

Only a fifth of the family heads (as distinct from household heads) who live in the quarter are from the Akhdar region. 13% are from the north (Fez, Rabat, Casa). Most of them are either teachers or soldiers. Five men are Soussi, and three come from the Rif: these are all soldiers. The largest spontaneous influx of population, many of them Berber-speaking Ait Morghad, appears to have been from the south, 40% of the quarter. Most of them are in service or craft occupations. All the owned houses are in the hands of local people or southerners. But the preference for house ownership is shared by local people, and seems to belong to a Berber culture pattern associated with a life-style in which insecurity has a constant influence. A house provides the

Table 8. *Housing and amenities in Aghzim*

Details of housing	No of households	Percentage of total
Adobe	31	91
Cement	3	9
	34	100
No running water or well in house	33	97
Well	1	3
	34	100
Rented at over 50 d./month	—	—
Rented at under 50 d./month	4	12
Owned	30	88
	34	100

Table 9. *Relation of population to housing in Aghzim*

No. of people/room	No. of households	Percentage of total
0–1	17	50
1 1–2	14	41
2 1–3	1	3
3 1–4	1	3
4 1–5	1	3
Total	34	100

Table 10. *Housing and amenities in the town quarter*

Details of housing	No. of households	Percentage of total
Adobe	18	27
Cement	50	73
	68	100
No running water or well in house	20	29
Running water	33	49
Well	15	22
	68	100
Rented at over 50 d./month	19	28
Rented at under 50 d./month	21	31
Owned	28	41
	68	100

NOTE: An unskilled labourer may earn 4 d./day, a mason 6–8 d./day, a *mokhazni* 250 d./month, a teacher (primary school) 500 d./month.

Table 11. *Relation of population to housing
in the town quarter*

No. of people/room	No. of households	Percentage of total
0–1	23	34
1 1–2	27	40
2 1–3	13	19
3 1–4	4	6
4 1–5	1	2
Total	68	100

minimum of security, being a focus of lineage solidarity. The professional northerners, being mobile, do not put down roots; as wage-earners they can be sure of being able to pay rent regularly, and kinship is not their chief source of security.

Of the spouses of family heads, a considerable proportion are local women. Apart from this bias, the proportions of the various regional components are similar to the pattern observed for men, with slightly fewer from the north. Several soldiers' wives come from Marrakech where one of the battalions now in Akhdar was recently stationed. Only two men who are still counted as members of households had emigrated to Algeria, but many more – whole families – left the town permanently when the Algero-Moroccan war broke out. Many of these emigrants were Algerian in origin, and several of the inhabitants of the quarter are of Algerian parentage.

Household composition

The birth rate is high throughout Morocco. Yet the 1961–3 census, 'Résultats de l'enquête à objectifs multiples', gives the average household size as 5·1 in urban centres (this includes *bidonvilles* where households are usually considerably smaller than in the town proper) and 4·9 people in rural areas.[1] These figures signify appalling rates of child mortality.

I have mentioned that the majority of households in Aghzim comprise only nuclear families. There is little sign of extended family

[1] 'Résultats de l'Enquête' (1964), 49 and 133. For an illuminating discussion of the significance of the extended family in an analogous context of progressive stratification within hamlet communities see 'Arab villages in Israel', by H. Rosenfeld in *American Anthropologist* (August 1968), 734–9.

arrangements. There is only one family which includes collateral kin and that belongs to a widow who fosters her mother's sister's son. This exclusivity restricts the number of people to a household. In Aghzim, 50% households have 1–4 members, 35·2% are in the 5–8 range and the remaining 14·8% consist of more than 8 people. This gives an average household size of 4·6 people.

In the town Akhdar, on the other hand, the average household size is 6·3, much larger than the Aghzim figure, in spite of the large number of young single men who have come to Akhdar as technicians or teachers; many of the houses contain a heterogeneous assortment of kin and even lodgers. The greater size of town households, coincident with their more concentrated distribution, must clearly lead to a style of domestic relations, and social relations in general, which sharply diverges from the rural one which is based on ascription.

In the town quarter only 34% of the households are accommodated in a number of rooms greater than the number of inhabitants. In 66% a person can rarely be alone, and in 27% there are more than two people to a room. In contrast to this situation, 50% of the houses in the *ksar* have less than one inhabitant to a room and only 8% more than two. The size of the household is not limited by shortage of housing, then, but by other social factors which do not operate in the town. They are associated with the fact that, in the *ksar*, the occupants of a house are members of a corporation with property rights. This group identity, with its accompanying obligations of mutual help, composes their most important resource since they have no skills by which they might earn a regular wage.

I have commented above on the fact that house-owning seems part of a rural-Berber cultural pattern, indicating the continuing usefulness of agnatic solidarity. Important also is the fact that to own a house is to be credit-worthy. As far as grocers and other suppliers are concerned, it is a risk to give goods on credit to irregular earners. A man with a house is another matter. It can be sold by its owner to pay debts, or appropriated by his creditor. All the widows who live alone own their houses. By this means they get credit until they can sell their spun yarn or carpets to pay off debts, or collect the proceeds of the harvest, if they own a plot or two.

The significance of the extended household in the 'ksour' and in Akhdar town

The stereotyped association, dear to many students of 'modernisation', of the large extended household with 'traditional'/rural social organisation, and the small nuclear household with the 'modern'/urban scene does not hold water in the case of the Middle Atlas (nor in many others) and deserves generally to be regarded with suspicion.

In the *ksar* Aghzim the small nuclear family was the rule to the extent of 72%, with an average household size of 4·6. Where extended households exist they are the result of complex social processes among which we must count the evolution of new forms of social stratification. They cannot be attributed merely to 'traditionalism', for, as I have remarked above (Chapter 1), even before the Protectorate the nuclear family seems to have been the norm in rural areas. In Aghzim and Bentaleb in 1971, there was only one married man living in the same household as his father, out of a total of 110 households. However, three rich men evidently intended to establish extended households, and had built enormous houses, so that (my informants said) if the sons quarrelled they could live at opposite ends of the house, and the agnatic group would survive. I interpret this behaviour as the first stage in the process of fission from the parent lineage, stimulated by the desire of a rich family to prevent the demands of kin from stemming the tendency to capital accumulation and social mobility which is manifest in all their behaviour.[1] To achieve an independent economic and political identity it is essential to establish a strong, autonomous agnatic group whose members are closely bound by their common residence, sense of exclusivity and need to co-operate.

This analysis is confirmed by the fact that the only extended households (two) I came across in the countryside had been set up when a family quarrelled with agnates and left them to start a new village in another area. Although rich families break away to escape the demands of their poorer kin, i.e. in order to act according to the tenets of the market economy, and poorer rural families do so in order to escape the control of agnates, the mechanisms are the same in both cases. In J. Goody's terms, the group established is part of a 'linear series' and not, like the migrant groups who maintain their shared political and economic identity, part of a 'merging series'.[2]

In the town, Akhdar, there was only one married son living in his father's house, out of a sample of sixty-eight households. He was there

---

[1] See Rosenfeld, *loc. cit.*   [2] J. Goody (1966).

only temporarily, having lost his job. But the average household size was 6·3 and only 43% of houses contained solely nuclear families. How is it then that town households contained more people and a greater range of kin than *ksar* ones? The majority of the kin were either school-age boys who lived with relatives in order to attend the only secondary school in the district; or women, the divorced or widowed sisters, daughters or mothers of salaried employees, who were better able to support them than their other relatives. This pattern may be a relatively recent one, for the number of salaried jobs available to Moroccans increased conspicuously only after Independence. The increase was due partly to the departure of French administrators, and partly to new forms of government intervention e.g. a policy of mass primary education.

A quarter of all households in the sample contained foster-children, generally girls who were maids-of-all-work. Many of them were kin of their foster-parents, for the fostering of children is another means by which geographically separated kin share resources and keep in touch.

The few attempts I came across in the town to set up extended households ended in explosive fission, for the group is not kept together by the need to stave off demands from poorer kin. In the households which included only the couple and the mother of the husband the crisis ended in her expulsion, but it was the young couple which left if the extended household was controlled by the father of the husband. In every case the split was blamed on quarrels between female affines, and there seemed to be every justification for this claim. However, it is clear that the interests of agnatic solidarity are classically served by avoiding an open clash between father and son, whatever the level of repressed conflict, whereas the women risk nothing by giving full expression to the tensions which they experience.

In all the cases I knew the parents were of rural origin and may be suspected of attempting to follow the pattern typical of rich *ksar* families which I have described above. However the son, and in two cases the wife, had received a Western education, and rationalised the split by expressing their preference for a 'modern' i.e. 'Western' conjugal household. Yet this is the most common type of Moroccan household, which might lead us to attribute their split to structural causes rather than to eccentric preference. Among these causes are the economic and social independence of the son from his father, and his reluctance to submit to the latter's control, even if he continues, on the ideological level, to regard the father's authority as paramount.

In fact, Western models of conjugal and family *behaviour* (as distinct from family forms such as the nuclear family which have been 'independently invented' in many parts of the world, including Western Europe and Morocco) have touched only a small section of the population, which could be labelled the Westernised professional élite, who are generally of city origin. Given the fact that family affairs are run by women who are barely touched by Western culture, it could scarcely be otherwise. As Germaine Tillion writes apropos of Algeria: '...les révolutions passent, tandis que les grand'mères et les vieilles tantes sont éternelles. Et les moeurs marchant moins vite que la politique, ce sont elles qui continuent à faire un nombre important de mariages.'[1]

Young modernists still expect to exercise considerable domestic authority. They deplore the difficulties of making a love match *à la Européenne*, because women are secluded and 'backward'. Yet they see to it that their own sisters are secluded and don't go to school. That is where girls learn to be flighty and insubordinate.

Many migrants, even the 'modernists', continue to be part of an extended family whatever their domestic arrangements. This is a group based on the children of one man who live in separate households but continue to have economic interests in common. The female agnates and affines co-operate to supply labour resources where they are lacking, and to prepare feasts and family rituals. The extended family in the town reflects a process of fusion in a hostile environment. The extended household in the *ksar* represents a process of fission in a too demanding one.

In the case of Arabised town-dwellers, the process of fission continues still further, stimulated by social mobility, as we have seen in the unsuccessful attempts to establish extended households. Agnatic relationships are reduced to their separate father–son components. A son may send his father half of his salary but maintain links only with selected siblings. When it is possible to ignore kinship bonds, lineage organisation can be considered to be on its last legs, already overshadowed by other principles of social structure.

[1] G. Tillion (1964), 127.

5
The cultural corollary: education and social stratification

The content and distribution of modern education in the Akhdar region prevent the majority of Akhdaris from becoming socially mobile. This is especially true in the case of women for the value system which reserves the 'public sphere' for men and excludes women from it also requires the training of women to be entirely domestic so that they are unemployable and economically dependent. They do not acquire a grasp of the principles on which is based the culture from which Moroccan education is derived. Their behaviour continues to be dictated by the ascribed status they occupy.

I was fortunate to be able to visit most of the schools in the administrative district of Akhdar. It will be useful to divide the social universe into the familiar categories of rural, urban, meaning Akhdar, semi-urban, meaning the *ksour* situated within 5 kilometres of Akhdar and closely integrated with it economically. The majority of the inhabitants of these *ksour* depend for their livelihood either on wage-labour, or on a combination of agricultural production and sporadic employment in the town. The first category comprises the rural *ksour* beyond the five-kilometre limit, whose economy may be considered almost entirely agricultural. Urban culture barely impinges on these villages. For them, the town represents a market for produce and a source of consumer goods, but not of behavioural models.

The main features of education in the area under study, which in this respect appears to be typical of Morocco as a whole, are these:

1. School attendance falls off drastically as the distance from the town increases.

2. Educational facilities in Akhdar, as far as the supply of building equipment and qualified teachers goes, are far superior to those in the countryside.

3. The curricula laid down by the Ministry of Education, which are meticulously followed by the teachers, bear little relation to the experience of Moroccan children in any other than a sophisticated urban bourgeois environment strongly influenced by French culture.

4. The number of girls attending primary school is nowhere more

73

than a third of the number of boys and is negligible at a higher level. The tendency for the education of girls to be disregarded is more marked as the distance from the town increases.

I will discuss the nature, possible causes, and implications of these facts in turn, as they relate to each other and to other aspects of the culture of Akhdar. I will stress particularly the way in which education has become a vehicle of the trend towards more striking and irreversible social inequalities.

Rural ambivalence to education

In a rural *ksar*, the government school is a focus of ambivalent feelings. It acts at once as the symbol of outside interference in village affairs, and so provokes hostility, and as the road to the prosperous world of the literate. On the one hand it evokes images of the redoubtable *Makhzen*, whose other manifestations are the policeman and the tax-collector; or the surveyor who heralds the take-over of tribal land, for sale to private individuals or for government building. The villagers of Aghzim stoned these personae, saying that they had not been asked whether they wanted to allocate ancestral property to the building of a school, public oven, or mosque, which, although intended for their benefit, would not be subject to their control. The authorities solved the problem by calling a 'democratic assembly of the elders', who voted in favour of the installations. It subsequently appeared that these elders had been mostly called from remote villages, which normally had nothing to do with Aghzim. Such incidents cannot dispose the villagers favourably to education, seen as an activity promoted by these same authorities.

On the other hand, the peasant has experienced a deterioration of his standard of living which, leaving aside the question of new wants, has corroded his sense of self-sufficiency. The annexation of tribal land over the past century, the development of a 'modern sector', has reduced the competitiveness of the peasant's products on the national market, and lowered their price relative to other consumption goods. Meanwhile, taxes on staple foods such as sugar have made the smallholder's budget impossible to balance. He is forced to recognise, on every visit to Akhdar, that he is on the bottom rung of the social ladder. Not only is he poorer than anyone else, but his social (i.e. cultural) personality has a negative value in the urban scene. He loses out in every transaction with the urban bureaucracy and communication is carried on through media (Arabic, writing, arithmetic) over

74

which he has no control. On the contrary it is clear that the governmental system is so organised that it will extend its control over a progressively larger area of his own life. Gone are the days of armed *siba*. It is by educating his children that he can improve both his own and their bargaining position vis-à-vis this culture.

So it was that villages without a school, such as two in the area of Umlil, sent a delegation of elders to the *caid*, asking that the Inspector of Schools for the Province come to witness that they could mobilise more than thirty children, the minimum required to justify starting a new school. And the men of the village supplied the labour for its construction. But hostility is deeply rooted. The history of rural schools is often tumultuous. I saw several whose windows had been wrecked by local adolescents. In a village near Umlil the teacher had been driven out, because they said he had beaten the children so severely that they refused to go to school. In another village of 550 inhabitants near Youmi, the school attendance had shrunk to twelve children, and the *sheikh* sent for the Inspector to discuss the lack of enthusiasm.

Teachers

The teacher must bear the brunt of the fear that the school may turn out to be the thin end of the wedge of authoritarian intervention. His position is sensitive for other reasons, one of the chief being that he epitomises the privileged outsider from the north. Because the Marrakshi, western coast and Fez–Meknes region have been the focus of commercial and industrial activity, their educational development is also far advanced relative to the southern half of the country. It is from these regions that most of the teachers come.

The relationship between *ksar*-people and teachers is further complicated by the subjective situation of the teacher. Teachers are among the most sophisticated and highest-paid civil servants in the Akhdar area. They take great pains to dress impeccably *à la Européenne*, and tend to keep the company of other teachers. It seems to them the corollary of their social status that they should enjoy the benefits of town life, and from time to time they show a fine bourgeois contempt for the uncouth villagers. However only *titulaires*, or those who have been enrolled as pensionable civil servants after passing a series of examinations over a number of years, have a choice of posting, or have accumulated a nest-egg and connections which are significant enough for them to obtain a position in a town.

On the whole, it is the younger and less qualified teachers who are posted to remote *ksar* schools. This is a great blow for an ambitious youngster who prides himself on his urbane image. He is probably unmarried, which makes life in a *ksar* a net of practical problems since domestic organisation is so labour-intensive. Most teachers appear to keep themselves to themselves, but this is difficult in a situation of practical dependence for domestic help on the people of the *ksar*. One teacher lived in Tislit, 4 kilometres away from the school which had been built at the midpoint between two *ksour*. He asked especially that a house be built for him beside the school, a striking request, considering the currency of fears of darkness and isolation.

In the semi-urban context, the villagers who are accustomed to working for wages may even consider themselves competitive on the labour market with the 'foreign' teacher. One teacher put the situation thus: '*Ksar*-people don't like teachers. They say they are paid a lot of money for a little work, and at the expense of the villagers. Teachers are all strangers. A villager says, "Why should he come from Meknes or Rabat or wherever and get a well-paid job here in my *bled*, where there is no job for me?" He will say this even if he is untrained. Teachers withdraw completely, each living for himself alone. They are afraid of the demands that poor people make on them if they are friendly.' This teacher's acquaintances in the *ksar* where he lived were the local *mokhazni*, the postman, and the other teachers.

Teachers expect to be treated in a particular way because they are outsiders. The degree of estrangement between teacher and population is radically reduced when the teacher is *mul-l-bled*.[1] Although teachers are encouraged to visit the homes of the children they teach, the only ones who did so were those with *mul-l-bled* 'insider' status. In these circumstances the teacher may become confidant, arbitrator and intermediary with the bureaucratic authorities. I have often heard teachers state that they hoped eventually to return to their natal village to teach if it proved too difficult to find a town job. Their distrust of outsiders is essentially the same as that of the *ksar*-people for most of them are of peasant origin with loyalties to their own village.

---

[1] *Mul-l-bled* (lit. owner of the land). This description applies only to people who are members of local communities by virtue of their rights in land.

The cultural corollary

Practical objections to education

Passing from the more diffuse antipathy to schools in the rural areas, which seems to arise out of uncertainty as to their political meaning, I wish to discuss the opposition to education on practical grounds.

When rural Berbers discuss education, they are referring only to the education of boys; education of girls is beside the point. If questioned about it, they express the view that the same arguments which prompt them to doubt the value of education for boys become incontrovertible in the case of girls. They amount basically to this: 'Education in the skills of another culture unfits peasants for their future roles! It is possible that men may be forced to earn a living in a different way, but girls? What can a girl learn out of books about being a housekeeper and mother, only to be hungry for unseemly clothes and expensive foreign goods.' As for their sons, the parents claim that they will refuse to farm just when their parents' strength is failing. They will leave the village, attracted by the glittering town glimpsed in their lessons, will be unable to find work and fall into bad ways.

Mobility in the educational system

These beliefs are held all the more tenaciously where the rate of social mobility is low. In the countryside, i.e. in *ksour* more than 5 kilometres from Akhdar, the probability that a man would replace his father as household head, or begin farming on his own account, was fairly high until the Second World War, and still today it is much higher than in the semi-urban *ksour*.[1] Here a family holding is not a viable economic unit, and its owner must have a supplementary source of income. The range of possible occupations is much greater than in the rural *ksour*. The most lucrative are those offered within bureaucratic *Makhzen* institutions. The headmaster of one school moaned 'Everyone wants his son to be a *petit fonctionnaire*, and that is his only interest in education.' However, the French mining companies also hold out promise to those able to acquire a technical training. So education and the army remain the main channels of social mobility. Yet here it soon becomes clear that the channels are more open to some than to others.

The disillusion brought about by poverty and lack of opportunity appears later in semi-urban and town schools than in rural ones. This

---

[1] One consequence of the return of Berbers from the French army, which used them to fight in World War II and in Indo-China, was the spread of dissatisfaction with traditional rural life.

is one index of the greater social mobility offered to pupils of the former through education. In the former, boys drop out in their second or third year at college (secondary school) ostensibly because their parents cannot afford the termly fee of 12 *drahem* and want their sons to bring in a wage. The real reason appears to be generally that, given the lack of powerful connections, the prospects of employment for such boys are hardly better after six years of secondary school than after three. In contrast, rich men will often pay for their married 25-year-old sons to be kept on in college, on a strictly illegal basis, because for them it is a definite asset. The training can be put to good use.

No marks for rural education

The odds of mobility within the educational system are impressively weighted against rural children. In 1970, the proportion of the candidates from rural schools in the Akhdar *cercle* who passed their *Certificat d'Études Primaires* ranged between 0% and 4%. In semi-urban schools the proportion rose to 10–20%, and in Akhdar it was 50%. These figures probably reflect quite accurately the availability of secondary education to the different categories of the population, and the relative accessibility to them of salaried employment and administrative positions.

The high failure rate in rural *ksour* can probably be attributed to:

1. The fact that the teachers are less qualified, and to their isolation from stimuli whether originating in the town or local population, and to low morale. The conditions in which they must teach are often discouraging. Theoretically there should be five levels or *classes* in the primary school. In the average *ksar* school there are often only one or two rooms. The teacher divides the class into two, and sets one half to read 'silently' (muttering) or solve problems, while he instructs the other half *à haute voix*. Since each group comprises children of various ages and levels, it is almost impossible for a child to progress systematically from Level 1 to Level 5, for he is always being taught together with those formally below him.

2. Learning conditions do not permit the child to work his way systematically through a curriculum.

3. In addition to the rural parents' view that education is compatible with their child's fulfilment of his *future* role, and partly as a consequence of this view, a child's present roles, domestic and economic, prevent him from attending school except on a sporadic basis.

The cultural corollary

A seven- to fifteen-year-old girl or boy makes an admirable and indispensable shepherd. One teacher told me how, in the early years of compulsory primary schooling, his father had sent a sheep and several cones of sugar to the Schools Inspector, so that his eldest son should be 'exempted' from going to school. In later years, the second son was similarly engaged in herding his father's flocks when the *mokhazni* arrived, to escort him forcibly to school. Peasants emphasise that the long training in agricultural traditions is a continuous one, and a boy who has missed some years finds it hard to catch up.

It is during the months of the maize harvest, in particular, when the older boys are cutting the stalks, and the younger ones stripping the cobs, that the priority of economic necessity over education becomes apparent. Barely half the class comes to school. Another deterrent is the sheer physical difficulty of getting there. Small children from distant *ksour* need to make a daily march to school of several kilometres. During the bitter winter months when the snow sometimes lies 1 metre deep, they stay at home, for the paths are blocked and their clothing is inadequate to protect them from the cold. In spring the roads are often flooded. Their school year is reduced to four months, October, November, May and June. October is maize harvest, June is wheat harvest. School can hardly play a prominent role in their lives.

The contrast with the town schools, where one teacher described the 97% attendance record of her class as 'below normal', is staggering.

4. An unsuitable curriculum; the most apt description of the attitude towards the school of both adults and children in rural and semi-rural, and to a lesser extent even urban environments, is 'diffident' or even 'uninterested'. The rigidity and inappropriateness of the educational programme seems to be the most important reason for this diffidence.

Although vast modifications have been made in the programme, its form as well as its content still correspond to the French model, to a remarkable degree. The fact that secondary schools are 90% staffed by French teachers and *co-opérants* (young graduates who teach instead of doing military service) is not irrelevant to the contortions of the primary curriculum. To begin with, nearly a third of schooltime from the third primary year onwards is devoted to the learning of French. Mathematics at this stage is also taught in French, which constitutes an obstacle for those not yet familiar with the language.[1] The French

---

[1] Before Independence, the fourth-year primary school curriculum consisted of twenty hours' French teaching, ten hours in Arabic. After Independence this proportion was changed to fifteen hours in each language. Madani Ali (1963).

texts concern Marcel and Denise, their *pique-nique, lits* and *lavabos*, none of which a rural child has ever seen, and about which a 'semi-urban' child has only a mild curiosity. The classroom décor depicts little fair-haired girls cuddling kittens, riding in trams or smiling in advertisements for toothpaste. The monotony is sometimes relieved by scenes of the Swiss Alps and the occasional map of Morocco. The other main item of classroom equipment, which is found in even the most remote school, is a 'museum'. For children whose consciousness is impressed with the scarcity of objects and their depreciation with age, such an institution has little meaning. This conclusion is borne out by the fact that a school museum always comprises imported plastic bric-à-brac, which has no domestic use. Far from serving to increase awareness of the significance and beauty of local artifacts, the museum becomes an arbitrary collection of lost property oddities.

Arabic

The greater part of the first three years at school is taken up in the learning of classical Arabic (language, script and arithmetic). The language is quite different from colloquial Moroccan Arabic, the relationship it bears resembling that of Latin to Italian. It is inevitably easier for Arabic-speakers than for Berbers to learn, although, once the initial disincentives have been overcome, Berbers tend to write more correct Arabic for they do not run the risk of confusion with their mother tongue.

Rural children are encouraged in the effort by their parents who regard Arabic as a sacred language, and its script is imbued with *baraka*. They ask their children to recite verses learnt at school and show their notebooks to guests. Rural villagers could hardly be expected to show the same enthusiasm for French, with which they are unfamiliar, and which they have experienced as the language of war and repression, even if its functions have become more varied on the tongues of Moroccans.

Taken at one extreme, then, the definition of education for a rural parent is the acquisition of skills (including languages) and concepts relevant to a culture other than his own. Moreover, the relation of these cultures to himself derives from a premise of hegemony which he does not accept. He has, so far and in the short run, viable alternatives. The semi-urban population has not, and must make a living within the terms imposed by the dominant culture. But even here there is little reason for small boys to show enthusiasm for school. Nothing in their everyday and immediate experience can find expression in literary Arabic, still less in French. That access to these skills is mediated by a controlling political authority is a fact of which Berbers especially are conscious, since they regard that authority as alien to their own interests. Townspeople feel this less keenly; for them the mastery of Arabic and, even more, of French has a visible pay-off in terms of status. For example, nearly all government officials speak French. The school curriculum is not so remote from experienced reality. They live in a world where cars, travel, commerce, the bank, the post-office, the cinema, do have a significance for which analogies can be found in the school text-books – which, however, make no mention of the Berber's mud-forts and mountains.

Koranic schools

The highest common factor of education throughout Morocco is the *madrassa* or Koranic school, which all children are obliged to attend for at least a year prior to their entry to primary school, and which often offers the only education which a peasant receives.

In Akhdar there is only one school, attended by about 150 children between the ages of four and seven. They are taught the rudiments of writing and arithmetic in Arabic, but spend most of their school hours learning to recite verses of the Koran. Their teachers are three *fuqaha* who receive government salaries. The children's parents pay 2 *drahem* a week for each child.

Every mosque is a centre of learning. The *fqih* at Aghzim has only ten to fifteen small pupils, whose parents make him an annual gift of grain, besides periodic *sadaqa* (alms) of *cous cous* or eggs. The mosque school is viewed as a kind of kindergarten, relieving the mother of the care of some of her children for several hours a day. It is also important as a centre of discipline. One father said of his son: 'The *fqih* will beat him if he disobeys or forgets his slate, and make him into a good Muslim.' This is another example of the belief, manifest in the institution of fostering, that a child is best socialised by a non-parent for certain periods of his life. People say, 'We are too indulgent with our own children.'

Many aspects of Koranic teaching, especially the authoritarian manner of the *fqih*, have crept into the style of primary school teachers. A teacher shouts his lesson, delivering ridicule and blows freely. The pace of recitation and fluency in reading Arabic are highly

81

valued, with the result that neither performer nor listeners can grasp the sense of the text.

Koranic school is, not unexpectedly, more highly valued in rural areas than in the town. To bring up your children as good Muslims is a religious duty, and earns you merit, or *a'ajr* – grace in heaven. But those who like to keep up with the times feel that opportunities are wanting for the traditional Muslim scholar.

Aziz the 'fqih'

Aziz, a *fqih* now living in Akhdar, was born in Casablanca. His father, a poor blacksmith, took him at the age of four to be a pupil in a mosque. Here he stayed for fourteen years, eventually qualifying to teach or to take charge of a mosque. He ate and slept at the mosque, but since at that time *tolba* (Koranic scholars) only got two pieces of bread a day, he used to go home for a meal every day. (He put down the poverty of the mosque to French discouragement of Islam, remarking that *tolba* live very comfortably now.)

Since he was trained only to teach the Koran, he was unable to find work in Casablanca. For a time he travelled around, visiting different *zawiat* (communities of religious scholars, under a learned teacher, or settled at the site of a saint's tomb or *saleh*). Finally he came to live in Akhdar, where he ran a small bookshop for an absentee owner, and on Sundays read the Koran to an admiring audience in the *suq*. He was disillusioned and cynical. 'What might I have achieved if I had spent fourteen years at a French school? But when I was young only the well-to-do sent their children to the new schools. The ignorant sent theirs to the mosque.' He comforted himself with the thought that a *fqih* takes all his family with him to heaven. He expected this to happen independently of the kind of life he might lead. His life had indeed taken a worldly turn. Sighing 'C'est le temps qui change', he remarked that he didn't go to the mosque more than twice a year – on religious feast-days – and that he didn't pray. He spends his evenings playing cards and drinking with his friends, and his neighbours laugh about the fact that he has married a local dancer.

Aziz is in some respects typical of many *fuqaha*, who have found it more convenient to 'be as other men are' and find a niche in the modern economy rather than seek to fulfil a faded religious vocation. There are far fewer mosques than there are *fuqaha* to run them, and popular faith in the *baraka* of such men has suffered a serious decline, especially in the towns, with a corresponding reduction in

82

material support. Many scholars have found jobs as accountants and clerks, in government and commerce, making use of their training in Arabic; others are salaried teachers in government *madrassat*.

Education of women

In the Province to which Akhdar belongs, 8% of girls of primary school age are at school. Akhdar provides the majority of these girl pupils, for it could be said of the southern half of the province that no girls at all go to school there. In the rural schools there is on the average one girl to four boys, but this proportion rises to one in three for semi-urban and urban schools. The proportion of girls to boys in the first year of secondary school (*classe d'observation*) is one to five; there is a sharp fall in the number of girls attending college after the first year relative to boys (one to seven) and only a negligible proportion carry on after the *Certificat d'Études Secondaires*, which is taken in the fourth year.

Rural Berbers laugh when asked why their daughters don't go to school. There are two main styles of response. The first emphasises that education is irrelevant to the efficient performance in the roles of wife and mother, and even of daughter; she makes bread, she cooks, she carries children on her back. There is no point in a girl's remaining at school if her mother needs her help in these tasks at home. The second is a proud statement of fact, 'We don't send our girls to school.' It is the Berber equivalent of seclusion, of preserving family honour intact. Schools are seen as a corrupting influence, giving access to the public sphere, 'the market place'.

If an urban bourgeois took part in the conversation, he would present no counter-arguments to these assertions. Education, in semi-urban and urban environments, is considered proper for women only if it does not disturb traditional relationships – '*ta-jn, ta-ib, ta-rkib ulad*' (she kneads bread, she cooks; she carries children on her back). But for modernist townsmen, a literate wife is a status symbol. One man used to boast that he and his wife had been to Koranic school together and that she helped him in his work, but all his neighbours knew that she was a peasant lass who knew only Berber, and was afraid to go to the *hammam* because she wouldn't know what to do there. Her home village had no such amenities. Education will push up a girl's bride-price, or dower, because she will know how to keep 'a modern home', how to knit and sew and pay attention to *vitamines*; how to count money, write letters, tell the time, and deal with medical prescriptions. There its usefulness ends. Most 'modernist' parents withdraw their daughters from school once they have finished the primary course. 'Now you can write a letter, that's enough' was the reported comment of many fathers.

The *Union Nationale de Femmes Marocaines* runs a number of *foyers* based on the more populous towns of the region. There is one in the district of Akhdar, one at Tislit and one at Youmi. They provide schooling in the main subjects taught at primary school with the addition of needlework and housecraft. At the post-primary level, girls learn more elaborate techniques in these fields, and produce embroidery and carpets which are sold through the U.N.F.M. *co-opérative* which provides the materials, and has a membership of older women who generally work in their homes. The *monitrices* of these centres attributed their popularity to the fact that many parents preferred their daughters to have an education which stressed homemaking rather than academic or professional pursuits, and were anxious that their nubile daughters should not attend the college which was mixed, and regarded by many as a den of vice. Older girls at the *foyer* were 'filling in time' until they got married. A few married women attended the *foyer* somewhat irregularly. All of them had children.

Contradictions: attitudes of men

The attitudes of educated townsmen, theoretically favourable to the education of women, are in blatant contrast with their practice, which reduces it to a minimum. The idea of reducing the economic and political dependence of women on their husbands, fathers or brothers seems to present an intolerable threat to the status quo.

One teacher *J*, aged twenty-six, after attributing the high divorce rate to the ignorance of women, stated that he wanted to make a love match, but thought he would never realise his ideal because women were so 'backward' in Morocco. On a visit to France he had almost decided to marry a French girl, but his parents, horrified by the idea, cabled him to come home. He returned immediately.

It then appeared that when, in the past, he has been posted to remote villages, he had always been accompanied by one of his sisters. He boasted that he had taught her to cook to perfection, 'so that she will be more useful to her husband'. However, none of his three sisters had ever been to school. I asked whether he didn't think that she, like himself, might derive satisfaction from book-learning. At this point he began vehemently to exclaim that educated women did not care for their children (although the examples in Akhdar strikingly belie this contention – as he admitted), that education was a guarantee that a girl would lose her virginity before marriage, that men with educated wives were always quarrelling with them, and that their wives were always wanting to 'go out' which in his view was tantamount to infidelity.

D, aged thirty-five, an educated man of Akhdar, claimed that marriages in Morocco were unsatisfactory because women were lazy and ignorant, and a man found the home atmosphere incompatible with his own interests. He was soon bored and angry. He was however opposed to education for women which conjured up in his mind associations of women smoking, of which he disapproved. 'Books and outside work are for men. Women were made for love.' His own wife was secluded but his small daughters went to primary school.

A, aged twenty-nine, a teacher who had recently moved to the region of Tamat, compared it unfavourably with the more rural village of Omar where he and his wife had been for eight years. The trouble with the new community was that it was composed of miners who had more ready cash available than their peasant counterparts, and this stimulated the greed for gold of their womenfolk, who entered into frenzied competition with each other. They threatened their husbands that they would leave if they could not have this bracelet or that *Iwiza* (gold coin which women wear on beads as a necklace and accumulate in whole chains). The teacher concluded angrily 'If they want gold, they should earn the money themselves. But women are not educated enough to work, and their ignorance is at the root of their wanting gold in the first place. They don't know how to spend money wisely.'

In a later discussion of the spheres of men and women this same man said that the woman's world extended up to the threshold and the man's was the sphere beyond, stating 'If my wife stepped over the threshold without my permission I would divorce her.' It is difficult to reconcile this attitude with his challenge to women to earn their own living.

Aspirations of women

Girls who as eldest sisters in a numerous family are taken away from school to help with household work feel a keen resentment. The excitement of meeting other children, of being active on their own account rather than serving others, seems to make school an enjoyable experience for girls, at least in the early years. But a girl is never allowed to forget that her school life is circumstantial, and that her real role is at home, making bread, washing up and looking after small siblings. Because of the lack of a special room for study, distracted by the activities around them, children are unable to do any homework. Some parents issue mild rebukes to their sons, but for girls study at home is unthought of. School for them is merely an interlude in the round of chores.

Most Moroccan girls do not expect the monotonous round to be broken by a change of activity, but they hope for a change of scene. They concoct fantasies about travelling to the big cities – Fez, Casablanca – or to France. They look forward to marrying, because this means that they will visit new parts of the country; – and when they are married they take every opportunity to visit their kin, or to take their children to spend the three months of summer with a rich relative in a distant town. Women and girls begin discussing where they will go in the summer before winter has set in. Few girls expect to shape their lives by their own efforts, but most intend to exploit as fully as possible the variety of stimuli offered within the limits of their network of kinship and affinity.

Secondary education

Girls who are educated to secondary school level are exceptional and are usually second and/or fourth in the birth order of girls, being relieved of most of the housework by the sister above. Their prospects are of three kinds: a girl can be a teacher, a nurse or a clerk. Every single girl in a class of thirty twelve-year-olds in Akhdar expressed the desire to be either a teacher or a headmistress. The choice was in a sense arbitrary since this is the only woman's profession they were familiar with, and suggests that they did not take a career to be a serious possibility. In the Akhdar area there is only one secondary school so that the possibility of many rural girls attending it is ruled out. A few girls from *ksour* Aghzim, Bentaleb, Ceima, Daoud, Elkbir and Fssa, attend, and parents from the more remote *ksour* have been known to rent a house in Akhdar during the school terms so that a daughter could attend the college. A town family then best illuminates the pattern of girls' education.

Hassan was a small trader of modest means. He was about fifteen years older than his wife, Fatima, who came from the same town as he did. The family had been in Akhdar for ten years, and comprised the parents and eight children, Zohor (girl aged 16), *B* (girl aged 14½),

C (girl aged 13), *D* (girl aged 10), *E* (girl aged 6), *F* (boy-twin aged 6), *G* (boy aged 4), *H* (girl aged 2). When Zohor had completed primary school, where she was very successful, her father took her away to help look after her small siblings. Then she spent a year walking 3 kilometres and back twice a day to learn embroidery and knitting and carpet-weaving at the workshop of a community of French nuns who lived in Aghzim. During winter the trek was too much for her and she gave it up. Although she had deep regrets and envied her sisters, she accepted her fate with equanimity as the logical one. Education was merely a frill to real life and hardly worth the rigours of a long walk through deep snow. All her energies were now applied to earning money at home, knitting and embroidering for casual clients who heard that she could sew. She had saved, after three years, enough to buy a treadle-machine. She wanted to be trained as a seamstress but could not find a woman to teach her, since most tailors are men and work in the open market-place, and it was impossible to learn under those conditions – '*hashuma!*' she said (shame!) It was a classic example of the way in which women are excluded from the market economy.

Her academic ambitions and resentment were displaced on to her younger sisters; the family had held out to send *B* to college, although it meant that she had to spend an extra year in primary school, having failed to obtain the *Certificat d'Études Primaires*. After the first year spent at this mixed school, it was decided that *B* should go to a military boarding school 100 kilometres away, for which she was eligible because her father's brother was a soldier. She saw herself as a teacher but Zohor wanted her to be a nurse. The importance attached to her education must have been considerable if her parents were ready to send her away, for her mother would cry if any of her children spent a night in hospital, and had often expressed surprise that my parents were prepared for me to live so far away. This emphasis on *B*'s education is perhaps related to the fact that as the children grew older their maintenance promised to become a real problem and the two boys would be unable to earn their living for another twelve years at least. Although *C* was successful at school she was more frequently called on to perform domestic tasks than *B* or *D*, and while there was humorous discussion of *D*'s studious tendencies and potential career as a teacher, no such remarks were made about *C*. *E*'s education was completely neglected but *F* went every day to the *madrassa*, even during the summer holidays 'so that he doesn't forget'.

The only acceptable paid work for women falls within the modern sector for which there is a high educational qualification, which, as we have seen, is very difficult for girls to obtain.

Educated women are often very feminist. Rabia, a young and brilliant teacher, often complained that she could not go to any man's office to arrange some bureaucratic matter without him exclaiming that it was a rare event to meet an educated girl and – the inevitable sequel – that he was bored with his wife who knew only how to cook and bear children, and why didn't she come and have tea with him one day. She took a sceptical view, remarking that at training college she had good friends among men, who valued being able to talk to educated women but would never dream of marrying one of the species. 'They want someone who will be content to sit at home and be their servant. They don't want any *contestation*. If a man who was late home every night were to claim to his uneducated wife that he had been "to a meeting", she would accept the explanation. An educated woman, herself accustomed to attending meetings, would look at her watch and say "Five hours at a meeting? There's something fishy about that."' Moreover she would have her own ideas about the spending of money, and would expect to be a discussant party to any project – such as the building of a house.

Rabia herself was wary of marriage and had refused several offers 'because I want to continue my studies'. In the one case where this would have been possible, her prospective husband even offering to arrange for her to go to university, she refused him because he was living with his mother and she didn't want to enter the mother-in-law triangle. Meanwhile, still intent on studying, she applied to take her *baccalauréat*, but her application arrived too late. 'Now I've missed both the cow and the camel', she wailed, revealing a certain ambivalence about the course she had chosen, for the pressures in favour of her marrying were strong. Yet educated women tend to have considerable self-esteem, and to hold out for the best bargain in marriage, the arrangements of which they conduct themselves. One, who was wooed by the mother of a tailor, refused to go and see her; 'Does she expect *me*, an educated girl, to marry *him*?'.

In 1969, the distribution of occupation of women in Akhdar educated beyond the level of *Certificat d'Études Secondaires* was as follows:

Monitrices (teaching housecraft) at U.N.F.M.   3 (1 married with children)
Nurses   6 (3 married, two with children)
Teachers   3 (5 in 1971, 2 married with children)
Notary   1 (married)

6

Religion and social stratification

I will show in this chapter how the operations of the market and the qualities appropriate to the successful entrepreneur or capitalist are legitimised by urban religion. I suggest that rural and 'proletarian' religion has the opposite tendencies, for it stresses rather the need to communicate with the Great Patron, and to placate belligerent spirits. Moreover it emphasises not the worthiness of the individual but attempts to preserve the solidarity of the segmentary unit, the *ksar*, by creating religious community among its most tenuously attached members, its women. I show, further, that women are considered intrinsically dangerous to men, and suggest that this belief corresponds to a real antagonism of interests. There is a structural conflict between the social necessity of marriage, and the superior rewards of kinship especially for women.

I mean to use religion in a general sense to refer to that sphere of action and belief where ideas of the supernatural intercept and account for the social and physical orders, introducing into each a symbolic and moral dimension. The symbolic and moral relationships brought thus into dialectic with these orders are conceived both as their cause and as their result, and supply a rationalisation for anomaly and suffering.

As in the case of Buddhism and Christianity, the generality of the statements of Islam and the vast superstructure of commentary make possible a plethora of interpretations. From such a variety of 'blueprints' (Gellner's phrase) it can be extracted that Islam has been everywhere easily syncretised with the pre-existing (spirit) beliefs and practices of actual social orders.

Nevertheless, in Akhdar there is a universal sense that if the possible solutions to a problem of explanation or moral conduct are contradictory, the prescription of Islam is definitive. Power therefore lies in the hands of those responsible for the definition of right Islamic conduct, for the definition will tend to serve their own political ends and emphasise the superiority of their culture.

Religion in the town

The towns, then, are points of reference for the Muslim community and, as such, tend to promote national unity. Yet the religious practices of the country are quite different from those in the town, while purporting to stem from the same belief-system. A Muslim in Akhdar observes the Five Pillars of Islam: he believes in one God and that Mohammed is his Prophet, prays five times a day, gives alms, fasts, and perhaps, if it is within his means, makes the pilgrimage to Mecca. If he is an artisan or even a salary-earner, he experiences prosperity as commensurate with effort. The corollary is that the more closely he carries out religious injunctions, the more he and other people will regard his prosperity as justly merited.

In Akhdar there is a close analogy between being powerful and conspicuously religious. Here too capitalistic and religious behaviour are characterised by rationality in Weber's sense. In particular, 'new men' from the countryside imitate the piety of their rich peers in the belief that they will acquire immunity from witchcraft and the evil eye of jealous people. Another factor in the mutual support of power, wealth and religion is the contention that a man who really keeps the faith risks contamination if he talks or shares meals with less worthy men. This provides a useful rationalisation for shrugging off relatives and the other parasites which batten on a prosperous man. Indeed, piety can be a precondition for 'rational' and materially rewarding capitalist behaviour

The setting of high personal standards results in the internalisation of sanctions, and many Akhdaris seem to suffer from a sense of guilt, of not having fulfilled their religious duty, of having failed.

The rich merchant's son

'No one ever keeps Ramadan completely, because to do that you should spend every moment thinking of God. Men should not talk to women, for it is bad to have sexual thoughts in Ramadan, though your desires are stronger in times of privation. You shouldn't even play music, as girls come flocking to hear it, and chatter flippantly.'

'A good Muslim should not drink, smoke or even sell things – and not only during Ramadan; you need to be a saint or a monk, but even if that's impossible, you are expected to try your hardest, and you aren't necessarily damned if you don't achieve perfection. My father is a good Muslim – he goes to the mosque, prays every day, doesn't drink or smoke, observes Ramadan strictly – but even he isn't perfect.'

Question: 'I met someone who said that Islam only forbids you to drink in excess.'

Answer: 'What is forbidden in its excess is forbidden in its minimal quantity, for God knows the weakness of men. We are forbidden even to smell drink, or to sell it to others – and that is mentioned in three places in the Koran.'

Question: 'But does that apply still today? After all, the Koran was written for people living in a different society from ours.'

Answer: 'The Koran is valid for all time – it is the word of God revealed to us through a human medium. Some people think they can get round it, like hypocrites who seem to carry out all the requirements of Islam, but miss out one – like Tartuffe. But God knows who are the real believers. People who compromise are condemned, and as for the pious types whom you see always talking to the *caids* and *super-caids* – they are just *profiteurs.*'

'I used to be religious at school, but when I was ill, I missed more than a fortnight's prayer – and now it is impossible to catch up so I don't try any more. Young men should try to be practising Muslims, but they usually fail because of the sensual character of youth. When they get married their sins are wiped away, and they start again with a clean sheet. Youth doesn't count – it is a time for learning the way of Islam, and for training.'

In spite of the fact that the speaker had a modern French education, this interview introduces many of the themes characteristic of urban religion. It is puritan, urging restraint, and suspicious of gratification. It condemns compromise with duty, and the stress on performance suggests that each person's fate depends on his own effort – no buttering up the *caid*. The written Book is crucial, and the exponents of religion are literate. Religious practice is significant only for those adults who create and become spiritually responsible for a household. Fatherhood and the propagation of one's line acquires a sacred dimension. Extramarital sex is a source of guilt.

Since women are always minors, in practice if not in law, they are ruled out of the 'spiritually responsible category'. Their religious practice is not so significant. Women appear as temptresses, reminding man of his animal nature, religiously irresponsible. The categories of people within whose culture literacy has no place, and whose life does not offer opportunity for choice between abstention and indulgence or examples of correspondence between effort and reward – which would inspire an analogously 'rational' approach to religion –

are country-people, particularly Berbers, and women. These are seen as people of little moral worth, second-rate Muslims. In this way the value-system of urban religion gives rise to, or legitimates, a system of social stratification.

In the *ksour* on the other hand, both semi-urban and rural, the central existential problem to be solved is not so much inequality, or the legitimacy of some people's relative wealth or political power, but the lack of control over the natural environment.[1] Unlike a shopkeeper or artisan, a peasant's goodwill or creditability with his neighbours can have no effect on his material success, which depends on fine weather and good health. Religion must account for, and provide some immunity from, recurrent suffering and disaster, especially illness, floods and bad harvests. These occurrences threaten his very life; the townsman is only minimally affected by them. The townsman sees life as a project, within which he makes decisions – rational, of course – and implements them, having a high degree of control over the outcome of his enterprises. Life itself, or the conditions of existence, are not perpetually at risk.

Spirits. It is arguable that the predictability characteristic of the townsman's life is a more favourable environment for the development of monotheism – the idea of a single being governing men's lives according to coherent principles – than is the uncertainty of rural life, whose vicissitudes are best conceived as resulting from the battles of contradictory beings. Moreover these ideas about the spiritual realm, with their respective emphasis on the concentration and the dispersion of powers, reflect to a certain extent the different political orders prevalent in town and country. The Berber supernatural is given over to *siba*, in which the behaviour of spirits and of men using mystical means to achieve their ends is conceived in terms of a kind of military strategy: aggression, retaliation, appeasement, protection, sabotage.

In the country, then, there is a strong belief in spirits, *jnun*, who jeopardise the success of every venture. They are creatures of arbitrary ill-temper, but they have some known traits which enable human beings to take precautions against their attacks. Sickness is usually caused by *jnun*, and many of the situations which are supposed to

---

[1] 'When one compares the life of a lower-middle-class person, particularly the urban artisan or the small trader, with the life of a peasant, it is clear that middle-class life has far less connection with nature. Consequently, dependence on magic for influencing the irrational forces of nature cannot play the same role for the urban dweller as for the farmer. Further, 'the economic foundation of the urban man's life has a far more rational essential character, viz. calculability and capacity for purposive manipulation', M. Weber (1966), 97.

make a person susceptible to attack by *jnun* are those which a Westerner, also, regards as unhealthy. For example, a person should not sleep on the bare floor, which is often damp, because the *jnun* will get him. You should not rake out the ashes of the fire at night, nor spill boiling water, because the *jnun* who live under the earth will be scalded and angry. Both these enterprises are also a focus of caution for Westerners but the hygienics argument is not in general adequate. Other beliefs operate on a more profound semantic level: the symbolic valency of redness, the darkness and light opposition, are cases in point. You should not beat a dog or cat (*jnun* live in animals; that is why their eyes shine red at night), nor tread on blood, which attracts *jnun*. You should not sleep with the lights on, for you are liable to see a *djinn* and die.

A 'live' light is a sign of *jnun*. They inhabit things which sparkle uncertainly, wavering between light and darkness, like flowing water, lightning, the stars, fire. It is possible that they are the element of darkness which disturbs the naturally steady light, for steadily shining objects such as gold discs, mirrors, candles, deflect the blow of spirits and the evil eye. Conversely, darkness attracts *jnun*. Black objects are called by euphemistic names which distract attention from their colour, e.g. the iron griddle for cooking flat bread over the coals is called *atumlilt* – 'the white one', and people always call attention to the colour of a black person, joking 'Isn't he white'. *Jnun* inhabit the world of fear and uncertainty: night, and 'thresholds', the beginning of a new phase of being, which people feel anxious about. Stepping into other people's houses, waking, the beginning of a task, or a journey, taking of food (into which a sorcerer may have infused a potion): all these hold dangers which should be neutralised by the formula '*Bi-smi-allah*' (in the name of God). If possible, the situation should be tested for favourable or unfavourable portents.

Many educated Moroccans, especially in the towns, say first 'Of course *jnun* don't exist', but then they say 'Well, the Koran mentions them'. One such told me about several personal experiences of *jnun*, who appeared to him mostly in the form of seductive women or negroes. For rural villagers too, spirit beliefs and Islam are quite compatible. God is remote and quiescent, while battles rage between *jnun* and their converse, *mala ika*, the good spirits who take possession of human beings and lift them into ecstasy in the *hedra*, or possession dance.

Women and property in Morocco

Hedra

The *hedra* is peculiar to religious brotherhoods, an institution which has had a glorious career among the Berbers. Drague in his study of Moroccan *confréries* defines them in this way: 'A hierarchical association of Muslims who, in order to be more deserving of divine grace, follow the special practice ordained by a saint, scholar, miracle worker or clairvoyant. The Sufi, by keeping to the severe discipline of the brotherhood, purifies his soul, freeing it from material bonds. In the state of ecstasy which he attains, he is in direct communication with God.'[1] As we shall see this is a life-saver for the people whom the temporal order relegates to the dung-heap.

In 1940 the seven largest brotherhoods comprised 200,000 adepts, not to speak of the sympathisers. The most important in the Akhdar is the Aissoua, whose *zawia*, or teaching and saintly community, is based at the great tomb of Sidi Ben Aissa in Meknes. The most important saint in the Akhdar region is Sidi Sherif, who is said to be the son of Sidi Ben Aissa and whose tomb lay about 2 kilometres from the *ksar* where I lived. Many maraboutic families and brotherhoods have a history of political militancy. One tribe of whom there are representatives near Akhdar declared war against the French in 1908. The *Kittaniya*, important in Fez, made a coherent attempt to oust the French in the early days of the Protectorate.

Apart from the politically disruptive potential of the brotherhoods, there is the threat that they represent to the whole structure based on Islamic orthodoxy. The charismatic *mrabten* (saints) present an alternative to the spiritual leadership of hereditary *shurfa*. The religious way, *tariqa*, aims first at purity, then at unity with God, and incorporates the use of superogatory prayers (*hizb*), that is, more than the orthodox five. All this is heresy. The *hedra* is worse.

It always takes place to celebrate a big religious feast, such as the end of Ramadan, or the commemoration of Abraham's sacrifice of Ishmael (*Aid-l-Kbir*), or the Prophet's birthday. The day after *Aid-l-Kbir*, for example, the members of the brotherhood burn candles at the tomb of Sidi Sherif and in the afternoon a huge crowd gathers covering the hill behind the tomb like so many ants. *Haratn* and Berber musicians play drums and *ghitar* (Arab oboes). A flag of red and green cloth is set on the perimeter of the dancing area, and people give money which is used to pay for the musicians and other

---

[1] G. Drague (1951), 278 (my translation).

94

expenses including those of the caretaker of the tomb who is supposed to be a descendant of the saint. Actually the tomb owner is a rich man living in Akhdar and working at the mines.

Everyone goes to the *hedra*, except the *shurfa* who say that it is a scene of licence and that their women should not be exposed to the wolfish gaze of the bystanders. It is clear that if anyone's interest suffers through this *maraboutic* display it is that of the *shurfa*, whose monopoly of the hot line to heaven is challenged. It is from *shurfa* that I have heard the most damning criticisms of 'maraboutism'. Although cultivated Arabs and Arabised Berbers come to Sidi Sherif from Akhdar, they regard the proceedings with explicit contempt and call them barbarous.

The circle is cleared by one of the members of the brotherhood who acts as master of ceremonies. The *ghitars* sound stirring and repetitive rhythms. One woman told me 'Whenever I hear that music I want to weep.' A woman stumbles into the arena and begins to dance; someone just manages to snatch the baby from her back as she enters the circle. Every dancer is 'made hot' by a particular melody, and calmed by another one which may have none of these effects on anyone else. No human agency can 'cool' a person,[1] and none would dare to interfere with the work of the spirit anyway. Not everyone can dance *hedra*. Some people have it 'in the blood', others don't. The capacity tends to run from one generation to the next, but perhaps only one member of a family will suddenly find that he is irresistibly drawn to a dance. They dance heavily treading on one foot, then the other, flinging their arms against their chests and away from their sides. Their heads jolt from side to side, they become more and more mesmerised till suddenly they fall to the ground in a kind of hypnotic trance, foaming at the mouth and rolling around. Bystanders rush anxiously to the prone figure, and cover him with a sheet until he has recovered consciousness.

At Sidi Sherif, some dancers perform sensational masochistic feats, to demonstrate their liberation from the bonds of the flesh and their union with the Spirit. I saw dancers in white *djellabas* cutting their scalps with sharp knives until the blood flowed down their faces – then lick and kiss the blade. People told me that they tore chickens apart and ate them. Since a Muslim should never taste blood, or meat which has not been killed in the prescribed Muslim way, the dancers are committing sacrilege. A gasp always goes up from the crowd

---

[1] *Henna*, the decorative dye used especially by women and at rites of passage, also has this two-edged property of changing a person's ritual state, by making him either 'hot' or 'cool'.

although they know exactly what to expect. The dancers are both men and women, the majority of them *haratn*. If a man persists for a long time in frenzied dancing, he may (it seemed) be accepted as a proselyte by the brotherhood. Once or twice members of the brotherhood will take the arena. They are mostly elderly or middle-aged, wearing white turbans and *djellabas*. They join hands and circle slowly in a dignified rhythmical dance. Sometimes the end dancer also takes the hand of one of the *hedra* dancers, who learns the rhythm.

Women and religion: women's 'hedra'.

Although adherence to a particular saint is important in determining political alignments – or has been in the past – it is the *hedra* itself which defines local solidarity, as far as women are concerned. The *hedra* typifies the way in which women's social relationships are independently structured from those of men. So although the two *ksour* where I lived, Aghzim and Bentaleb, are both Ait Sidi Sherif (people of Sidi Sherif) the women hold *hedras* separately. This is on the twenty-seventh night of Ramadan, when the Angel Gabriel revealed the Koran to Mohammed. On this night, called *fdela* which means grace, all the angels are supposed to come to earth, and the women of Aghzim assembled in the disused mosque. Everyone is supposed to keep a vigil till sunrise. That night I visited several families, and noticed that the men who had talked about the necessity of the vigil most emphatically were all asleep. But the women, who are uneducated in religion and excluded from the mosques, are innately impure and distract men from their pious duty, have a great deal to gain by superogatory religious practices. Not one closed an eye, and the majority attended the *hedra*.

At this assembly the older women were very serious and reproved the young girls for larking around. Tea was continuously handed round, and two women were beating *tara*, a third clanking the handle of a bucket which contributed to volume if not to tone. The music sometimes reached deafening proportions, with everyone clapping and repeating refrains like 'pray to God and the Prophet' or 'Mohammed, Messenger of God'. A *hartaniya* danced, burning twists of paper under her chin, or putting the flame in her mouth. When she had recovered after her eventual collapse, she went round the room kissing the hands of all the people present. Among the other dancers were two widows, the village gossip who is herself the object of scandal for 'going with men' between marriages and for controlling her

96

husband, and an adolescent with deformed feet and severe astigmatism. One of the widows, an elderly woman, frightened her friends by persisting in dancing for nearly an hour. Both her daughters refused to intervene, but one finally remembered the song which would 'cool' her.

The social personalities of these dancers give a clue to the meaning of the *hedra*. Apart from their psychological propensities (they are all exceptionally intelligent and independent) they are all people who experience the ambivalence of others. They fail as social beings according to the dominant ideology. The main prospects for an adolescent girl are to be married and have children, but the cripple's future with respect to these criteria of the good life, looks very uncertain. *Haratn*, as we have already seen, are discriminated against in a number of spheres. Blackness is considered both ugly and sinister. In stories of *jnun*, the evil spirits who live under the earth, the spirit appears two out of three times in the form of a woman, the third as a *hartani*. Many Berbers and Arabs have *hartani* friends, but there are many elements of a joking relationship and other signs that the association is conditional. The profligate or scandal-monger is regarded with the same ambivalence. As for the widow, there are two possible reasons for her appearance in company with these other social invalids. She had borne one son, who never helped or visited her, and five daughters, too many for any woman to feel that fortune smiles on her. Without a man in the house, she was forced to undertake many tasks in the public sphere, on behalf of her old mother and her daughter. She was active in male-specific roles to a point which would be considered indecent for any married woman. It is only by acting in a mystical context where her social attributes were irrelevant that she could recover a sense of personal validity.

I think that the *hedra* as a whole can be viewed in this light, as an assertion of the validity of Berber cultural forms, which wherever they come in contact with Arab values are demeaned. A Berber in a town, Berbers say, feels like a little twig. At home in the *ksar* he is like a great tree. The hegemony of the *Makhzen* powers does not grow weaker. It seems rather that the prospect of country people, including Berber country people, sharing the profits of the national productive system grows more remote. Self-esteem is threatened by an economic structure which offers plenty to a few and nothing to many. The significance of having an alternative context in which to nourish these necessary emotions by outlining a different frame of reference must increase rather than diminish. Certainly, to judge from the huge attendance at the *mussem* of Sidi Ben Aissa of Meknes, on the Prophet's birthday, the Aissaoua brotherhood for one is as vigorous as ever.

Women's saints

Women also have recourse to the help of saints, many of whom are supposed to be good at getting husbands for people, or conferring fertility or sterility where appropriate.

Itto, an unmarried girl from Aghzim, went with two other girls from her *ksar* to ask for a husband at the tomb of Sidi Mendri on three successive Fridays. The tomb is about 6 kilometres away. Before they left, they collected contributions of sugar, bread and tea, from women in the *ksar* who wanted to make *sadaqa* (alms), and they were joined by two women from Daoud who brought two chickens to kill. This was to place an *ar* on the saint, a compulsion to grant their request. All day they stayed at the tomb playing *hedra* music. The chickens were killed by two men, one of whom had brought a calf to kill but refused to give them any of it. Itto's mother pronounced on him 'Shame! Everyone knows that hunger brought those women there. What kind of *sadaqa* is that?...'[1]

Local saints are especially important for women, for they are the *rjal-l-bled* – the men of the place – the sacred validation of women's continuing rights in local resources. 'What attaches people to their home are the *rjal-l-bled*', one woman insisted in an argument with her husband, who maintained that a woman should be prepared to go wherever her husband wished. Clearly, he had no interest in conceding that his wife's attachment to her natal village had divine sanction.

Signs of salvation

Poor people cannot point to any material sign of favour from God as a proof of their spiritual or political worth. Strict fulfilment of the Five Pillars may be followed just as often by illness and disaster as by prosperity. A person can only have a subjective proof of salvation. The first lies in a release from the senses and therefore from suffering and finally translated into ecstasy – which is interpreted as possession by an angel. This has Islamic precedents – Mohammed was possessed by Gabriel who revealed the Koran to him – but orthodox Islam frowns on these excesses, which are more rarely found in the town.

---

[1] Her reaction *points to the multiple functions of sadaqa*, which operates to some extent as a system of mutual aid, utilised and practised by women more than by men.

Religion and social stratification

Sadaqa (Alms)

The other proof of righteousness is selfless action, through which a person acquires *a'ajr* or merit. This was described to me by Berbers in Aghzim as a quantifiable attribute which was stored in a heavenly account and which served to pay off a person's sins on the day of judgment. Merit is earned in the performance of many different acts of piety, defined according to 'folk' rather than Islamic ideas of the 'good action'. The former lay stress on generosity and lavish hospitality, on devotion to parents and the diligent performance of family roles, on provision for one's children particularly in the matters of circumcision, arranging for their marriages under auspicious circumstances, and for their religious education.

Finally it is possible for a person to make *a'ajr* for himself or on behalf of another by giving alms, or *sadaqa*. Just as ecstatic religion exercises a special attraction for women, so too does alms-giving. The most common occasion for *sadaqa* is at the funeral rites of a kinsman. A huge *ks'a* or pottery tray full of *cous cous* is placed in the centre of the women's room in the dead person's household, and all the *mesakin* or poor people are invited to come and eat. In the *ksar* this usually means the entire community, but only a few women and the children who are playing outside generally come. They are pressed to show none of the modesty which usually accompanies eating, but to eat their fill because *sadaqa* confers *baraka* (blessing) on the receiver. The *fuqaha* who have been singing the offices of the dead for several hours are similarly served. In the town a *sadaqa* is generally offered to the children playing in the street, and only friends of the family are called into the house.

Someone who is suffering from a serious illness or a difficult childbirth may also give a *sadaqa*. The implication is that illness and difficult childbirth may signal neglect, however involuntary, of a religious duty. *Sadaqa* is one way of erasing the offence, or of obliging the powers that be to bless the sufferer. This view bears on the meaning of the funeral *sadaqa*, which is a way of appeasing the spirit of the dead person, so preventing it from molesting the household. The *sadaqa* is an indication of the guilt felt by the survivors, a compensation for neglect and the resentment and turbulence that frequently marks the relations between dependent elderly parents and their adult children.

Again it is women upon whom falls the main burden of caring for the sick and elderly, and to whom are attributed sinister powers of witchcraft, who have most to gain by offering *sadaqa* both to establish their innocence and to calm their sense of guilt. When a woman makes *sadaqa* she throws open her house, normally a secret hidden place, for inspection by her neighbours. They demonstrate their confidence and solidarity by eating liberally of her food. Once again a relation to the community is exchanged in orthodox Durkheimian manner against an offering ostensibly meant for God.

Purity and impurity

The source of all increase and prosperity is *baraka*, a kind of energy inherent in certain people (*shurfa* or saints), conditions (pregnancy, extreme age, trance), animals (horses, sheep, bees) or objects (healing springs, milk, seedcorn, dried fruit, lightning and thunder). But all *baraka* contains dangerous elements which may harm their possessor or cancel the good effects of other *baraka*. The danger intrinsic in sacred objects is attributed to the *jnun*. Thus, water as a neutralising agent in one context may purify from evil spirits (it is used to 'cool' grief and epilepsy) but in another (e.g. a marriage) it may destroy the *baraka* (of the bride, whose situation is dangerous and whose person is sacred).

All food is liable to become the home of *jnun*. Its *baraka* is sensitive to certain kinds of impurity peculiar to women – pollution by menstrual blood or sexual intercourse, bodily dirt, and spiritual impurity. Because spiritual impurity is a function of the kind of religious conduct which is specific to Muslim men (ablutions, prayer, fasting), women (as well as Jews and Christians) are a constant source of danger.

The combination of the stigma of impurity and the responsibility for the well-being of the members of the household has a profound effect on women's religious needs and attempts to satisfy them.

Their sense of a lack of religious worth gives to their conduct a masochistic, compensatory aspect. The ordinary positivist gestures of piety are not enough for people whose very being is an offence against religion. Salvation is only available through self-obliteration (hence the frequency of fasting and submissive behaviour among women, both within the family and towards *shurfa*); or through self-transcendence, in the form of the ecstatic *hedra* dancing, and possession by spirits (women say 'by angels', men say 'by devils'). These tendencies become less marked among *shurfa* women, and the rich bourgeoisie, who follow the more orthodox Islamic practices. Poorer women always pointed out the piety of their rich patronesses, 'You see, she *knows* how to pray.'

Preoccupation with impurity and its relation to sexual anxiety

Stephens, in his cross-cultural study of the 'Oedipal Complex',[1] has suggested that a long post-partum taboo on sexual intercourse gives rise to a strong sexual interest between mother and son (he does not attempt to consider the case where the child is a girl) and consequent rivalry between father and son. This situation is at the root of anxiety about sexual intercourse, and is associated with physical types of punishment, dealt out by the father to his son-rival. (Circumcision is an institutionalised form of such punishment.) Stephens further suggests that the idea of physical injury following on sexual intercourse lies behind the belief that menstrual blood is dangerous to men and he uses the linkage in folk tales of such injury (wounds suggesting castration) with menstrual taboos to support his hypothesis.

The coincidence of his three main variables (post-partum taboo/father–son rivalry; sexual anxiety; and menstrual taboos) in the Akhdar area, together with some of the correlated factors, such as stress on physical punishment by the father, and circumcision, favour his hypothesis as a possible framework of interpretation for Akhdari behaviour.

Father–son rivalry can be discussed in connection with their competitive relation to property, and to the services of women. Sexual anxiety is indicated in the rituals surrounding intercourse which is polluting and should be preceded and followed by ablutions, in the prohibition on premarital intercourse, the obsessional fear of adultery resulting in the seclusion of women[2] and the elaborate *rites de passage* – circumcision for a boy, marriage for a girl.

The exclusion of men from scenes of childbirth, and danger to them of blood of childbirth, their expression of pique and of rival claims at the births (e.g. being ill or absent) and during the child's early months – all these are adequately explained within the Oedipal framework. As far as menstrual taboos are concerned, monogamy appears to be the limiting factor. Menstrual complaints appear to be aggravated in

---

[1] W. N. Stephens (1962).

[2] Adultery appears, in fact, to be a male prerogative and the recipients of men's attentions are either prostitutes or temporarily unmarried women (divorcées or widows), never, as far as I know, married women.

households where a women's tasks can be taken over by her co-wives, sisters, or mother. The mitigation of the taboo in the case of a one-woman household, where *someone* must cook and clean, i.e. where the taboo would act against the practical interest of men, suggests that it is more closely linked to fears aroused during the early socialisation of men than to the psychology of women.

Women should bathe in the *hammam* after menstruation and not before, for any attempt at purity is rendered void by menstrual blood (the *hammam* features in pre-wedding rituals and confers ritual as well as physical purity). According to the same principle, it is useless for a woman to fast during the days of her menstruation in Ramadan, for her impurity makes it impossible to approach God. She must fast extra days later in the year.

Power, purity, and witchcraft

Where membership of the Islamic community, the *umma*, confers rights of citizenship, women as second-rate Muslims are at a political disadvantage, and this fact is relevant for all aspects of the relationship between men and women. Lacking political control of their own lives, lacking religious worth to give their judgment weight, women are forced to turn to intrigue and attempt to redress the balance of power, on a personal level, by means of witchcraft.

S'Hur (witchcraft) is the power by which a woman binds her husband to her, in spite of the opposition of her affines; by which one woman entices away the husband of another, or a co-wife secures the exclusive attention of her husband. *D*, a woman teacher, told me of a case where two women, married to the same man, concocted a charm which would make him impotent every time he went to see a girl whom they suspected he wanted to marry. With them his powers returned.

Accusations of witchcraft are often levelled against a wife by her husband's female kin, which supports the hypothesis that witchcraft is a weapon presumed to be used in a power struggle between husband and wife. Since spells are normally dropped into food, cooking and the household in general are sensitive areas.

Naima, a wife from another town, had been married for less than a year, and lived in lonely seclusion in Akhdar, very unhappily. Her husband fell ill with hepatitis, and in his delirium was unable to recognise his sisters who had come to visit him. They accused his wife, their father's brother's daughter, who was weeping helplessly, of bewitching him. Finally, Naima's parents came to fetch the couple away.

There are also male witches who may give a man a potion to deal with a girl who persistently refuses him. She will begin to rave about him and roam the streets in search of him. Midwives and women of 'personality' who have some medical expertise are especially liable to bewitch people.

In Aghzim there was an old black woman whose knowledge and treatment of women's complaints were well-known. She even gave secret and conditional 'contraceptive treatment' to a very few deserving women whose families she had known for many years. Once she accompanied a woman to her new husband's home, to ensure the success of the marriage. The young woman refused to pay her price, whereupon the 'witch' put a charm on her to make her barren. She related that three men had already divorced the girl because she did not bear any children...

The habits of witches are the inverse of purifying, or social. They are believed to make their pathogenic potions in cemeteries on nights when the moon is reddish, cooking *cous cous* with parts of a corpse. They jeopardise the safe ascent of spirits by charming their graves.

Protection against the attacks of witches and *jnun* is secured by the wearing of amulets containing Koranic verses, *hajab*, which are written out by a *fqih*. Some *fuqaha* are known to be more skilful than others and are especially sought out because their *hajab* are known to be effective, or because they deal in medicines. It is above all women who use *hajab*, both for the protection of children, who are always adorned with protective beads and gold discs, and to cure women's maladies, such as pains connected with childbirth or menstruation, sterility or sheer exhaustion.

7

Conjugal roles, kinship roles and the division of labour

In this chapter I discuss men's and women's work, pointing out that women's work is very labour intensive. Child-care, for instance, is entirely in the hands of women. They cannot take advantage of the technical innovations of the public sphere to relieve the burden, for this is the province of men. On the other hand, women who are closely confined to the home and its concerns, townswomen especially, are often more concerned about how to spend time and effort than how to save them, so that labour-intensive techniques have the function of combatting boredom.

Women depend on other women for company and for labour in times of peak activity, the latter especially in the *ksar*. They have little formal authority in their conjugal household and none in the community at large, so that their relationships with other women become a source of self-esteem and social support.

In the next chapter I pursue the organisation of women's relationships, and point out that uterine kinship bonds provide a safety-net for casualties of the social system, that is, those who do not enjoy full rights in their agnatic kin-group because they are women or the offspring of a broken marriage. Because these people constitute a high proportion of the population, if not the majority, matrilateral relationships assume such social-structural significance that they constitute a threat to the arrangements made according to the principle of agnation, of which virilocal marriage and control of property and services by men are the most important. Seclusion signifies the attempt to ward off this threat, an attempt which can never be entirely successful given the instability of marriage, and the emotional and practical dependence of women on other women.

I have taken especial pains to document these chapters on women with extensive case-studies. The empirical detail of women's activities and attitudes, especially in societies where men and women are strictly segregated, have not often been accessible to the anthropologist, generally male or unacquainted with the 'dialect' spoken by the women in such a society. Yet such detail is crucial to our understanding of such social phenomena as marriage and divorce. Without considerable case-illustration of this perhaps unfamiliar material, analytical statements concerning the significance of 'seclusion' or of a woman's 'kindred of co-operation' can hardly be appreciated at their true value.

Children and contraception

The diacritical factor in the division of labour between men and women is that the care of children falls entirely on women and girls. Until they are adolescent, children spend a much greater proportion of their time with their mother than with their father.

Women spend most of their lifetime tending or bearing young children; most women I knew who had three or four children, had borne eight or ten, many of whom died in infancy. It is understandable that they appear more relieved when their children do not die, than concerned about the 'population explosion'.

A recent government enquiry into Moroccan attitudes to family planning came to the following conclusions with respect to Moroccan towns.[1] Only 29% of the women (married and under fifty) had heard of the pill or loop, so that it is difficult to assess the significance of the survey. 60% of women were in favour of birth control, 32% against and 7% hesitant. 69% of those with five or more children were in favour, and 57% of those with fewer. 74% of women whose husbands had received more than a primary education were in favour, compared with 57% of those whose husbands were less educated. 75% of women thought that five children or fewer was the ideal number, yet 31% of women had borne five or more, and 67% of women who had borne four or more children wanted no more. Although the percentage who intended to use contraceptives was 49%, taking Morocco as a whole, it varied regionally from, for example, 77% in Rabat to 13% in Tetouan.

Husbands were generally less favourable to family planning than their wives, but at least half of those in the sample were keen for their wives to know about contraceptive methods and 75% thought the ideal family was composed of fewer than five children.

It is clear then that a large proportion of the population would limit their families if the means were available, and this tendency is especially marked in the *ville moderne*, and in those sections of the

[1] 'Enquête d'Opinion sur la Planification Familiale au Maroc, 1966', *Bulletin Economique et Sociale du Maroc* (1967).

population who are most involved in the market economy. A maximum of five children might still predicate a high rate of population expansion, but the attitude of the interviewees cannot be regarded as unreasonably '*nataliste*', if we take into account the high rate of child mortality (186/1000; 70% of all deaths occur among children under fourteen, see note p. 138). Thus the average family size is 5·2 (3·2 children). Moreover Pascon points out the functional importance of large families in 'patriarchal' southern Morocco, at least until three generations ago. Given primitive technology the numerical strength of the family determined how much agricultural terrain could be exploited and defended. Children were necessary members of the productive unit, and at five years old yielded important returns (as herders) on the slight investment made in their upbringing. The same principle may still govern the family policy of migrants, who seek to place their children in as many different economic niches as possible in order to spread the risks and maximise the opportunities of the agnatic group. The process may begin by sending their children to be fostered by wealthier kin, maintaining or creating links of clientship. Thus 'Il ya au niveau du présent aucune incompatibilité entre la fécondité et la croissance économique au sein des familles.'[1]

Although economic planners claim to believe that there is no such compatibility at the level of the national economy, the distribution of newly released (ex-colonial or state) land is in practice organised according to family size, so that large families remain profitable. 'Une telle attitude,' comments Pascon, 'pleinement consciente ou non, prouve que la norme est patriarchale, et jusqu'au sein de la société qui se veut industrielle.'

To turn to the local level. Even if the ideas and methods of contraception are becoming more diffused, they are rarely taken up by women in the *ksour* or Akhdar, except as a last resort. They complain of the discomforts and expense of the pill, for a woman rarely has a chance to take a pill adapted to her physiological type. They also dislike the loop, which proves useless for women who have had three or more children, i.e. those most likely to wish to limit their families. Some turn to traditional methods, but are dependent on the good offices of the few old women who know the secret. The practitioners consent to treat only their most trusted friends, since, one told me, if 'the men' found out, they would stone her or take her to the *mokhazni* who would imprison her. The rate of infant mortality does not appear

[1] P. Pascon, 'Le problème demographique au Maroc', *Bulletin Economique et Sociale du Maroc* XXIX (jan–juin 1967).

to have been affected by the availability of medical services, contrary to the claims made by Malthusian social scientists. Most of the deaths can be attributed to the malnutrition of mother and baby, and the unhygienic conditions in which both are forced to live. It is probable that if the problems of low productivity, unemployment, lack of appropriate education and social services were realistically tackled, paradoxically the rate of population increase would slow down although infant mortality would drop. People would have fewer children. The family's fund of physical labour power would become less significant than the quality of the skills it could offer on the labour market, and the role of those skills in the national economy. The upbringing of children would require a greater investment, yet the child would remain unproductive for much longer. Children would no longer be regarded as the chief family resource nor the only means to secure a comfortable old age. But these are as yet pipe-dreams.

Today in the Middle Atlas contraception is rarely practised, and a woman's children may range in age from three to twenty, so that there are always children around her, dependent on her for care and attention and greatly reducing her mobility. So it is that most of her activities must be carried out within a severely circumscribed space, and the upkeep of the house is the woman's duty, in the execution of which she employs the services of her children.

A girl's mother-centredness persists until she dies, and all her childhood activities are conditioned by a working-relationship between them which begins at a very early stage in the girl's life. Young girls play repetitive, singing games near the houses, so that care of their younger siblings and frequent interruption from mothers can be integrated with their play. Adolescent girls are almost entirely absorbed in domestic activities and child-care. Their favourite sport is to wash at the stream with other girls.

A boy in adolescence spends more time with his peers. Indeed the relationship with peers rather than family is suggested by the fact that four informal age-groups are recognised for boys, those at the Koranic school (age four to six), those who are still small boys who play marbles and hide and seek (aged seven to ten), those who spend their evenings outside playing hide and seek, or telling stories in the old mosque, or trap birds and play cards and learn to smoke (aged eleven to fourteen). Then the bigger boys who control their younger siblings, and go to the cinema, make experiments with batteries and light bulbs, play football in the evening with their unmarried elders who are at college or spasmodically at work.

107

Women and property in Morocco

In the later stages of adolescence, clashes with the father are common, since a boy is considered to be physically mature enough to undertake many of the father's duties, such as harvesting and marketing, so that there are also elements of a struggle for authority within the home for the services of mother and sisters. Moreover while relations with the father have always been loaded with tension, they become even more charged because of the possibility that the intimate relation between mother and children might be brought to an end by an arbitrary action on the part of the father. The mother is subordinate and peremptorily treated; the father has the legal power to disrupt mother–child relations.

The emotional allegiance of children to their mother is a conspicuous element in all family crises. The following case is an illustration of this fact.

Fatima, a youngish woman married to a small shopkeeper Hussein, had eight children, four of them under six. Her husband, an enterprising and shrewd man, travelled frequently to other towns and often stayed away for weeks at a time. Fatima would often declaim bitterly on the evils of divorce and polygamy, sometimes making explicit in a joking tone her apprehension that her husband had a wife somewhere else. She was a humble and industrious wife, but would often give her opinion on matters concerning the family in no uncertain terms. Hussein had promised to instal a new pipe for the stove because winter had set in, but remarked casually that he couldn't find the pipe. A heated argument ensued during which mutual insults were exchanged in the hearing of the children, who seemed to feel menaced by their father's intransigence as if his anger was directed at them in the person of their mother. Fatima threatened to leave, and discussed this with her eldest daughter Zohor. Zohor told me that she would go with her mother to stay with a woman friend in *ksar* Ceima, and the rest of the children would follow leaving her father alone. 'Then he will have to plead for us to come back.' The rights and wrongs of the case were not clear, but the alignment of the children was...

The behaviour of Berber men and their children is very relaxed while they are young, when a father will play with them with great kindliness. However the abrupt and sometimes violent rejection which a child experiences, when at around two years old it is decided he should be weaned from his mother, is endorsed by his father.[1] From this experience the child learns to regard with apprehension the father who may punish him with blows and violence, and the foundation is

[1] See A. Radi (1969).

laid for a gradually more strictly observed respect-relationship between father and son. This seems to be connected with the initiation of the child into productive activity. He will be used by his father to run messages, or he may help his older brothers as he watches them cutting hay, marketing or harvesting barley. He learns to be silent in front of his father, to act with dignity, never joking or laughing. He greets him respectfully by kissing him on the forehead and obeys his every order.

The Koranic school to which he is sent between four and five is seen by many fathers as teaching the child obedience to authority rather than instilling knowledge. Certainly the severity and discipline to which children are subjected in the learning of Koranic *surat* in classical Arabic, and elements of arithmetic, reinforces the general pattern between men of proximate generations. But the values which the father attempts to inculcate in his son, namely the rightness of hard work under his father's eye in the service of the household, are almost impossible to demonstrate in practice. Clearly the father, often unemployed for most of the year, is unproductive, and the son's orientation is affected by his school life, however remote it is from reality. Father needs son in bureaucratic procedures and the contradictions in the relationship are only aggravated by the attempts of the father to deal with his son in a despotic way, and activate traditional privileges such as the right of the household head to take the clothes and possessions of his family to sell or wear at his whim. The child, feeling that his parent's behaviour is unrealistic, will come to depend more on his mother and his peers for guidelines. The age gap between father and son is often as much as forty years, and the father's memory of a hardworking peasant childhood leads him to make bitter reproaches to his sons, whose prospects of employment, unskilled as they are or with only primary education, are nil.

This only increases the strains. A teacher in Aghzim told me that in this situation fathers have approached him saying 'You're his father now. I don't know anything about this new education.' Zeghari also notes that the teacher becomes a buffer between the parties to this relationship. 'L'éducateur, à l'extérieur de la famille, apparaît revêtu d'un rôle sociale extraordinaire; enfants et parents attendent de lui la solution des difficultés que leur suscite la complexité de la vie politique, economique et sociale.'[1] The awareness of teachers does not always rise to this.

The relationship of fathers with their daughters is hardly more

[1] M. Zeghari (1962).

relaxed; a girl should never dance or sing, laugh or joke in front of her father. Generally a girl is entirely educated by her mother, and the need for her to earn money to support the family is not a factor in her relationship with her parents which is less ridden with anxiety. It is not to their daughters that parents look for support in their old age, as they do to their sons. However the daughter/sister may become the focus of conflict between father and son. Since the household head is often away on a job or looking for one, he is not in a position to defend the *hurma*, or intimacy of the household. This failure gives rise to competition between father and sons for responsibility for the activities of the women of the household and then for control of resources. This seems to take the form, in the few cases I have met, not of confrontation, but of the son keeping back a part of his earnings, or spending them on himself or on other members of the family without consulting his father.

Domestic duties of a ksar-woman

A *ksar*-woman is expected to fetch water morning and evening from the stream, which is rarely more than a few hundred metres away, to bake bread twice daily, and cook simple meals for the family, mostly of the stew variety, or a soup of pulses. During the winter from November to early March, *ksar*-people warm themselves by woodstoves which are also used for cooking. Chopping the wood is a major feature of the day's work, and a mother hands it over at the earliest opportunity to her adolescent sons and daughters. She is also responsible for washing and repairing the clothes of her family. But clothes in the *ksar* approach the European kind, a far cry from the woollen cloaks and *djellabas* of the Ait Hadiddou, and it is not unusual to see the paterfamilias sewing on buttons. If a woman has many children her sons may do their own washing and that of their father. Men always pound the clothes with their feet, thus distinguishing their activity from that of women, who crouch over the lid of a petrol drum, rubbing the clothes with their hands. Asked to characterise a woman's activities, an Aghzim Berber said they were those performed '*aghjdim*', sitting down.

The keynote of a young woman's relationships with her children, husband and male kin is care and self-effacement. She brings them cushions to make them more comfortable, fills and refills braziers with glowing coals so that they may warm themselves, covers them with blankets as they go to sleep, reserves for them choice morsels of food, denying herself in their favour, fetches everything they ask for. The scene is one of people lying propped on their elbows talking and laughing; occasionally one issues an order to the girl or woman who flits in and out at their whim. She settles now and then to listen to the conversation if it is among members of her family, or to giggle and whisper with the women and children in the next room if the guests are unrelated men. To recommend a girl highly, people say of her '*ka-tnud*', or in Berber '*da-tkerr*', 'she gets up', meaning that she is always submissive and ready to serve. The typical order to stir a girl to action is '*Nudi!*' or '*Kerr!*' repeated in rising tones if she looks sleepy or unwilling. In significant contrast is the stressed invitation to a guest or senior member of the family to sit down, '*Qim*', indicating that he should relax and allow all his needs to be supplied. Women guests are also waited on hand and foot.

A woman is expected to prepare fastuous banquets for the guests of her husband, and often if she is many years married and the mother of children, she will invite guests of her own. She will eat with her guests but never with her husband's guests who are always men (or close kinswomen, whom she can eat with). She darts about for several hours, bringing water to wash their hands, carrying in and clearing dishes from which they eat communally. After they have finished she will reheat what remains for herself and her children and kinswomen, to eat in a room apart. A considerate husband will wait for them to finish before calling for tea.

'*Tajma'at*'

Men are responsible for all activities of the public sphere, *tajma'at*, and the Arab-speaking town, *tamdint*. This applies to dealing with the various bureaucratic institutions, the post-office, the schools, the registry to register births and marriages. But frequently in these contacts he needs the services of his sons who are literate in Arabic, and who are thus implicated in the father's adequate performance of his role. Less prestigious are the men's marketing duties which a father may leave to his sons or even daughters, though he may undertake such weighty tasks as enquiring about the price of sheep in view of impending feasts which the family must hold. Many Berbers from the country buy the fabric for the clothes of their womenfolk and take it to a tailor to be made up, but in the *ksour* it is usually the women who choose their own clothes.

Similarly, many women go to market to choose their own fruit and vegetables, considering that they know better how to market than their husbands. Many townswomen go, especially those of Berber origin, chiefly because their husbands are working, but they regard these sorties, like their visits to the *hammam*, as a welcome relief from their humdrum routine existence, and a chance to talk with friends. However, no women sell in the market, except for poor widows who sell such products as eggs or *ifssiyn*, a kind of scrub used as a sweeping brush, which needs minimal productive resources or none at all. For a woman to sell is '*hashuma ghur rbbi*',[1] shameful in God's eyes, I was told.

A man who spends too much time with his family, or where women are working, is ridiculed. If time is heavy on his hands, he will meet friends outside the walls of the *ksar* and spend hours talking and commenting on the goings-on in the *ksar*. A younger man will walk around the town or while away the evenings playing cards in a café. It is this prohibition on the associational and spatial relationship of men with the hearth and women which prevents them from sharing women's tasks except in exceptional circumstances. But there is no intrinsic taboo. I have seen men baking bread of barley for a stomach ailment, and making coffee in their wife's absence.

When services normally performed by women are commercialised, they are taken onto the public market by men. There are several cafés in Akhdar where men cook and serve. All the hospital cooks are men. There are workshops where men weave *djellabas* with the help of small boys who twist the thread. There is a laundry and a bakery, both entirely operated by men. Most of the hospital nurses are male, but because there are women nurses also working there this occupation carries a slight stigma.

It seems that *ksar* men have a more detailed knowledge of the techniques used in women's activities than have townsmen, and more readily gave me information about them. This is consistent with the greater degree of economic co-operation between the sexes in the *ksour*, and the extreme segregation of the activities of men and women in both time and space in the town. The fact that *ksar* men would profess ignorance of women's work if strangers were present is one index of the degree to which urban culture is given higher status.

[1] *Hashuma*, used even more commonly in the town than in the *ksour*, means 'shame' in the sense of 'dishonour', and in the sense of those feelings which are prompted by a proper modesty and observance of the norms of one's role (e.g. as a guest, man, woman, son etc.).

Roles, and the division of labour

Fieldwork

The bulk of fieldwork is usually said to fall on the shoulders of men. However, in the *ksour* fieldwork is not a necessary component of the role-set of household head, but it is of that of a field-owner's wife, unless her husband is rich enough to seclude her, and employ labourers to do her work. Many field-owners rely on the services of *khammesin* (labourers) to carry out the specifically male tasks. This happens when the household head is in full-time employment, or when he has no mules or plough. Four of the full-time peasants own these instruments and are hired at a rate of 5 *drahem* per day for a mule and 5 *drahem* per day for a worker with a plough. Other peasants cultivate land of others in exchange for half the harvest if the owner provides the seed and the worker the tools. The *paysannats*, or government agricultural centres, hire out tractors with drivers at 15 *drahem* per hour, which in an hour cover roughly a *juj*, or the area covered by two mules in a day, but only two peasants used this facility. The ploughing begins after the end of the maize harvest, that is in the second half of October.

During November the *fellah* transports animal manure to the fields, and those who own no animals buy manure at 75 fr. the cartload from those who do. Most *fellahin* also make use of phosphates. They sow the wheat using a broadcasting technique, then cover up the seed. Each *fellah* has his own preferred Islamic formulae and songs designed to bring his fields to fruition and protect them against the elements, chiefly floods and summer hail which frequently destroys the wheat-crop just before harvest. This song is known only to the *fellah*'s sons, and not to women, who don't take a regular part in the sowing – that is they sow only if there is no kinsman to sow for them. But although women are considered less efficacious because they don't learn the techniques and formulae in childhood, widow Bedda preferred to sow her own wheat rather than confide this crucial task to someone outside her family who might work evil on it.

In December the *sequiat*, or irrigation channels, are repaired and the fields flooded with water. January and February are months without work.

In March the maize and kidney beans are sown, and when the women have harvested the *fava* beans they are taken to market by the men, usually when the family needs cash to make a specific purchase, but not too long after the harvest because of the hazards of storage. In April and May while the women weed the wheat and cut hay, the men

113

have no agricultural work. In June the wheat is harvested by hired labourers who travel hundreds of kilometres from the mountains and the Tafilalet. They are Ait Hadiddou and Ait Seghrouchen, whose only qualification is the ownership of a sickle and a strong right arm. Just as the husband is responsible for hiring a labourer, so it is he who seeks out one of the *ishiwal* from the *kissaria* where they stay, and asks him to bring a group of so many to harvest his wheat. The wife of the field-owner cooks for them, and they are paid 4 or 5 *drahem* per day. Sometimes they must also sleep beside the stacked wheat to prevent it from being stolen.

During July the men are engaged in threshing, but as there is such a shortage of instruments of production, in this case mules to tread the wheat, the time actually spent threshing by each field-owner is negligible. Usually several field-owners pool their mules and place them in the charge of a labourer, who is paid a fee by each owner. The mule-owners may be given a portion of straw by those field-owners who don't own mules, but no other payment seems to be involved. The *ishiwal* do not take part in the threshing. The women winnow and transport the straw. Between the wheat harvest and the renewal of the cycle in mid-October the men have nothing to do and their children often travel to stay with kin and friends in other towns. In October they cut the maize, and co-operative groups are formed to beat it. Sometimes these groups are made up of the owners of neighbouring fields. More often the threshing groups have a kin basis, with non-field-owners helping. The grain is divided up among the field-owners, and those who do not own fields are paid 2 *mouds* per day of 7 *drahem*. It is heavy work. The threshers stand in a circle and raise stout sticks above their heads bringing them down together with a gasping shout '*halla, halla*'.

Widows with fields generally hand over men's work to a labourer, but in some circumstances the head of the household has a direct responsibility which he cannot delegate. This is true of sowing. Widows even arrange to thresh their own maize. To do this a woman invites kinswomen or friends to help her and holds a threshing party on the terrace of her house. It appears then, that although the *control* of certain productive activities remains vested in the household head, the actual performance of those activities is in some cases transferred to hired labourers, or machines, in others to women. Women have more limited recourse to outside help because of the restricted compatibility of honour and association with men. Under modern conditions, the workload is generally redistributed in a way which increases the number and range of tasks women must perform, while reducing those of men.

Women's field work

The tasks of women fall essentially into two categories, the care of animals and the processing of animal and plant products. The former is the most demanding. The woman must look after the few sheep, perhaps a cow and mule, belonging to the family, which is regarded as fortunate in possessing such stock. Most families have chickens, whose eggs the wife is entitled to sell for pin-money, but they are not regarded as a significant productive asset. During the warmer months the animals of the whole *ksar* are taken to the hills to graze, by a shepherd who is paid 15 fr. per day per animal, and earns about 150 *drahem* per month. Some families prefer to send their animals with a small daughter when it is not too cold. (They prefer to send sons to school.) For an hour or more every morning and evening in spring, summer and autumn, a woman must cut hay and lucerne for fodder. This is dried and stored to feed the animals in the dry summer and barren winter. If the supply is too large for the family's needs it may be sold at 40 fr. a bundle, which takes about half an hour to cut. This high price reflects the prevailing shortage of fodder.

The women also weed the wheat from March to May, feeding the tares to the animals. In June, they winnow the wheat. Women are responsible for stripping the maize-cobs in the fields in October. They are helped by their children of all ages. The maize stalks are gathered into enormous bundles often nearly 2 metres in diameter. The bundle is tied with a rope so that a wide loop remains, which the woman passes over her head and pulls down with both hands against her chest, in what appears to be a desperate effort to avoid strangulation. The charge of carrying these large burdens on her back always seems to be the woman's. Women go to the mountains to fetch wood, sometimes carry baskets of manure and bundles of hay in similar fashion. A man usually uses a beast of burden. Among the Ait Hadiddou, according to Bynon, a bride was expected to bring no more than her rope and sickle (*tamgurt*) at marriage.[1]

At the end of every wheat harvest there is a residue which is gleaned by poor women, generally indoors, who hand over the straw to the *fellah*. After the maize harvest they collect the bare cobs, which they use to light fires.

[1] Personal communication.

115

Table 12. *Agricultural activity of men and women compared*

Jan.–Feb.	Mar.–April	May–June	July–Aug.	Sept.–Oct.	Nov.–Dec.
			MEN		
	Sow maize		Irrigate lucerne	Cut maize	Manure fields
		Harvest barley		Plant beans, chick-peas	Flood fields
			Thresh wheat with *khammes*		
		Harvest wheat with *ishiwal*		Thresh maize	
				Ploughing	
			WOMEN		
Feed animals	Harvest pulses	Cut hay and lucerne	Cut hay and lucerne	Cut hay Maize: strip cobs and trans-port stalks	Feed animals
	Weed wheat				
		Winnow barley	Winnow wheat Pick fruit		Collect cobs
		Process grain, dairy products			

In March the women and children harvest *fava* beans and chick-peas, in July they work for the owners of the orchards, harvesting apricots, plums, peaches, apples and pears in turn. They are paid by the task, and consume quantities in the process. Women are in charge of milking cows and goats. Anyone who has helped to cut fodder acquires a right to *aghu*, milk generally curdled, so that this is a favourite occupation for old people. The housewife sometimes makes *udi*, butter, by shaking the cream in a goatskin for hours. But the recent influx of surplus French dairy products which are sold at very low prices makes this effort hardly worth while.

Economic decision making

It is the woman who decides to give up a traditional domestic activity and to spend cash on a manufactured product. It is clear that as a woman plays such an important economic role she will have a say in the allocation of resources. In the semi-urban context, few of a family's needs are supplied from their own fields, and as we have seen above, only half of the inhabitants of the *ksour* own fields. Their appetite for consumer goods is continuously whetted by the possibility of buying on credit; by the range of commodities available in Akhdar, and the demonstration effect of urban consumption patterns, adapted to, or the product of, a completely different ecological context.

Secluded women

Married women in the town do not work unless they are *hartaniyin*. Their pattern of life is entirely domestic, and so lacking in variety that I have known young strangers without children and strictly secluded to suffer severe nervous breakdowns after their marriage. In later stages of a woman's married life she has more opportunity to visit, and is entertained by her children. But the tendency to spin out each domestic task, performing it with exquisite care, persists throughout the townswoman's lifetime. Elaborate cuisine, embroidery and knitting, spring-cleaning at every feastday, the radio – these are the pillars of the existence of the bourgeoise. Less fortunate and accomplished women may sit idle for hours, occasionally turning to sort *henna* and decorate their hands, or perhaps they may have learnt how to distil perfume from rose-petals. The mutual dependence of women for company, services and resources described in the section on patron–client relations is demonstrated in a concrete way in the pattern of intervisiting. It will be seen that the main difference between *ksar-* and townswomen in this respect is that the former see more of their own kin more often.

The activities of the husband determine those of the wife to an extreme extent when the wife is secluded, preventing her from maintaining contact with the social network to which she belonged before marriage. However this network is always available. For example, when the husband was away from the household whose

Table 13. *Articulation of husband's and wife's activities*

	Husband	Wife
Day 1		
7–11 a.m.	Breakfast with guest. Worked.	Prepared breakfast. Ate alone, washed up.
11–3 p.m.	Lunch with guest, went to town with guest.	Folded clothes and swept and washed up. Prepared
3–7 p.m.	Walked up and down streets, had coffee.	linen. Played with child. Mother came. Prepared
7–11 p.m.	Returned with guest, supper and sleep in living-room.	supper, mother took child. Slept in kitchen, after washing up for guests. Own supper alone.
Day 2		
7–11 a.m.	Breakfasted with guest. Worked	Got up at 5 to prepare coffee. Slept till 9. Played and fed baby.
11–3 p.m.		Prepared lunch and washed up.
3–7 p.m.	Went to visit parents in another city. Stayed away for two weeks.	Talked to anthropologist. Visit from neighbour with children.
7–11 p.m.	Also visited WZH.	Mother came and left. Fed child, prepared supper. 10 p.m. went to sleep.
Day 3		
7–11 a.m.	Husband absent	9 a.m. got up, made coffee,
11–3 p.m.		prepared lunch, swept and
3–7 p.m.		washed floors. Sent for
7–11 p.m.		ZD to look after baby. 11.30–3.30 stayed in *hammam*. Talked to woman visitor. Slept. Mother came. Supper to which she stayed. 9 a.m. bed, ZD stayed the night
Day 4		
6–11 a.m.	Absent	Prepared breakfast with ZD.
11–3 p.m.		Washed floors. Sat playing
3–7 p.m.		with child. Prepared
7–11 p.m.		lunch. ZD washed up. Made coffee for visitor. Mother came. Z came. Slept till supper. Prepared supper for self, Z and ZD. Bed at 8.30 p.m.
		Ditto for two weeks until husband returned, bringing wife's ZS to stay, so that he could be made to study under the eye of his MZH.
Day 5		
7–11 a.m	Coffee with wife. Went to market to buy vegetables.	Prepared coffee and washed. Wife washed clothes. Mother came; sent ZS to baker's with loaves.
11–3 p.m.	Lunch with wife.	Prepared lunch and washed up. Continued washing, made coffee. Mother came wouldn't stay.
3–7 p.m.	Worked.	Prepared supper, washed up.
7–11 p.m.	Supper with wife. Woman came to sell carpet, bargains with her. Marked books. 11 p.m. bed.	Sat with baby, talking occasionally with husband.

Table 14. *Visiting patterns of women*

Status of ego	Townswomen			Ksar-women		
	1 *Sherifa,* married, poor	2 *Sherifa,* married, Fassi elite	3 *Sherifa,* unmarried, father a merchant	1 Berber, married, landless migrant	2 Berber, widow, small landholder	3 *Sherifa,* divorced, father employed
Others residing in household	H, 8 chil- dren	H, foster- D	M, F 2 B 1 Z fiancé's B	H, 3 S 1 D 1 DS	M, ⌀ D	M, F 4 B 1 Z
Intervisiting with uterine kin	1	—	8	1*	4 D 4 DS 4 D children	1 MMZS 4 MM
Living over 30 km away	—	3	—	1	—	—
Agnatic kin	—	—	—	—	—	1
Living over 30 km away	—	—	—	—	1	1
Affines	5	—	8 fiancé's Z 15 fiancé's ZS	—	6 DH	—
Living over 30 km away	2	—	—	2	—	—
Others	4 DFr 1 MFr 4 Fr	3 HClW 9 H fe- male Cl 2 Fr	MMFr 1 Fr 3 ⌀	16 P teacher's W 4 P, not- able's W 5 P, from own region 2 Fr region	W 2 suitors for D	5 Fr 1 notables W
Living over 30 km away	—	1 HClW	—	—	—	—

This sample was taken over a period of three weeks, in winter.
4 P means 4 visits to or from patroness.
* Mother stayed 16 months before this period, 1 month immediately after it. Daughter visited twice soon after.

M = mother	⌀ = divorcée	W = wife
F = father	B = brother	Cl = colleague
S = son	Z = sister	Fr = friend
D = daughter	H = husband	P = patron(ess)

119

timetable is given in Table 13, the wife began to see her mother, sister and another sister's daughter every day and for long periods. When her husband returned, these contacts became flying visits or ceased altogether.

The husband was a teacher living in a government house in his wife's village. She was the only girl in her family to have had some secondary schooling, or indeed any schooling at all. She was secluded, with one eighteen-month-old child.

Secluded women cling to the chance visitor. '*Gelsi maya*', 'Sit with me.' Invitations from one woman to another are always couched in this form: 'Come and sit with me.' And, indeed, simply being there is one of the main purposes of the visit, which may last several hours, most of the time being passed in relaxed silence or talk of the most desultory kind. Women who are less secluded have by far the jollier life. Some of those who are widowed or divorced weave carpets for the co-operative or may even attend the housecraft classes run by the Union Nationale de Femmes Marocaines.

In this situation the head of the household is its focus, and the authority of the paterfamilias, who is generally employed and rides the crest of the wave of 'progress' and modernity, is conserved to a much greater degree than in the *ksar*.

8

Relationships among women

Whether Moroccan women are secluded or not they need the company, services and material support of other women, since those of men are not available to them. These women tend to be kin, especially in the *ksar*, but as I have pointed out in Chapter 3 they may be patronesses or clients of various kinds. They demand of each other severe standards of behaviour. Educated or working women and even dancers adhere to these norms when they are interacting with other women, and come equally under the sanction of rebuke from those women vested with authority, or of withdrawal of support. Most women belong to several overlapping co-operative networks. If a woman loses her place in one, she has others to fall back on, but in the last resort only that based on her own 'kindred of co-operation' is indestructible. Even if she herself falls out with her kin, her children's relationship with them is not affected.

In the pages which follow, I discuss first of all how the allocation of authority among women is related to the division of labour, and move on to point out the structural importance of uterine kinship

Division of labour and allocation of authority among women in all social milieux

Within groups of co-operating women, domestic tasks are allocated in a way which reflects the status of its various members. In this way some tasks come to be associated with low esteemed status, others with highly esteemed status. In an *ad hoc* action-set, there is an already established mode of distributing tasks, and performing them; women express symbolically their acceptance of the authority structure which has emerged for the time being. The roles assumed within the group are inevitably of a multiplex nature, and the authority structure is more durable and valid on every occasion of interaction. The most important criteria in the allocation of status are:

1. Relation to the head of the household. This gives a man's mother priority over his wife, but his wife priority over her mother if the

context of activity is his own household. It also gives own children priority over foster-children, or the child of the wife by a former husband.

2. Marital status. Wives with children have the upper hand over those who have none, and women who have only boys or many boys appear to enjoy the deference of other women on that account, but this is a barely tested perception. Married women are more highly esteemed than divorced or widowed women, and the latter more than single women. A divorced woman will often insist that she is *tam Tut* (a woman) if you refer to her as *tarbat* (girl or virgin).

3. Seniority. Age is used to rank people who would be of equal status according to the other criteria. Thus, older women have precedence over younger ones, and unmarried siblings are ranked in birth order. This gives the eldest daughter a power over her younger sisters which she uses in a conspicuous and tyrannical way. They may protest but always end up doing her bidding.

In a household where there are tasks of fieldwork, household work and child-care to be done, there is usually a graduation from older to younger women down from the performance of tasks involving skill and responsibility for resources towards those which merely involve expenditure of energy and the removal of dirt.

An analysis of the distribution of domestic tasks in thirteen families living in Akhdar, and another thirteen drawn from Aghzim and Bentaleb, all of whom I knew well, revealed a consistent association of tasks with status, and the assumption of authority within the group. However, this is not to claim that this distribution is unaffected by the personalities of the actors. A strong-minded daughter may rule her mother, especially in unstructured situations, although she may observe the forms when there are strangers present. The tasks selected as carrying status-specific significance are the following, in order of esteem: cooking, making tea, making bread, working in the fields, marketing, washing and washing-up, fetching water, serving meals, running errands, playing the fool to amuse the company.

Where two combined statuses, e.g. wife/mother are mentioned, this means that a woman with children would perform them most often in her capacity as wife, but although still entitled to perform them as mother, would tend to hand them over to her daughters. Where mother precedes wife, as in tea-making, this means that a woman as mother would perform this task more often than as wife. If a woman bearing the relation of wife to the head of the household and a woman

Table 15. *Distribution of tasks*

Task	Performed by
Cooking	Wife/mother, eldest daughter
Making tea	Mother/wife, husband/father
Marketing	Eldest daughter, husband/father, elder sons, foster-child (only sent for specific item)
Making bread	Wife/mother, elder daughters
Working in fields	Wife/mother, eldest daughter, husband/father, sons, daughter-in-law (*ksar* only)
Washing	Wife/mother, any of daughters, foster-daughter, daughter-in-law, peripheral persons (*hartaniyin*, widows and divorcées, i.e. non-kin)
Washing-up ⎱ Washing floor ⎰	Any of daughters but usually younger ones, foster-child, peripheral persons
Serving at meals	Daughters, foster-child, peripheral persons (younger daughters, foster-child) (*ksar* only)
Playing the fool	Younger daughter, foster-child

who was his mother were both present the latter would be more likely to perform this task than the former.

Behaviour

Women performing esteem-carrying tasks tend to control the activities of other women. Thus a woman who is cooking calls on others to supply her with needed utensils, to bring her water or light the fire. In a more general sense she can distribute tasks, but as girls grow older they will automatically perform the work expected of them. Adult outsiders also take up specific roles, generally subordinate ones. But this relationship of subordination is all-pervading in that women holding little-esteemed status expect to be the servants in every respect of those more favourably placed, and to consider the needs of the latter before their own. Their seniors, however, having been through a lifetime's training in altruism and deference tend not to exploit their position unduly. The ideal is that mothers should cherish their children and put their needs first. This conditioning tends to counteract the inducement in the structural situation for women of highly esteemed ascribed status to act despotically towards their juniors. In fact this may be one reason why women seem always to act with exaggerated politeness and modesty towards each other, as their

123

altruisms clash. Each swears that the other must sit still while *she*, the speaker, does the necessary. Each vows that she is not hungry if supplies are short, or that she has no great passion for meat if there is only a cubic inch in the stew, to be shared among four people. This kind of behaviour is especially common among peripheral members of the action-set, such as divorcées or *hartaniyin* who are not members of the kindred of co-operation and who tend to perform low-status tasks. By acting towards them with extreme consideration, the kindred of co-operation secures their service for future occasions, and attempts to create in them an emotional attachment to the group. There is often a great show of affection among all the women of the group.

Close relationship among uterine kin

All the Moroccans I met laid great emphasis on the importance of the mother, but this sentiment was especially stressed when the relationship between daughter and mother came under discussion. A motherless child is in Moroccan eyes the most wretched creature on earth. But a girl is particularly *meskina* (poor, wretched) if her mother dies, because in this event she stands to lose her father as well. A man usually takes only his sons into his new marriage, leaving his daughters to be brought up by their maternal grandmother or mother's sister.

The significance of relationships among women related matrilaterally is indicated by the frequency with which they foster each other's children, either 'voluntarily', or more often in times of crisis such as the remarriage or death of the parent (see Chapter 9). Uterine relationships persist in spite of acute personal conflicts. Relationships of lesser structural significance such as that between a girl and her father's wife (step-mother) are not expected to stand the strain. In the following account of matrilateral relationships in three generations, the structural factor is seen to win out over the personal one.

Baha (see page 43 above) who had had twelve children, only six of whom survived, was a living example of the strength of obligation and sentiment which attaches mother and daughter to each other. Her daughter Aisha had married an elderly *fellah* from her parents' region, and the couple with three children lived about 35 kilometres away from Akhdar. Baha fostered Aisha's eldest son so that he could go to school in Aghzim. She visited her daughter about once a month, and the latter kept her parents supplied with maize and wheat. Visiting Aisha one winter's day, Baha, who always maintained a slightly amused and patronising air when faced with the rude conditions in which her daughter lived although she herself was much poorer, took off her dress and cardigan to give to Aisha who was complaining of cold. She put on her daughter's thin and worn clothes remarking to me: 'You see what it is to be a mother; she is my daughter, so I gave her everything.' In the spring, Aisha with one of her children fled to her mother from her *ksar*, where the floods were so severe that roofs were caving in and it was impossible to reach the nearby market. Although she was the one in danger, she told her mother in the purest convention: 'I was worried about *you*, in the floods.'

Although Baha's relations with her own mother were ambivalent she always attempted to act towards her according to the social ideal of mutual devotion. She sometimes showed scorn for her mother's ineptitude and lack of craft skills, saying that she herself had learnt all she knew from her father's sister and not from her mother. Nevertheless, it was with her mother that she left the child of her first marriage, when she married again after her first husband's death. The old lady, who was between seventy and eighty in 1970–1, would often travel from her home, some 100 kilometres south of Akhdar, to stay with her granddaughter whom she had fostered and who lived some 100 kilometres to the north of Akhdar. She seemed to prefer her company to that of her somewhat domineering daughter, with whom she nevertheless remained for more than a year, both of them suffering the turbulent atmosphere because of the reciprocal obligation traditionally attached to the mother–daughter relationship.

Moreover, this relationship had sustained some buffeting over the years. Indeed, none of the old lady's relationships had been plain sailing. For two years she had lived with Baha's brother in his late father's house. However, she quarrelled with his wife, eventually forcing her son to divorce her. The wife had two children, one of whom was so grief-stricken by her departure that he ran away from home and had not been heard of since. Baha's mother then chose another wife for her son, a hard-working *hartaniya* from a village near Akhdar. Baha, who was very conscious of the fact that her father had been a *sheikh*, and who often stressed her white Berber ancestry ('Women in our *bled* will marry old men rather than marry *haratn*' she said with great vehemence) was scathing about her mother's choice. Her behaviour towards her sister-in-law verged on the offensive. She insisted that her brother had been very attached to his first wife, and that her mother had damaged the family honour. Both daughter and son had therefore serious reproaches to make to their mother. Nevertheless, not only did the son obey her in this matter but she continued to live in his house, until she declared herself put upon by his children. Selling two small houses which she had inherited from her husband, she bought another in the village nearby, where she lived, abject and alone, refusing all offers of help from her children.

Baha, being distressed to hear of this arrangement, made the long journey to visit her brother. They decided to visit their mother and to attempt to persuade her to return to Baha's house in Akhdar, where she could be cared for.

It was spring and the village in which the old woman was living was surrounded by a deep moat, filled by the heavy rains. Her children refused to allow the encounter to be on her terms, saying she was *wa'ar* (difficult), and they would not go into the village, although she was so weak that she had to crawl out on her hands and knees. Baha had brought her some sugar and tea, and they sat down behind a wall to talk. The mother set up a wail ' *A-illi, a-illi!*' (My daughter!) being apparently very moved to see Baha. Baha used her mother's loaded appeal to demand why she refused to come and be looked after. She tried to persuade her that it was shameful for them all, that she should be living alone, uncared for. She should come home to Akhdar, where she could be clean and nourished, where she could sit on a dry cement floor in the sun. She should spend these years in prayer, to prepare herself for death, and not in strife with her children. But the old woman was adamant, attempting to get her way without estranging her daughter. Baha grew desperate at her mother's stubbornness, repeating that this was not the way for a woman with children still alive to spend her old age. Finally, she swept off weeping, leaving her mother to call weakly after her.

Both mother and daughter experienced acute distress at this contravention of the norms governing the mother–daughter relationship, although such a contravention was made inevitable by the mother's personality. This is one clue to the significance which women attach to the mother–daughter relationship. More telling even than this is the strong apprehension, apparent in the attitudes and behaviour of both men and women, that a woman's attachment to her female kin, notably mother and sisters, will wreck her marriage. Mothers are supposed to connive with daughters and arrange for them to meet lovers, when the girls are still living in their father's household. Men blame mothers, too, for giving their daughters such a welcome when the latter run away from their husbands, a common preliminary to divorce.

This fear corresponds to a reality. In the *ksour*, where no bride-wealth is paid on marriage, and to a lesser extent in poorer town marriages when little bridewealth is paid, a woman maintains economic bonds with her kin, especially if she inherits property in land which most women do not claim. This shared economic link with kin will reinforce and legitimise the tendency for female kin to render service in each other's households, where there is always a labour shortage in times of peak activity. Moreover, there are circumstances, such as childbirth or illness, in every woman's life, when she activates the close relationship with female relatives. When a woman gives birth she likes to have her own kin around her, informants say emphatically. A woman's mother often travels hundreds of kilometres to take care of her daughter. Married sisters are also welcome aides, since they introduce none of the elements of respect which tend to intrude on a woman's relationship with her husband's sisters and above all with his mother. Similarly when a woman is ill or unable to do heavy work because she is pregnant, she calls on her own kin to help her. It is as if she were responsible for fulfilling certain specific obligations towards her husband, and if she is for some reason prevented from doing so, she should find a substitute from among her own kin.

Standing aside

If a woman's kin consider her marriage to be an advantageous one, either to her and/or to them in that it holds out prospects of help for other members of the family, they will do all they can to prevent her conflict of allegiance from destroying it. However, they will not fail to rescue their kinswoman from a painful situation. Where the wife has received no dowry, her kin, not her husband, are liable to supply any extra clothes, jewellery or medical treatment which she may want. However, if a woman has remained with a man for many years, and has borne his children, it is considered honourable for him to see to her needs, as if she were one of his kin.

The divergent attitudes of a single person (admittedly a widow playing the roles of both mother and father) towards her daughters' marriages are described below. They give some indication of the social implications of marriages in which bridewealth has been paid – in the one case she intervened, in the other she remained aloof. To pay bridewealth is a sign of a man's cultural advance and his equality with town Muslims, which he will fiercely defend. To receive bridewealth is a sign of a woman's social advance, but it is also a sign that she abdicates reciprocal obligations of maintenance and service with her kin, submitting to strict control of her activities by her husband.

However, it should be noted that in order to claim genetricial rights in his wife a husband must take entire responsibility for maintaining her during pregnancy and the nursing period, even if he has paid bridewealth. He should also pay for the services of a midwife and provide the child's keep. A woman's kin hold more than residual rights with respect to her children.

Marriage or kinship?

Yamna's mother, Bedda, a strong-minded widow who owns fields in Aghzim, is on bad terms with Yamna's husband, who never visits her house. Bedda has a range of criticisms to make about her son-in-law: his failure to buy his wife contraceptives although she has nine children and is still only in her late thirties; his tendency to keep his money – and he earns a good regular wage – for himself, and to buy what she considers excessive quantities of meat when the children are badly clothed and housed. The quarrel which resulted in rupture was over his refusal to buy a new and larger house which was on sale in the *ksar*, when his own was damp and small, aggravating his wife's attacks of asthma, and rheumatism in one of his sons.

When Yamna had her last child she was in some danger, but her mother had to find a taxi to take her to hospital. Yamna's husband arrived in hospital the same day, complaining that he was very ill and no one was there at home to look after him.

When Yamna had an acute attack of asthma, her husband was away; she had been ill and overworked for some time, but he showed no interest in her receiving treatment, and she felt she must stay and look after the children. Bedda at this crisis said she was not going to let her daughter die, but hesitated for a long time to take matters into her own hands fearing that Yamna's husband would interpret her actions as an attack on his conjugal rights. 'He will say that I am trying to take his wife away from him.' She resolved to sell a field and see to her daughter's treatment, sending her to her son's home to convalesce. But she knew that by this means she was in effect abrogating the husband's conjugal rights. 'When she comes back she must choose between bringing her youngest child and coming to live with me, and we can get a divorce, or if he pleads with her to go back she can if she wants to.' In the event, Yamna stayed only a few days with her mother before returning home.

Relationships among women

Kinship or affinity?

When Yamna's sister Fadma (see Chapter 7) was in her last month of pregnancy, her parents-in-law came to see her from a town 500 kilometres away to persuade her to have the baby in their village, but could not stay because of the demands of their farm. Bedda put herself in an increasingly peripheral role, leaving Fadma's married sister Khadouj to do Fadma's heavy household tasks (Khadouj was married in Rabat, and was encouraged by her husband to come for this occasion). Finally when Fadma went to hospital, her mother did not come to visit her, leaving that task to Fadma's husband Ali and to Khadouj.

Ali, a teacher in Aghzim and therefore uxorilocally married, was sensitive to the implications of his position, and often made it clear that he was not subservient to his mother-in-law by casually forgetting to help her with a particular task, or by forbidding the children of his wife's sister to come into the house. He often waxed eloquent on the evils of divorce, which he believed to be due to two factors: first to an attachment of the wife to her mother and siblings, second to the fact that her wishes were not consulted by her father when he went about choosing a marriage partner for her. Her conjugal situation amounted to an enforced coexistence with a possibly antipathetic stranger.

Since Fadma was born in Aghzim, she had many kinship ties there, which could endanger her commitment to her marriage. Her mother explicitly recognised this when the couple moved into their own house, saying 'We won't visit you much now, so that you can get used to living on your own', and her conspicuous absence from the birth scene was a further recognition of the precedence of conjugal ties, and the alignment of the new baby with his father's group, although born in his mother's village.

The necessity for such tact varied according to the stage which the couple had reached in the developmental cycle. Many old women lived with or near their daughters in Aghzim and Bentaleb, relying on them for a measure of help and company. At this stage in the marriage when the wife had borne several children and contributed largely to the smooth running of the affairs of the household, her husband was likely to view the prospect of supporting her mother with equanimity. However, the mother was never assertive. Many mothers would frequently baby-sit for a daughter and son-in-law and keep the daughter company in the absence of the household head. But such a woman would rarely stay long when the son-in-law returned, preferring to stay in her own house nearby (see Table 13).

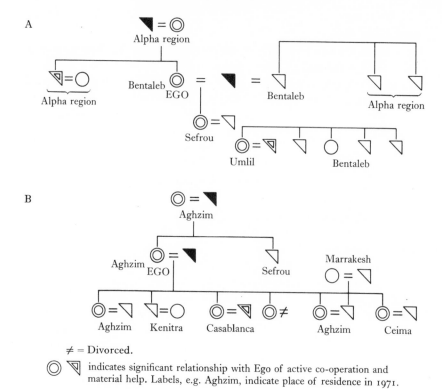

$\neq$ = Divorced.

◎ ◥ indicates significant relationship with Ego of active co-operation and material help. Labels, e.g. Aghzim, indicate place of residence in 1971.

Figure 1. Matrilateral solidarity: A. Baha as Ego; B. Bedda as Ego

It appears then that where the stakes in the conjugal relationship are high in terms of wealth in goods or children, the wife's kin will take care not to present themselves as a threat to this bond. Where the marriage is newly established or precarious for other reasons, the husband will attempt to prevent his wife from renewing contact with her kin, for fear that the departure should become definitive. He will encourage the wife to form co-operative relationships with her affines, rather than her kin, effecting her more complete incorporation into his kin group. To take these measures is to recognise the latent strength of a woman's ties with her kin, particularly those to whose 'kindred of co-operation' she has belonged all her life, her mother and sisters.

Further, if a woman has married a man with a salary or capital, she will have received dower. Dower gives rights of bride-removal to the husband. He will attempt to replace his bride's kin by his own in the roles of household helpers and friends, thus achieving a greater

130

degree of 'integration' of the wife into the husband's kin group than is possible in the *ksar*.

The exchange of children (for fostering) among women kin is the life-blood of a woman's 'kindred of co-operation'; it is a means of communication for virilocally married women whose days would be played out within sight of their hearth, but for their links with female kin.

9

Fostering

Children who, as a result of misfortune or design, come to live with people other than their parents, are frequently fostered by their mother's female relatives. This is especially true of girls fostered in crisis and constitutes one more indication of the structural importance of uterine kinship, which acts as a safety net for the casualties of a discriminatory social system which tends to work to the advantage of men, though favouring some men more than others.

The arrangement which places children with their mother's kin also avoids the conflicts over inheritance which might break out if a child were fostered by an agnate. Such conflicts might be of two forms, those between the rightful heirs of a man and his foster-child agnate, or those between a person fostered in crisis and his agnate-guardian who might attempt to steal his inheritance. Both these situations might arise in fostering but the threat to kinship rights would be greater if adoption were possible.

In this chapter I discuss the meaning of fostering and the prohibition on adoption, the reasons why children are fostered, and their distribution among kin and others.

The importance of the category 'others' leads me to deal with the social situation of foster-children. The foster-child's disadvantages complement the need of many women to improve their position in the women's status-system by acquiring 'false kin' and clients, among whom are children.

The presence of a child in the household of adults who are not his parents may come about for different historical reasons, and carry only one of a range of possible social meanings. Behind the variety of relationships subsumed under the category of fostering lies the common assumption that children may be reared away from their parents at the convenience of the adults concerned, and that they will suffer no damage in this process that is not socially tolerated. In spite of this common denominator it is important to recognise that the precipitating causes are various – from the breakdown of a marriage necessitating alternative arrangements for children (crisis foster-

Table 16. *Distribution of foster-children*

| | I. GIRLS | | | | | |
| | Agnatic kin | | Uterine kin | | | |
Sample	M	F	M	F	Others	Total
(1) $n = 87$	0	0	3	2	5	10
(2) $n = ?$	1	4	1	8	4	18
Total	1	4	4	10	9	28

| | II. BOYS | | | | | |
| | Agnatic kin | | Uterine kin | | | |
Sample	M	F	M	F	Others	Total
(1) $n = 78$	1	1	1	1	2	6
(2) $n = ?$	2	1	2	2	3	10
Total	3	2	3	3	5	16

n = Total number of children in sample.

ing), through the recruitment of domestic helpers, compensation for sterility, maintenance of kinship bonds to mutual advantage, or co-operation among kin in the schooling and other provisions for children. (All the latter category I will call voluntary fostering following E. N. Goody.[1]) Several of these factors may contribute to the decision to foster a child, but my impression is that on the whole they work in favour of the adults and their mutual social arrangements, rather than in the child's interest.

The advantages for foster-parents

In many cases of voluntary fostering the foster-parent takes the initiative for the child's transfer. The arrangement is not always between kin. In fact the category of 'others' (i.e. non-kin) cannot be considered, as in Gonja, a 'residual' after fostering by matrilateral and patrilateral kin has been considered. It forms such an important proportion of total fostering that it has a profound influence on the content of kinship fostering, which acquires elements of a conditional and contractual relationship.

In a sense, the foster-child is always a necessary addition to the foster-parents' household in that he allows the members to fill the socially valued complement of roles. A barren couple will foster a

[1] In Association of Social Anthropologists' monograph 8, 1970.

child to satisfy their need to be parents, and to provide the wife with a servant to help her with necessarily co-operative tasks. In this way the husband is able to seclude his wife more efficiently, since she can send her small minion on missions to the outside world, and his own status is thereby enhanced. This appears to be in contrast with the situation in Gonja, where fostered children 'would have been equally useful at home'.[1]

In Morocco, a woman without children rouses compassion mixed with scorn. Her childlessness is her most significant characteristic, and is immediately mentioned if she is under discussion. Even women without husbands may assume a foster-mother role to avoid such attention.

Bedda's third daughter, a woman who had been five times divorced by the time she was twenty-five, three times because she had borne no children, became the nominal 'mother' of one of her sister's sons. He remained at home, and his mother would often come to stay with his parents, between her own 'marriages'. She would take charge of him, carrying him with her, supplying all his needs. She insisted that he called her 'mother'.

Two children of sample (1), and four of sample (2), were fostered by couples who had been many years married without having children.[2] A further two of each sample were fostered by widows who had had no children of their own and did not expect to marry again. A child fostered by a childless couple tends to keep in close contact with his or her parents, chiefly for the contact with siblings. Except for one widow in sample (1) who adopted a *hartani* orphan and a Berber orphan originally fostered by the French Franciscan nuns, the children are those of friends or neighbours whom the child can visit more or less frequently. Except for orphans adopted by childless people children are generally fostered at an age when they can be useful to their foster-parents, that is, over six years old. Girls appear to spend more years in the fostering household than boys, and the foster-parents will arrange for the marriage of a teenage foster-daughter.

Boys may stay on if they have employment or training prospects. In one case a man's brother's sons, aged sixteen, helped his uncle to prospect for minerals. In another, the fostered boy, whose brother was employed by his foster-father, became in turn his shop assistant,

---

[1] E. N. Goody (1970), 60.

[2] 10% of married women in Morocco, compared with 25% in Britain as a whole, were childless, 12% in urban areas and 8% in the country. Syphilis has been suggested as one cause of sterility but others may include malnutrition and lack of sexual adjustment. The high rate of marriage and divorce among younger women must also be a factor. (Résultats de l'enquête (1964), 69.)

Table 17. *Circumstances of various foster-children*

Living with	Father dead	Mother dead	Parents dead	Parents divorced	School or training	As servant/ companion
			SAMPLE (1)			
Mother and uterine kin	1 boy, 1 girl	—	—	2 boys, 2 girls	—	—
Uterine kin only	1 boy, 4 girls	—	—	—	—	1 boy, 1 girl
Agnatic kin	—	—	—	—	1 boy	—
Others	—	—	—	—	—	2 girls
Total	7	0	0	4	1	4
			SAMPLE (2)			
Mother and uterine kin	—	—	—	—	—	—
Uterine kin only	3 girls, 2 boys	—	3 girls	3 girls	1 boy	1 boy, 2 girls
Agnatic kin	—	—	3 girls, 2 boys	1 boy	—	2 boys, 1 girl
Others	—	—	—	—	1 boy	3 girls
Total	5	0	8	4	2	9

Alternative to fostering: 2 children live with their working *hartaniya* mother; 1 girl lives with her remarried mother; 2 boys with their remarried fathers.

and a third brother married the foster-father's daughter. One boy was fostered by his Koranic teacher and stayed at the mosque for several years.

Samples

Sample (1) is drawn from the sample quarter of Akhdar town. Here, out of a total of 165 children under sixteen, 16 were fostered. 23 % of households contained a fostered child. Sample (2) is composed of all the cases of fostering in Aghzim, Bentaleb and Akhdar which I encountered, apart from those in the Rising. The limitations of this kind of material are evident for the nature of the population is unknown. It can be regarded as useful in that it gives insights into the nature of the foster-parent/foster-child relationship and the relations of both parties with the foster-child's parents, rather than indicating the significance of fostering in the society as a whole. This sample provides a total of twenty-eight cases. Other samples which provide illustrative and confirming instances are the final class in the girls' primary school, the second year[1] in the mixed secondary school in Akhdar and the penultimate class in a mixed *ksar* primary school.

Informants' model

Asked about fostering, men talked about kinship fostering. Brothers might bring up each other's children, or a brother those of his sister. When asked if a sister might bring up her brother's children they said it could happen, but were unable to bring a case to mind. This is consistent with the ideal that women should be wards rather than guardians but my findings suggest that the majority of kin-fostered children are reared by female kin. However, these are more often relatives of the mother than of the father. They are mostly girls. The fostering of girls by female kin is one aspect of the strong but unacknowledged association among women, which tends to undermine the political control of men. The presence of a strong sibling bond can also be inferred from the actors' view of fostering.

The prohibition on adoption

It is consistent too with the actors' emphasis on fostering among kin that adoption should be heavily censured. It is shameful for a man to give away his children, even to kinsmen. Firstly, foster-children are essentially servants, and, secondly, to foster a kinsman's children is to allow kinship rights of usufruct, as it were. After one's kin it is one's close friends who may enjoy usufruct as a privilege, but this is an individual affair rather than a social norm and is ignored in the actors' model. Moroccans often make claims on the resources of other people in the name of kinship, but the understanding is that if the parties are classificatory kin, there is no obligation to satisfy these demands. However, the ideological infrastructure for mutual help between remote relatives does exist. A man who transfers the kinship rights and duties of his child to another person takes no account of the latent network to which the child belongs, extending through space and time. In allowing someone else to appropriate his child he is also alienating the rights and duties by which a large number of people are linked to the child. He has no right so to deal with the property of other people. Hence the strong social opprobrium.[2]

[1] What is nominally the second year is actually the third year spent at the school, the first one being a probationary year, spent in a *classe d'observation*.

[2] Note also: 'Allah n'a pas permis deux coeurs dans l'intérieur de l'homme. Il n'a pas fait que vos fils adoptifs soient comme vos propres fils' and 'Appelez-les (vos fils adoptifs) du (nom)

Fostering

Kinship rights cannot be transferred. Adoption, that is simulated kinship and fertility, must be viewed in the light of ideas which people hold about real kinship and fertility. Briefly, they are beyond the control of the individual, and ordained by God. In important ways, these two factors govern the life-chances of individuals in Akhdar. A man's kin are ideally his economic helpmates; he derives his most significant political status from their standing in his community, their ancestry and their wealth, their numerical strength. With the help of his kin, he acquires socially valued domestic statuses, those of husband and father, control of the services of wife and children and future security. Chance plays a big part in all this. What if he is born a *hartani*, or his wife is sterile or bears all girls, whose husbands will not be obliged to support their parents-in-law in later life? What if she is so prolific that the family becomes impoverished and children die? It is the will of God. A man who attempts to create or cancel kinship by giving his child for adoption, or taking one born to someone else, refuses to recognise what is ordained. A man's kin are a part of his personality and they will help him make good the deficiencies to the best of their power, by financial aid, lending him children, at the same time keeping an eye to their own interests.

The first obligation of a man is to his children, and by reason of the care and the patrimony they receive from him, they incur reciprocal obligations. Baha told me, 'We must work to bring up our children. Then they will look after us.' The ideal behaviour on the part of a salaried son, for example, is to halve his earnings with his parents, whatever his own needs or wants, and this expectation continues after he is married. Increasingly this norm, with its strong Islamic backing, is resented by the young sophisticates, and to escape such extreme family pressures some salary earners cut all contact with their kin. A foster-child does not have such duties towards his foster-parents. His position is essentially that of dependant, but were he adopted, given kinship and property rights with respect to his adoptive parents, they would be entitled to exact the performance of reciprocal duties.

Although nearly half of voluntarily fostered children are non-kin, sometimes orphans, they are never adopted by their foster-parents. My informants said that however poor a man is, and however many children he has, he would not have it said of him that he gave away his

de leurs pères; cela est plus juste, auprès d'Allah. Mais si vous connaissez pas leurs pères: qu'ils soient vos frères et vos clients' (Koran: soura 33; verset 4 & 5 cited from A. Faibi, *Revue algérienne des sciences juridiques, économiques et politiques* (1968), 1140).

children. And the foster-parents prefer 'to live at peace with society' than 'to be accused of taking another man's child from him'.

I only heard of two cases of adoption, and my informants' first reaction to questioning was to say that it never happened. One involved a boy whose father died. His mother sent the child to her brother to foster, but when she fell dangerously ill allowed him to adopt her son, changing his name to his own by legal process. The mother died shortly afterwards, but her action was not excused in the light of the circumstances. She was held to have done something terrible. Her son eventually became headmaster of a school, successful in career terms, but his biography was still anomalous.

The other concerned three orphan girls and a boy who were raised by their deceased father's sister. She gave one girl to a woman in another village for adoption and earned lasting social opprobrium. The strict sanctions on the legitimation or formalisation of child-transfer suggest that fostering is a function of the 'underground', as it were, the informal women's sphere, in which relationships have no politically regulated dimension, but persist independently of the formal political organisation, controlled by men.[1]

Apart from the taboo on the disruption of the kinship order discussed above, there are three associated factors which may explain why not a single child is dispensable. One is that the habits of thought associated with a high infant mortality rate,[2] appreciably reduced for only some sectors of the population within the last twenty years, have not been abandoned. The second is that children are an assurance for the future, but, third, their success in a context of generalised unemployment and uncertain agricultural yields cannot be ascertained in advance. A family, by keeping all its children, maximises its chances of support, and spreads its risks. Children mean a potential not actual plenty and none can be spared for outsiders.

Boys and girls

The fact that the productive potential of boys will be more continuously available to their kin than that of girls, and the fact that women do not hold political status, are two reasons for the fostering of

---

[1] E. de Gaudin de Lagrange points out that in Tunisia before adoption was legalised, people resorted to numerous subterfuges in the attempt to lay more definitive claim to their foster-children. This sometimes lead to disputes between real and foster-children over inheritance. 'Cependant l'adoption faisait figure d'institution de fait, non *de droit.*' Ibid (1968), 1143.

[2] *Maroc rural*: Zones arides et de montagnes 186/1000; *Maroc urbain*: 100/1000. This includes all deaths of children under 1 year old. 70% of all deaths in the rural population occur among children under 14 years old. (Résultats de l'enquête (1964), 76.)

Table 18. *Distribution of children fostered voluntarily*

Sample	Agnatic kin		Uterine kin		Others	Total
	M	F	M	F		
I. GIRLS						
(1) $n = 87$	0	0	3	2	6	11
(2) $n = ?$	0	1	1	1	3	6
Total	0	1	4	3	9	17
II. BOYS						
(1) $n = 78$	1	0	1	0	0	2
(2) $n = ?$	2	1	2	0	3	8
Total	3	1	3	0	3	10

girls in much greater numbers than boys. In both samples (1) and (2) they comprise 64% of the totals. A girl will leave home. It is her husband's kin who stand to gain most from her services and productive skills. By fostering a girl a couple avoids the suspicion that they will try to adopt her definitively, because she is only a temporary asset. Her own parents are less anxious about the transfer of her loyalties: they will lose her anyway.

The other main reason has to do with the 'functions of fostering'.[1] Girls are fostered voluntarily in the town more frequently than boys, since a woman cannot manage without a helper and companion in the performance of her daily tasks. A man without a son is not so handicapped; he can employ a labourer and in the town he will not be engaged in co-operative work anyway. The psychological disadvantages of childlessness for a woman are also greater than for a man, since bearing and rearing children is considered a woman's primary role. The range of acceptable activities for men is much wider.

While noting that fostering of girls for the purposes of foster-parents is important, it must be pointed out that crisis fostering of girls, that is the rearing of children from broken homes, is even more common, but mainly in the *ksar*.

Voluntary fostering

There are two modes of voluntary fostering. Brothers or a brother and sister may agree that the child of one should be raised by the other. Although this seems casually to represent the 'strength of the

[1] E. N. Goody (1970), 59.

139

sibling bond' and the desire to maintain an effective tie, there seem to be concrete mutual advantages. A foster-father always derives service from his foster-child and his authority is likely to be more absolute than that of the child's own parent. It is the wife nevertheless who most needs extra hands and small messengers. A boy not infrequently is sent to kin who are richer than his own parents, or who have fewer children, or live in an area with a good school. A girl is always useful, and from the parents' point of view may have better marriage prospects with her foster-parents.

Apart from fostering by the siblings of the parents, there are many cases where the grandparents of a child may foster him in order to maintain relations with their own children whose services and other resources they wish to claim.

Mohand, whose son is a *mokhazni* with eight children (five of them under twelve), fosters one grandson. In this way he relieves his daughter-in-law and assures himself of the services of the family on his fields from time to time, and his wife can call on his granddaughter's help.

Baha's daughter (see p. 43) is married to a large field-owner, living about 30 kilometres from Akhdar. This daughter has four children under seven. Their grandparents are very poor and depend on supplies of wheat and maize from their son-in-law's farm. In turn they foster a grandson, who is thus enabled to go to a good school, for his grandmother is the client-friend of the headmaster's wife. If he stayed with his parents he would not be able to go to school, or would have to walk a great distance to a very poor one.

Foster-children as servants

Many children are fostered by non-kin. Most of them are girls. Since it is only poor people who would, in the last resort, send their child to an unrelated family, these girls tend to be of lower status than their foster-parents. Sometimes the foster-child is the real daughter of an employee of the foster-parents, and is thus bound in a relation of clientship. This type of fostering occurs mainly in the town.

The situation of foster-children might be ranged then on a continuum, with, at one end, those who enjoy high kinship status because they are descended from close patrilineal kin, through children of matrilateral kin (the majority), and, at the far end, the children of 'others' who, because of the servant status of their parents, can claim no rights but are bound to a life of service and dependent clientship (see note p. 25).

Fostering

Haratn sometimes send their daughters to acquaintances in other towns where they are said to 'work'. There is no doubt that such children are sent in order to relieve the family of financial burden, and to forge links with richer families who may, by virtue of the service they have received, and the total nature of the relationship, prove to be a source of economic help. Sometimes the girl may be treated quite harshly. I heard several stories of girls who had run away from their foster-parents. If she is a *hartaniya*, her position is particularly unenviable, for she is unlikely to become a daughter, even in classificatory terms. One widow who had fostered a *hartaniya* since she was a year old described her as *abid*, which is a generic term sometimes used for *haratn*, meaning 'slave'.

On the other hand, an educated couple who had no children and fostered their *hartani* employee's daughter gave her everything any bourgeois girl could desire. She lived a glamorous life, accompanying the wife to the celebrations of rich people, speaking French, doing fine embroidery. However, she was expected to wait on her foster-parents and their guests. Unlike daughters who often, in their security, protested that they were tired or that it was someone else's turn, this girl never demanded any consideration of her wishes or needs. Her parents and brothers lived in a two-roomed house adjoining that of the foster-parents but never came into it. Their daughter often visited them, but her mother was slightly awed by her sophistication, and felt more at ease with her sons. The daughter had derived her social identity from her foster-parents, but she was their dependant and subordinate.

Psychological effects – some hints

Since the majority of foster-children are found at the low end of the continuum, their status is bound to affect the self-image of foster-children as a whole. They, like 'peripheral members' of women's quasi-groups, tend to be more than obliging, to perform low status tasks like cleaning and fetching water. Their behaviour is 'rationalised', never impulsive. They are generally silent and serious, sweet-natured. Sometimes, especially for boys, because this behaviour is imposed by external constraints, it turns into its opposite when these constraints are removed.

The boy fostered by his father's father (Mohand above) was acknowledged by his own family to be wild. His actions, when he visited his parents' home, were violent and uncontrolled. He fought with his siblings. Three out of the eleven fostered boys in sample (2) seemed

141

confused and violent when they were away from their foster-parents. In none of these cases had the boy been sent away because he was 'difficult'. When a fostered boy returns home, his efforts to establish his place among his siblings are probably more desperate than if he had been able to work out these relationships in the process of growing up. As an outsider he is handicapped.

The same behaviour is not apparent among fostered girls. This may be because their context of action is less competitive, nor, given their domestic role, are they likely to meet outsiders. The need to establish an identity among people to whom they or their parents are unknown is less urgent for girls than for boys.

Children after the divorce of their parents

Legally the father of a woman's child should contribute to her subsistence expenses during the gestation period, should pay medical expenses at the birth, and should continue to make her an allowance until the child is weaned if he intends to claim it. In poorer milieux I have been told that a husband usually helps with medical costs and little else, but even if he did not and refused to give up his claim to the child he could probably take it away. In fact most husbands relinquish all claim to their daughters, but appear after three or four years to take away their sons unless a formal agreement has been made assigning custody to the wife and her family. The method usually employed to make agreements ratifiable when they have no legal backing is to call witnesses, ten or twelve, who will stand by the original arrangement if the husband returns and attempts to take his children (a residual function of the Ait Ashra'a. See p. 11).[1] However, arrangements about children are usually informal, casual even, resting on the whim of the parents.

It is usual for the wife to take the children of the marriage if there are one or two, especially if they are young. A greater number of children tends to constitute a strong disincentive to divorce, but the couple will often split the children between them if the wife has means to support herself, the husband taking sons and the wife daughters. The problems arising between children, especially girls, and their stepmother are legendary. The remarriage of the father also reduces the likelihood that their mother will have access to them. All these

---

[1] A similar system of witnesses operates in the case of a wife who wishes to be freed from her husband when she has not seen him for a year, and for the transfer of title to land which has not been officially surveyed or registered, and whose extent is known only to other field-owners of the same village.

Table 19. *Distribution of children fostered in crisis*

Sample	Agnatic kin		Uterine kin		Others	Total
	M	F	M	F		
		I. GIRLS				
(1) $n = 87$	0	0	0	0	0	0
(2) $n = ?$	1	3	0	7	0	11
Total	1	3	0	7	0	11
		II. BOYS				
(1) $n = 78$	0	0	2	1	0	3
(2) $n = ?$	0	1	0	2	0	3
Total	0	1	2	3	0	6

factors persuade women to take responsibilities which are often beyond their means, and which force them to rely heavily for assistance on their kin. A woman who remarries cannot take her children into a new marriage, and leaves them with her parents or matrilateral kin so that she is assured that she will not be definitively separated from them.

Crisis fostering

Thus, children of marriages which have come to an end through either divorce or death tend to be parked out with relatives when the mother marries again. Usually a divorced woman has custody of her daughters and of her sons too if they are very young.

The circumstances of the ex-spouses may influence the allocation of children. In sample (1) the boys who were fostered in crisis were all sons of divorced women. Two of these women had salaried brothers with whom they and their sons went to live, the brother later fostering the child of one of them when she married again. The third woman had a wealthy father. So there were advantages for the children in being allocated to their mothers. However, it is more usual for daughters only to remain with their mother. When she marries again, a likely event in the life of any woman under forty, her new husband will not maintain her children by another man. She must leave them with her kin. This accounts for the fact that the majority of children from broken homes are fostered by their matrilateral kin – all three boys in sample (1), nine of sample (2); that most of them are girls, and are fostered by women.

Women and property in Morocco

Sometimes it is a mother's parents who foster her children. Women say 'I left her with my mother', a phrase I heard so often that I began to recognise it as a formula referring to a 'social custom' – 6/28 cases in sample (2). More often she leaves the child with one of her siblings.

Relations with foster-parents

Bassou, an orphan fostered by his father's sister and her husband, quarrelled with his foster-parents. They wanted him to work in the local lead-mines, but he refused. He left home to take up a job in the laundry in Akhdar. In so doing he virtually sacrificed his inheritance, saying that he would leave the house and carpets of his parents to his father's sister and his sisters on the condition that no one came to pester him or beg him for money once he was earning his own living.

Boys who have been fostered by their patrilateral or matrilateral kin after a marriage broke down sometimes return to their father in adolescence. However, I heard one mother making efforts to strengthen the relationship between her son and her brother. Visiting the house where the son was living with her brother Mohamed (see Love and war case on p. 213), an educated man with a salary, she counselled him to call her brother *bba*, father, rather than *habibi*, mother's brother, the name to which he was accustomed. She was still married with six other children.

Sometimes a mother may take her daughter into her new marriage. The two girls who were in this situation talked of their stepfather in the same terms as people speak of foster-parents, '*rrba-ni*', 'he fostered me'. This relationship is clearly distinguished from the case where a women has suckled the child of another. This creates kinship and marriage is forbidden between milk-siblings. The child will call the woman who suckled her 'mother'.

Societal position of fostered children

Fostered children are regarded as less fortunate than children who live with their own parents, and are even, as we have seen, liable to be taken for servants. As with other 'peripheral members' of women's quasi-groups, it is unclear at what point the kinship fiction ends and the servant status begins. Those women or children who have kinship rights in the household where they live and work have a more pleasant life than those who have none. To be without kin is to be dependent on the good graces of other people.

144

Fostering

I do not know to what extent people fostered as children are socially impeded in Morocco, but they are not conspicuously so. Certainly the five fostered women I knew had made marriages as advantageous as any in terms of stability and material comfort. They are attractive marriage bargains, if their parents are dead, because they will have come into an inheritance. However, I would suggest that such women may divorce less frequently, not because they perform their conjugal roles more satisfactorily, but because they have a lower economic and emotional investment in their family of socialisation than home-reared children, and because marriage improves their social position to a greater degree than it does that of other women who must forego the statuses of daughter and sister.

E. N. Goody has shown for Gonja that as far as access to high office and marriage are concerned, i.e. performance within given social institutions, fostered people are not at a disadvantage. They have a capacity as great as that demonstrated by home-reared people to control their social environment in accordance with conventional ideals. However, such a conclusion cannot reveal what the content of these social relationships is. In Akhdar the stability of a marriage seems to be strongly influenced by the advantages it offers in status terms over the home situation, towards which women appear to have a decided tropism. The emotional relationship of the spouses does not appear to be significant because most of their activities are carried out independently of each other. If fostered women do not divorce, it is because they do not feel a strong attachment to 'their' families. If men are 'successful' it seems to be partly a result of the tenuousness of their kinship ties. The four fostered men I knew were more mobile than other men, more likely to seek paid employment rather than helping with co-operative tasks. Their earnings they would spend on themselves rather than to the advantage of kin or foster-kin. There were few demands on their time or resources. They were also unhappy people, who complained of neglect in childhood.

The assessment of Akhdaris may be the right one. That in spite of their apparent success, foster-children are not as well off as others. There is a tendency for foster-parents to attempt to do the right thing by their foster-children, to send them to school and dress them well, as if in compensation for the affective lack and identity problems they experience.

Women and property in Morocco

Women as child-takers and child-givers

The importance of women as foster-parents is associated with the Moroccan version of Goody's third function of adoption (for Western Europe), 'to provide homes for orphans, bastards, foundlings, and the children of impaired marriages'.[1]

That is, the children must be brought up and cared for. Women are responsible for the socialisation of children, especially for rearing girls. In their role as cherishers-in-chief, female kin are best fitted to look after a man's or a woman's offspring if the parent is unable to do so. Although there is room for manoeuvre in that the child may be sent to the kinswoman who can make most use of him or her, the arrangement is intended essentially to provide the child with a mother-substitute. A child without a mother is the most wretched creature on earth, a child in the house of his step-mother is only one degree less pitiable. It is usually easier to arrange for a child to visit her mother from her mother's kin than from the house of her mother's ex-husband, for divorced spouses in Akhdar avoid each other like the plague.

In accordance with the view that a child's first need is maternal care, women neighbours will take it upon themselves to care for a child in the custody of a divorced father who has not yet remarried.

The role of women in the circulation of children is impressive. From the samples it appears that women tend to foster children both for their own ends and for those of other women to whom they are related matrilaterally for the most part.[2] However, men who are attempting to integrate their 'dowered' wives (for whom they have paid bridewealth) into their kinship group explain the presence of their own brothers or sisters as an asset to their wives. Generally the initiative to foster a child or have one fostered is taken by a woman. It is on her female relatives that a woman depends to foster her children in crisis. This is especially true for women in the ksar with their close links with kin, and their frequent remarriages.

[1] J. Goody, 'Adoption in cross-cultural perspective', *Comparative Studies in Society and History*, Vol. II, no. 1 (January 1969).

[2] After coming to this conclusion on empirical evidence, I found the following statement. (In the case of divorce) 'la tradition musulmane considérait en effet la garde comme un droit exclusivement réservé à la branche maternelle, présumant en sa faveur une meilleure aptitude à prodiguer des soins maternels.' (A. Becheur, *Revue algérienne des sciences juridiques*, 1154.) Why agnatic kinswomen are not so good at this is a moot question. The 'sentimental' explanation is less satisfactory than that in terms of access to children on the part of the mother, and the structural importance of relations among matrilaterally related women, providing a form of social insurance.

Table 20. *Circumstances of foster-children at school*

Living with	Father dead	Mother dead	Both parents dead	Parents divorced	To go to school	Servant/ companion
	Town primary school girls ($n = 30$)					
Uterine kin	1 girl	—	—	—	—	—
Agnatic kin	—	—	—	—	—	—
	Class from town college ($n = 29$; 23 boys, 6 girls)					
Uterine kin	1 boy	—	1 girl	—	—	—
Agnatic kin	—	—	—	—	2 boys	—
	Ksar primary school ($n = 49$)					
Uterine kin	1 girl	—	1 girl	—	2 boys	—
Agnatic kin	—	—	—	—	—	—
Total	2 girls 1 boy	—	2 girls	—	4 boys	—

Alternatives to fostering: 3 *ksar* boys live with their mothers and siblings only.

This seems a further illustration of the close relationship between a woman and her mother and sisters. They, however, are separated from her in different parts of the country wherever they happen to have married away. She, for her part, is unable to travel frequently because of her domestic commitments and lack of control over resources. To exchange children is to guarantee that contact is maintained, particularly as her husband becomes indebted to her family, which provides his household with extra resources. In the latter case her domestic power position is improved.

Where a woman sends her child to her brother she is claiming rights in property and rights to support which, if she received 'dower' she may never enjoy in person since she is considered to be the responsibility of her husband's family. Where she sends them to her mother she creates an obligation to help her mother in old age. In sum, the exchange of children among kin prevents the lapse of kinship bonds, where these are socially considered desirable for emotional or material reasons. This tendency is more marked in the *ksour* than in the town, because of the greater tendency in the town for dower to be paid and for a woman to be integrated into her husband's kin-group.

Considering this emphasis on fostering by women, or through ties mediated by women, it is interesting that the preferred marriage, that between the daughter and son of brothers will nearly never be between children who have grown up in the same household. So a man will not be marrying someone who has been assimilated in affective terms to a sister.

It is through children as well as clients that adults attempt to acquire for themselves status and service.

The social facts that the school samples in Table 20 represent are the following:

1. The girls who go to school in the town are generally the daughters of the well-to-do and 'progressive' members of the community, who do not send their children to be fostered.

2. Girls who are voluntarily fostered are usually taken as servants and are therefore unlikely to go to school.

3. Girls are more frequently fostered in the crisis created by the divorced mother's remarriage, since boys will have been taken by their father.

The second set (in the college) may be analysed as follows:

1. Boys are frequently fostered by their kin in order for them to go to school.

2. Girls who have been fostered in crisis go to college (secondary school) proportionately more frequently than girls who have not been fostered. Of six girls and women in Aghzim and Bentaleb who had been fostered, four of them had spent at least one year at secondary school.

The third set (in the *ksar*) indicate:

1. The tendency for matrilateral relationships to be utilised in the *ksour* at least as often as patrilateral ones, and perhaps more often.

2. Widows in the *ksour* appear to keep their children. They are able to resist the pressures to remarry (a) because they inherit from their husbands means of production which they can exploit with the help of their children; (b) they play an economic role which enables them to support themselves, unlike townswomen; (c) they are more likely to have kept up strong links with kin on whom they can rely for support. This is linked with the kind of marriage, dowered or not, which they have made.

10

Marriage

My approach to the discussion of marriage in Akhdar takes as its premise the existence within this society of different economic and social environments, giving rise to different behaviour patterns. It seems appropriate to consider the various aspects of marriage in each setting in turn before attempting to assess its significance for the social structure as a whole.

This latter phase of the analysis is legitimate in so far as Moroccans of different milieux, when talking of marriage, assume that they are referring to an institution to which everyone subscribes. They recognise the same elements, more or less, in the establishment of a new union – that the marriage is arranged on behalf of the young couple, not by them; that they are consequently often strangers, and any familiarity between them before marriage is shameful; that the groom's female kin must assess the bride; that a great deal of *nif* (honour, face) is involved in this mutual sizing up of the families; to safeguard this the services of an intermediary come in useful; that a material settlement is made on the bride by the husband or her parents – to be paid on divorce; that a written contract stating the conditions of the marriage should be drawn up by a notary and witnessed; that the bride's virginity and fidelity carry a heavy load of *nif* for both families; that extravagant ceremonies help to assure the fecundity and popularity of the new relationships set up through the marriage, and that within it the husband's authority should be paramount and the wife's submission ultimate, but that all kinds of countervailing forces are at work to prevent the realisation of this ideal. Further, *shurfa* should marry *shurfa*, and *haratn haratn*, and marriage with Jews and Christians is anathema – especially marriage of Muslim women to Jewish and Christian men.[1] All Moroccans are aware of the existence of the frequency of divorce, the conflict between conjugal and kin ties,

---

[1] I knew of four Jewish women who married Muslim men but all of them had been converted to Islam. Most of the Muslim men who had married Christians lived in Europe, returning periodically with their wives to see their families. One Jewish man converted to Islam and married a Muslim woman in Akhdar. A French engineer fought for two years for the right to marry a Muslim girl, but it was never ceded.

the importance of marrying 'a social equal', and of certain endogamic preferences with respect to estates, regions, and kingroups. Finally it is assumed in all milieux that the main personae in the performance are women, who busy themselves about enquiries, assessments, demands, forging new affective bonds, and sabotaging existing ones. The success or failure of relationships among female affines, for example, may make or break a marriage.

Age of marriage

The age of marriage for women in the Akhdar area is considerably lower than that for men, although there does not seem to be a significant discrepancy between the ages of marriage in the town and those in the *ksour*. The average age of first marriage for women was 188 years in the town and 179 years in the *ksour*; the corresponding age for men was 252 in the town and 239 in the *ksour*.

These are only rough estimates since many of the sample had not had their births registered and their 'estimated' ages were a compound of their own guesses, mine, and those of the government officer who completed their *Carnet Civil*. My impression was that women recently married tended to over-estimate their age of first marriage, because the official lower limit is fifteen, and the French consistently condemned early marriage. On the other hand a woman 'advertising' her daughter for marriage, would set her age at thirteen or fourteen as if this was the ideal and would boost her chances of suitors. This was especially common in the *ksour*.

In effect, people think that girls should be married young in order 'to prevent accidents', and boys should be married before they start 'going with women'. No longer does a man marry in order to provide extra labour on his father's land-holding: on the contrary, his marriage is often delayed because he is unemployed and neither he nor his family can provide for a wife.

Although it would seem that the pressures for early marriage of women were greater in the *ksar* than in the town, for *ksar*-girls are more 'exposed' when working in the fields, things in the town are changing. The majority of townsmen are too poor to seclude their daughters too severely, it is more urgent to seclude their wives, who therefore need to send their daughters on errands or to the stream to wash clothes, whereas richer women may send a servant or foster-child. Even more important is the fact that many girls in the town (and certainly the daughters of rich townsmen who would otherwise seclude their daughters) go to primary school but few *ksar*-girls do. Town-girls are therefore just as 'exposed' and probably more familiar with the 'public sphere', the male domain, than *ksar*-girls. This probably induces their parents to find husbands for them before they resort to self-help.

More interesting as an index of the social assumptions concerning marriage is the large age gap between husbands and wives. The average discrepancy in age between husband and wife in the town was 108 years and in the *ksar* 144 years. Marriage especially in the rural areas is seen as an enterprise undertaken by the kinship group in its own interest. According to this view, marriage for the girl is merely one of a series of temporary unions, and the sooner she embarks on the career which assures her future – the bearing of legitimate children – the better.

Girls who are pawns in the economic relationships of their elders, in the establishment of work-associations with neighbouring field-owners for example, are liable to find themselves married to men who are closer in age to their parents than to themselves. This situation is only one of the factors which make for tension between spouses.

Men and women in Akhdar have different opportunities. Men derive their social identity as much from their relation to the labour market, their marketable skills, their wealth and their public achievements as from their kinship status.

But ascribed status is fundamental to the social identity of women. Men and women are likely, therefore, to pursue their political and economic interests in different ways, but these interests are competitive and bring them into sharp conflict with each other. Only when the husband manages to restrict his wife's freedom of action, thus impeding her association with kin and status-based networks such as those based on regional groups or patronage, or when the wife has borne several children, do the interests of one partner become dominant, or do they begin to have common interests.

In this chapter I discuss the antagonism of husband and wife, and how marriage arrangements in the richer milieux tend to mitigate it. Marriage has a different and lesser significance in the *ksour* than in those groups whose male members have a secure income and can provide an alternative source of economic and social support to that provided by kin.

A girl should be married by her late teens. If she is not it reflects on the status and prestige of her family, for no one has sought to be allied with them; and on her own status, for it suggests that she lacks the qualities desired in a spouse.

Yet the conjugal relationship has limited relevance in the *ksour*. The standard bridewealth paid at rural and *ksar* marriages is a merely nominal one – 500 *drahem*, half to be spent on clothes for the bride *during the marriage*, the other half to be paid in cash at divorce. The cash payment is a hypothetical one, and never realised. A wife knows then that the material stakes in the marriage are low. A woman is never economically self-sufficient, for her material assets must always be under the management of a man, unless she is widowed or lives alone. Her rights within the marriage contract, and sanctioned by social norms, correspond to only the most elementary requirements for physical existence – food, shelter and essential clothing. A man's obligation to his spouse is specific rather than diffuse, and the wife has a reciprocal attitude towards her husband especially during the first years of marriage. (She does not act in this way towards her children however.) For the satisfaction of contingent needs a person must turn to his or her kin, where therefore his major allegiance lies. This is true for extra clothes, jewellery, fares to visit kin, and even medical attention. I have heard the question of a husband's obligation seriously discussed when his wife, Yamna, (see p. 128) to whom he had been married twenty years and who had borne him nine children, was ill with asthma and exhaustion. He refused to take any action and told her to go to her mother (a widow of much slighter means than himself). His daughter, on the other hand, came home when she needed a tooth seen to, and her father paid the dental fees. She also hoped to persuade him to pay for her two eyeteeth to be gold-plated, a customary adornment among rural women and older women in the town.

The limited relevance of the conjugal relationship is further demonstrated by the fact that divorce is not considered a serious problem in rural areas, although the rate is higher than in urban areas. In the semi-urban *ksour*, this nonchalance tends to be the dominant attitude, but when the other party to the divorce is a townsman, and considerable economic restitution or losses are involved, faces are graver. However, the reaction tends to occur *ex post facto*, whereas in the town divorce is continually discussed and its frequency regarded as deplorable. The older *ksar* members tend more towards the former than the latter viewpoint. Their outlook is that the pattern of frequent divorce and remarriage is an inevitable one for the first few years of a young person's adult life, especially for a young girl away from her kin. The matter of importance is not that a girl should remain married but that she should have married status, thus safeguarding the family *nif*.

Analogies from the Ait Hadiddou

Among the Ait Hadiddou, first marriages are celebrated collectively. (It should be remembered that the majority of the inhabitants of Aghzim, as well as many in Hassan, Inurar, Payu, Umlil, and the Youmi area are second generation migrants from this area.) The word *tamghra* refers originally to this *rite de passage* which is celebrated every five or so years. The word is used in Aghzim to indicate any individual marriage of a virgin. I call it a *rite de passage* because few of the marriages made at these collective festivals end in the establishment of new domestic and reproductive units.

According to Dr J. Bynon, and Zaid, girls and boys who fall into the marriageable category (ten upwards for unmarried girls, fourteen upwards for boys) are paired off by their parents, often their fathers. The easiest and most honourable match is that between patrilateral cousins. The fathers of the grooms keep open house for seven days, when any of the tribespeople, who come from far and wide to dance and feast, can eat with them. Because many of them are also doing the honours for their own sons, the guests are thinly spread. The young couples must stay together for this seven-day period, but may separate immediately afterwards if they wish. After the first marriage many men as well as women may remain unmarried for several years. The second marriage is generally more under the control of the respective spouses than the first, and is celebrated between their respective families at their own convenience, though some of the marriages contracted at the collective *tamghra* are also 'seconds'. No bridewealth is paid, apart from the gift of a set of new clothes – white *izar*, embroidered belt, slippers, *sirwal* and one or two *tfinat* and *tshamirat* and a kilo of *henna*.

The first three daughters of Bedda, for example, were married at twelve, which, in retrospect, they regretted. Such early marriage has something of the character of a nubility rite, which accustoms a girl to the idea of marriage and prepares her for a more long-term relationship. Since the parents came from the Ait Hadiddou homeland, where this was definitely the meaning attached to first marriage (by the women), the condemnation of early marriage by the girls themselves should be seen as the result of the intensification of urban influence in the Akhdar area over the last thirty years. In the town the first marriage is meant to last, and divorce is considered to be a social problem. Thus it was consistent with their town-influenced value system that the women mentioned above should condemn early marriage because it led, they claimed, to divorce – an outcome which their mother, in contrast, took for granted and about which she had no strong feelings.

However, within the semi-urban value system marriage is always a positive and commendable undertaking; though in retrospect, when a disastrous marriage ends in divorce, people will always have a battery of reasons why the couple should never have married in the first place. This approach of retrospective rather than predictive analysis tends to obscure the possible risks in a match. A striking feature of *ksar* marriage is that it is often based on only the slenderest knowledge of the character of the spouses, particularly of the husband, or even of his real economic circumstances. The assumption is that the relationship of the spouses is a largely formal one of mutual convenience, and that there is no knowing whether it will last or not – if there is no clearly negative circumstance such as madness or alcoholism. But even these things may be hidden.

In the first case that follows, a sense of the fragility of the conjugal bond, of the intrinsic antagonism of interests of husband and wife, is conveyed in the mutual accusations, the information which each spouse gives about ambivalence to this match.

Only after a long testing process, described in the second case, and the birth of children, do husband and wife acquire any confidence, and it is tenuous at that, in the loyalty of the other. The antagonism of husband's and wife's interests is taken for granted. It is muted only when one party to the conflict agrees in advance to give up certain rights as in a dower marriage, or when the nature of kinship relations do not threaten the union but rather reinforce it, as when the families of the spouses have pre-existing mutual commitments e.g. in business.

The antagonism in marriage: Case of Safiya and Moulay Hassan

This case demonstrates the limited knowledge which a woman and man may have of each other before they marry and the tendency to regard compatibility as a matter of luck. Marriage is undertaken in an experimental and apprehensive mood. The atmosphere in which the spouses first set up house is therefore one of mutual suspicion and caution.

Marriage

Moulay Hassan is a *sherif* from Goulmima without any kin in Akhdar. He has spent some time in the cloth trade in another town before settling in Akhdar about two years before the marriage we are about to discuss. He is around thirty, a good talker with a sense of humour. Safiya is also a *sherifa*, (a status inherited from her father only although her mother's mother is a *sherifa* from Ksar-es-Souk) who was married once before to an elderly sherif of Akhdar whom she left within a month. She had been living in her father's house in Bentaleb for nearly three years, strictly secluded. She was about twenty-three to -five, but self-conscious about her single status so claimed always to be nineteen. Her father was a *mokhazni*, but his salary scarcely allowed for luxury after providing for the needs of his seven sons and two daughters.

Moulay Hassan knew the widow Aziza, who went to his tailor's shop and chatted with many of the shopkeepers in Akhdar. She lived in Bentaleb, with two daughters of her sister and two of her own. The French nuns gave her an allowance for the two orphans, who attended their workshop. But Aziza, a lively and intelligent woman, spent most of her time running from benefactor to benefactor in Akhdar and the *ksour*, saying 'People like me and ask me to come, and what could I do without their help.' Moulay Hassan asked Aziza if she knew of a suitable girl for him to marry, and she put the idea to Safiya who was favourable. She then arranged for Moulay Hassan to meet Safiya in her parents' home. 'It was a hit immediately.' Safiya's father who was away in another town, came home for the marriage dinner, and Aziza took Safiya in a taxi to the new house rented by Moulay Hassan on the outskirts of Akhdar.

Two weeks later Safiya came home with her husband to visit her mother at *Aid Mouloud*. Her nonchalant backchat to her husband embarrassed the other woman. Aziza was there and Moulay Hassan addressed much of his conversation to her, his flirtatious attitude to his wife resembled a joking relationship in some respects. (Safiya drew me aside and somewhat anxiously asked if I thought her husband was a good man.) Later Aziza was invited to a meal; Aziza acted very warmly to Safiya, and Moulay Hassan and his wife acted in a very boisterous way towards each other. Moulay Hassan joked that he had a lot of other wives that he hadn't told her about, and that he would repudiate her because she wasn't a virgin. Safiya between ogling her husband and threatening to hit him, said that if he divorced her she would be desperate. The pitch of the joking/dispute rose until Moulay Hassan got up and hit her hard on the back, apparently in

155

fun, but Safiya became very angry and hit him back, cursing loudly.

The other prominent topics of discussion were whether Moulay Hassan should allow Safiya to go out, about which he referred to Aziza for an opinion, hoping apparently to get some clues as to his new wife's character, but neither she nor Safiya made serious arguments in favour of her having this freedom, assuming that it was for him to decide. The other subject was the recent divorce of an acquaintance of Safiya. Moulay Hassan was enraged by it and said that the girl should be made to return to her husband or sent to prison. It seemed that his exaggerated reaction would not be separated from his fears about his own marital situation.

Two weeks later Safiya left him definitively. She at first reported 'we quarrelled' but later it appeared that he had another wife and two children in another town whom he proposed to bring and establish in the other room of his house. Safiya said 'How could I stay? *Hashuma*,' (shame), and her mother and grandmother, while deploring the fact of divorce agreed that to act otherwise would have been dishonourable, and lacking in self-respect. She said 'I didn't have any luck' and her grandmother said 'We must just pray God to send her another husband.' The exploration of the limits set by each spouse to the other's activity had ended in disaster.

Bedda's fourth daughter, Fadma of Aghzim (see p. 129), who had married a man from a town described the 'testing' process (under similar conditions of mutual apprehensiveness). When she first married Ali he would not let her go out at all, even to see her mother, and then he would go with her; she muffled up to the eyebrows in *jellaba* and veil. 'Gradually as he saw that I went about my own business, and stayed peacefully working at home, that I didn't spend my time chatting on the doorstep, and I didn't look at other men, he began to say "Now you can go here or there if you wish".' (The range was still limited, she went only to the *hammam* and to the house of one neighbour.)

He would also leave money in his pockets to see if she would take it but she knew that trick and would replace it carefully. Finally he reached the point of giving her his entire salary as soon as it was paid, and if he needed money he would come and ask for it. (I knew that this was an idealised picture and that she was often asking him for money.) She took this as his way of showing her that he was careful with money too, and that he didn't go after prostitutes nor spend it in the cafés drinking. She said 'I would not sit here peacefully if he did. Now I have borne his child, I see our lives as carrying on together, and I would rebuke him for wastefulness.'

She considered that she treated him honestly, in spite of the fact that she was always involved in intrigues to go out, or sell her clothes to get pin-money, in which plots her mother was a key accomplice. Yet she said 'Some women don't know how much their husband earns, and others are always plotting to get pin-money.' (It was nearly two years before she found out that her husband was giving a half of his salary to his parents and not a third as he told her.) 'For example, a woman might hide away the remaining half of a bottle of oil and tell her husband to give her money to buy some more. She then brings out the hidden oil and spends the money on herself.'

The marital scene, because of its inauspicious beginnings, in terms of mutual knowledge, and the segregation of activities, is generally riddled with half-truths and deceit, until the couple either divorce or with the passage of years and evidence of loyalty become more or less *mtafqin* (mutually trusting, or agreed). Given the view, misleading in my opinion, that Moroccan marriage is a matter of trial and error, it would seem that one way of reducing the probability of error would be to make more extensive enquiries into the suitor's character and circumstances. However the fact that the strong preference for intra-neighbourhood marriage does not provide immunity to divorce (in Aghzim 50% of marriages but 58% of divorces over three generations, took place between people who lived within 2 kilometres of each other), suggests that marriages are arranged less with a view to conjugal happiness than to serve the temporary interests of those who arrange them, the parents of the spouses and the intermediaries.

Intra-neighbourhood marriage

The importance of intra-neighbourhood marriage may in fact make transparent the contradictory interests maintained by husband and wife: that a man needs a wife to work for him, but that her kin-interest disposes her to divide her attention and commitment.

In Aghzim, of the total number of women in generations, first ascending (A1 born approximately 1890–1905) Ego (born approximately 1918–25) and first descending (D1 born approximately 1930–50), 75·61% married husbands from villages less than 5 kilometres away, and 58·8% of the total number came from less than 2 kilometres away from Aghzim. 44·61% of men in these generations married women from less than 2 kilometres away.

157

Out of all marriages made by people born in Aghzim, 28·6% were made within the *ksar*. Most of these were marriages between kin (21·8% of all marriages contracted). Of these 10/26 were between patrilateral parallel cousins, and a further 10 between classificatory patrilateral cousins. Three related factors appear to influence the preference for marrying locally, on the one hand, and for marrying patrilineal kin on the other (bearing in mind that these patterns may overlap on the ground). They are (1) rural poverty, (2) the importance of links among female uterine kin, (3) the need for agnatic solidarity.

Rural poverty (here semi-urban) is manifest in the shortage and unequal distribution of the factors of production; land, water, working instruments (ploughs, animals for traction and transport) and labour resources. Since few families in the semi-urban region are self-sufficient in all of these factors, they find it necessary (in the absence of agricultural credit) to go into working association with a neighbour who owns complementary resources. Marriages tend to be made with a view to setting up a mutually advantageous working association between members of the bride's family and the groom or members of his family, or may be used to cement an alliance already in existence. However these arrangements seem to be of a temporary nature, and it is difficult to tell whether the instability of marriage in the *ksour* is to be attributed partly to the fact that the work association is under normal circumstances governed by an annual and renewable contract i.e. is easily made and broken; or whether it is the fragility of the marriage tie which undermines the work association.[1]

The second factor combines with the third to keep an out-marrying woman as close to home as possible. Since it is women who concern themselves with marriage arranging, they will tend to take into account when choosing a groom the possibilities of preserving the bride's links with mother and sisters. Moreover her status as an agnate gives her rights to inherit one part of the patrimony for every two inherited by her brothers. If she can be 'bought off' with rights to usufruct rather than claiming a share of land which will pass under the control of her husband, the agnates' interests are well served: and hers too, given the instability of marriage.

A lawyer from Nifaddn working in Akhdar estimated at 80% the

---

[1] R. Joseph (1970) 61, points out that in the Rif there are strong predisposing factors which would tend to give rise to such associations. 'Despite the weak claim that daughters exercise over their inheritance, there are certain legal restrictions over their property. A brother cannot sell his sister's land nor construct on it unless he has obtained the prior permission of his sister's husband. Likewise a husband cannot sell his wife's inherited property unless he has consulted with the woman's brothers who have first option to purchase the land.'

proportion of women field-owners who act in this way, regarding their natal village as their real home between and beyond marriages. He cited his own case somewhat bitterly.

His wife's father had died when she was a baby, leaving considerable property in the form of date plantations in a Saharan oasis. His only kinsman, living in Mrabet, had cunningly married his widow, then he divorced her so that he remained sole trustee of the daughter's property which he exploited for many years, continuing to do so even when she got married. The income she eventually derived from the property usually amounted to less than 200 *drahem* a year. Her indignant husband tried to persuade her to sell it and realise 10,000 (nearly £1,000) but she was appalled. She said that it was ancestral property and interpreted his suggestion as an attempt to appropriate it for himself.

An ideal situation occurs when the property interests of the spouses are already closely linked through kinship and inheritance expectations (hence the importance of father's brother's daughter marriage), but intra-neighbourhood marriage works almost as well, in so far as it enables the bride and her husband to draw benefits from the association without tempting them to claim land. Of all marriages in Aghzim, 39/58 men in generations A1, Ego and D1 had married women from the *ksar* of one of their parents or one of their grandparents. The corresponding proportion for women was 43/66. These spouses were not necessarily kin, but most of them were classificatory kin. (A person's *ksar*-members are often called father's brother's sons.)

Although these marriages were often described as taking place within the same *nikwa*, or named clan (a putative agnatic group, descended from a single ancestor) what is remarkable about them is that the connection was often traced through or by a woman, more evidence of the role of women in marriage arranging. Because of the tendency of *ksar*-endogamy, her *ksar* was often also the *ksar* of her husband. It is possible that in stating the connection in patrilateral terms, the parties to the marriage were recognising or attempting to reactivate a common interest in property and asserting the common political destiny of the agnatic group. It is an index of the importance of patrilineal and local endogamy in the past, that women can arrive at what are generally believed to be agnatic alliances by utilising their uterine connections.

When we come to examine marriage outside the neighbourhood as well as within it, it becomes clear that alliance within this field is not arbitrary, nor dictated by sheer economic interest.

Interest, of both an emotional and an economic/political kind, has two foci. The first is in the rural area from which one's forebears recently migrated. Most of the A1 generation in Aghzim migrated from three areas, Zwur in Ait Hadiddou country, Kibrit and Mrabet. Similarly Bentaleb was founded in about A4 by migrants from the southern Ait Izdeg around Rich and has been continuously replenished since then by accretions from their area of origin as well as by absorbing local elements. People can choose between marrying local 'kinsmen', local strangers or distant 'kinsmen'. Many inhabitants have claims to fields in their region of origin, and marriage is a way of maintaining contact with the relatives who work them, and preventing the amnesia which would cause their claims to lapse.

The other focus of interest is the modern economy on which the semi-urban *ksour* have become increasingly dependent. In the D1, 13/31 spouses came from villages over 10 kilometres away compared with 14/64 in the previous generation. On the one hand this may be regarded as the result of a new mobility due to improved communications and pacification; on the other hand the mobility itself must be examined in the light of dramatic migratory movements which reflect the impoverishment of the countryside.

This is not to say that people marrying into distant villages do not marry into their agnatic lineages. The third factor mentioned above, the political need to consolidate the patrilineage by endogamy was, in times of *siba*, a measure to ensure the loyalty of agnates in war and transhumance. Today it provides uprooted tribesmen with a minimal guarantee of mutual help and security in a situation of chronic unemployment and generalised impoverishment.

However true to pre-Protectorate tradition, judicious alliance outside the lineage as a means to improve one's individual lot (by marriage or clientship) is considered a perfectly legitimate, if less honourable practice.[1]

The decline in intra-neighbourhood marriage may be explained in part by the decreasing importance of local working associations as the

[1] Jamous, writing on Arab marriage, but concerned particularly with understanding parallel cousin marriage in the Rif mountains of Morocco, points out: 'Une manipulation de la parenté et de la segmentarité est possible par le choix entre la solidarité ou la fission, l'opposition ou la fusion....Plus qu'un moyen de définir une structure, cette manipulation est au contraire un moyen de jouer sur elle, plus qu'un moyen de définir son appartenance à un groupe, elle permet de jouer sur plusieurs groupes. Elle peut d'un côté (avec le mariage endogamique) pallier au défaut de solidarité lignagère, et d'un autre côté (avec le mariage exogamique) ouvrir un champ d'alliances renforcant les chances politiques d'un individu ou d'un groupe.' R. Jamous, 'Réflexions sur le Segmentarité et le Mariage Arabe,' *Annales Marocaines de Sociologie* (1969), 25.

chief focus of economic interest. Now that wage-employment and consumer goods bulk large in the semi-urban economy, the marriage net must also be spread to catch fish in those seas, in the shape of government employees (the only secure living is to be got by working for the government or in a skilled capacity for industrial enterprises) and traders who can provide cash and credit. *Ksar*-people want their sons to be *mul-l-daf* (salary-earner), and to have helpful links with salary-earners. But even the loyalty of kin is suspect. One way of reminding a *mul-l-daf* relative of his obligations to his kin is to reinforce the link with an affinal one. Both these possibilities presented themselves to Baha.

By the time Baha's daughter was fourteen, Baha (who was always the dominant influence in her family, although she held strong opinions about the primacy of men, and of the domestic role of women) began to receive offers of marriage. One man even went so far as to present the *henna* and bridal gifts of a *kaftan*, a *tfina*, some shoes and a belt, but he disappeared and was never heard of again. He was a peasant from her *bled* who had recently become a miner, and Baha said she was quite glad that he hadn't come back because he had shown himself in time to be unreliable. Two other men, one a radio repairer from Akhdar, the other an unemployed man from her *bled*, had asked for her daughter. The first she had put off because 'I don't know anything about him', and the second because he was unemployed. At this point it became clear that she hoped to make an alliance which was useful from the politico-economic point of view.

When I accompanied her to visit her elder daughter, married to a man from her husband's *bled* who had settled near Tislit town where he had a 25-hectare farm, she remarked on the fleas, the recent floods which had destroyed many mud houses in the village, the lack of running water and electricity, the distance to the market, the burden of work which her daughter had to carry, the remoteness of schools – and swore that she would not marry her second daughter to a *fellah*, but to someone with a *mandat*, who lived in the town – preferably a teacher or someone who worked in the 'biru'. Next best came mechanics, carpenters and substantial shopkeepers. She held this view in spite of the fact that her daughter's husband supplied her with almost all her needs in wheat and maize, in exchange for which Baha fostered his eldest son so that he could go to school in Aghzim.

At this time her main *ksar* patrons left the district and Baha began thinking in earnest about marrying her children. When D's husband left her alone with her sister E, D having just borne her first child,

Baha helped them out. E, a widow's daughter from Rabat, suggested that her brother, a plumber of a bourgeois family, should marry Baha's daughter. Baha, half aware that this suggestion was a function of E's temporary situation of dependence on her, didn't know whether to take her seriously, but the discussions proceeded even to the point of E having a photo taken of the girl and sending it to her brother. Baha said to me that she would rather marry her daughter to a man from her *bled* than to people from the *medina*, from whom she had experienced harsh and humiliating treatment when she had occasionally undertaken to do paid work for them. However, she was impressed with the thought that her daughter was eligible, and began to seclude her, forbidding her to leave the house even if it was to help her mother.

As far as her son was concerned, her enquiries were more circumspect. He was an apprentice mechanic earning an uncertain 150 *drahem* a month, with no prospects of improving his earnings. When her husband's father's brother's daughter came with her husband to stay in order to attend the hospital in Akhdar, Baha discussed the possibility of marrying her son to their daughter, who was then fourteen. The discussion was not carried to any definite conclusion because the girl's parents pointed out that the boy could not yet support a wife. However they foresaw the prospect of his moving to a big town and marrying her when he had adequate finances. Both young people were absent. When I pointed this out, Baha and the parents of the girl laughed uproariously and said it was none of their business. This was an affair for adults.

When the electrician's wife came to visit her one day with Malika her cousin, Baha half seriously suggested to Malika, then seventeen and living in Akhdar, that she should marry her son. Malika threw up her hands in horror and said 'But he is poor, he hasn't got a job'. Baha said bitterly 'You don't want to have anything to do with us poor people. What about your brother (the teacher) marrying my daughter?' Malika replied, 'He wants to marry an educated girl, not one who can't even read.'

Baha's most serious effort to finalise a marriage for her son came when she went to visit her full brother in her natal village. The family was very poor, but her brother was a travelling salesman and had some useful connections in the towns, such as the *sherif* who had found her job. She suggested that her son should marry her brother's second daughter, aged fourteen. 'Should I have a son to marry off and leave my own [relatives] out of the affair. If I can marry him to them I should.'

11

Marriage and the market

In this chapter it becomes clear that women play the major part not only in choosing brides for their kinsmen and acquaintances, but in carrying out the marriage rituals. This is because a girl's change in status has far-reaching implications for her female network, but a man's relationships are not affected by his marriage to nearly such an important extent. This is not to say that they remain the same but that his relations with men and with women too are governed more by his achievements in the public sphere, and his position in the labour market, than by his ascribed status. It is noteworthy, in this connection, that in the countryside, where a man's marriage means that he can set up a household which is viable in terms of labour resources, it also implies a new independence of his kin. Significantly, men participate very actively in rural weddings.

After an account of a townsman's betrothal to a *ksar*-girl, I discuss town marriages of various kinds, concentrating on the significance of dower as the mark of Arab status and economic autonomy. Dower entitles a man to replace his wife's kin with his own. For this reason, soldiers are generally unacceptable as husbands and affines, because a girl and her kin do not know whether, marrying a soldier, she is actually acquiring a respectable kin-group or simply being deprived of her own, for she will inevitably leave the area.

I go on to discuss the circumstances of courtship which establishes not so much the compatibility of the spouses as the readiness of the wife to renounce her kin if necessary in exchange for social and economic advance. Among the élite, marriage generally takes place between people whose kin already have interests in common. The wife's social network does not present such a threat to the marriage as it does in other milieux. Moreover she receives a large dowry which gives economic self-sufficiency; the dowry as well as her interest in education, employment and the public sphere reduce her dependence on her kin. The conflict of interest between spouses is therefore less intense than in other milieux.

How people get married

For the sake of exploring the most complex sequence of events, I will assume that the families of the spouses are unacquainted with each other. In this case the intervention of an intermediary (see Chapter 3) is necessary.

Once an intermediary has fixed on the girl she believes to be a suitable mate for a wife-seeking acquaintance, she will broach the subject with the parents of the girl. If the girl has been married before she will often consult her, rather than the parents. In either case the intermediary will carry back news that the parent or the girl is willing or not to consider the match. She may then arrange for the girl's family to meet acquaintances of the boy's family and vice versa, to supplement her own judgment with external opinions and thus to insure herself against being held entirely responsible if things go wrong.

If the man has female kin, they will come to visit the girl's family. The wife-seekers would never risk this visit unless they were determined to make an offer. The visit is sometimes omitted altogether, other occasions being sought for appraising the girl. The father and father's brother (or in the last resort the man himself) come to ask for her hand, explaining their unusual call by introducing themselves as *dif-l-llah* (guests of God) to which the household head, understanding the reason for their mission replies '*mehrhaba bi kum*' (welcome). They bring gifts of sugar and tea, and a meal is prepared. In Berber this delegation of men is called the *imsnayn*. The bridegroom to be and the girl meet for a short talk, and decide whether they wish to marry. Only a firm refusal constitutes an objection and in most families it would be heeded. Silence is translated as consent. There are few *ksar*-girls who would consider it their prerogative to go against their parents in the choice of a husband. A well-connected young man may have watched a girl over a long period and even talked with her. He may himself suggest that his parents propose to so-and-so. This pattern is more common among educated men, or those whose father is dead or far away.

Once the girl has been asked in marriage, the terms of the contract are discussed, a process which has often gone far, through rumour, counter-rumour and the agency of the intermediary, before the parties meet. For a marriage with a townsman who has a fund of moveable property or cash income the bridewealth may amount to about 500 *drahem*, generally paid partly before the marriage so that the bride can buy carpets, and wool for cushions with which to furnish her home. He will also make her a present of clothes whose cost might amount to another 500 *drahem*. Before the wedding the bridegroom brings provisions for the feast. Our man, worth 400 *drahem* per month would bring a sack of flour, a gallon of oil, half a sack of sugar cones, a ram costing about 100 *drahem*, several packets of tea, and a symbolic presentation of dates, almonds[1] and *henna*. The main burden of the feast and its preparation falls on the man's family, but the bride's family make a considerable expenditure for their end of the feasting, for the sake of their *nif*. I was frequently told, 'you shouldn't *sell* your daughter'. Men stated openly that they had been deep in debt for a year after their daughter's marriage.

In the town it is common for a betrothal ceremony, the *henna sgher* ('the little *henna*') to be held. This happens when it is necessary to postpone the wedding until the employee husband has a holiday, or has accumulated the bridewealth. Below is an account of one *henna sgher* which took place three months before the wedding.

Marriage between Saleh and Rashida

The match was made between Saleh, whose mother came from Aghzim, had lived with his Algerian father in Ceima, and later moved to Akhdar: and Rashida, who lived in Bentaleb with her mother's parents. Her parents were divorced, her mother having married a man from Kibrit, her father living in Gwali. Rashida often went to stay with her mother but never saw her father. Her mother's sisters had made profitable and prestigious marriages and her mother's brothers were all educated to secondary level and one beyond, and had salaried professional jobs. Rashida's grandparents were prosperous land-owners and had built their house away from the main bulk of the *ksar*. She went to secondary school, which had made her available for the attentions of Saleh. She was reputed to 'go with men'. Saleh's father was dead, and he lived with his elderly mother and older brother. He was a *fonctionnaire* and very 'modernist'. He dressed impeccably. The house which he had furnished for his bride had several armchairs and hard chairs, a rarity in any Akhdar house. His own room was decorated with pictures of boyish French and American innocents, some bikini-clad, and some of stylish French dandies.

---

[1] Dried fruit and nuts represent fertility, the sweet things (honey and dates) more specifically sexual intercourse. In rural Berber weddings the dried fruit and nuts are called *amzid*, and the groom's male guests obstreperously demand that the bride's mother distribute them, before the journey to the groom's house.

After the wedding it leaked out that the couple had known each other for some time and that they used to meet at the house of Rashida's mother.

At Saleh's request his mother had gone to Rashida's grandparents' house to ask for her hand. They said '*mehraba*' and decided to let the two meet to decide whether to get married 'so that they don't divorce'. Rashida said that she had decided to marry him 'because he is handsome' and said that all she knew about him was that he was young and a *fonctionnaire*.

Fadma and her mother, Bedda (see p. 128), were close friends of Saleh's mother, and Zaid was a colleague and friend of Saleh. This couple played a prominent part in all the proceedings, which was considered all the more auspicious for the marriage because Fadma was several months' pregnant.

Guests at the bridegroom's house

Fadma came earliest and shared a meal with Saleh's mother, who showed off the two cases of clothes, including such modern items as nightdresses and a handbag, besides two gallons of olive oil, eight cones of sugar, a sack of flour, and several pounds of the best tea, and a kilo each of *henna*, dates and almonds, and a ram valued at 150 *drahem*. The whole '*henna*' had cost about 700 *drahem*, as the groom boasted when he came in later to greet the guests.

The guests were all women and included only the kinswomen of the boy's father, mainly of Algerian stock who had settled permanently in Akhdar, but had ongoing connections with Algeria, e.g. sons who worked there. Among them were two *sherifat* who sat silently shrouded in their *izarat* against the glance of the profane musicians who came to amuse the company. Prominent among the dancers was a graceful *hartaniya*, who asked their *sherifat's* blessing before and after her dance. Rashida's mother also came and danced with abandon, even opposite one of the musicians who was smoking *hashish*. The *henna* was brought and displayed by the *sherifat* amid shrill *youyous*, which are the shrill tonguing sounds which women make to express ritual joy, or to raise an alarm. Tea was served continuously.

Someone asked why none of Saleh's mother's kin were there. She said that she only had kin at Elkbir now and that she had quarrelled with them.

Marriage and the market

Procession to the bride's house

This was called 'taking the *henna*'. The *henna*, including the ram, was crammed into the boots of two taxis, into which the musicians and guests piled, to make the slow journey up to the *ksar*, pausing at intervals in public places, and outside the bride's house. Here the bride's 'sister' (actually her mother's youngest married sister) and a kinswoman of the groom to be, each took a case of *henna* and danced with it surrounded by clapping women and children from the *ksar*. Then the ram was taken in and slaughtered and the guests received by the bride's grandmother and married aunts. The women set up a beat of the *tara* (big tambourine) and a *hartaniya* acted as mistress of ceremonies encouraging solo singers. The younger girls and pregnant women would from time to time get up to dance opposite each other. The bride's mother helped a *hartaniya* woman to distribute tea and generally care for the guests. The other guests included women from Bentaleb, mainly *sherifat*, and Bedda the mother of Fadma, and a number from the town and from the *ksar* of the bride's mother, Kibrit. *Ahrir*, the wheat and butter gruel which is served at *rites de passage* in the *ksour*, was offered to the guests. The bride meanwhile was talking to young friends in a room apart, playing records to herself and them.

The men arrived at about nine in the evening, and set up their own Arabic music making, using the lute-like *eud*, played by a professional entertainer. They motioned the women, who were divided from them by a curtain, to be silent. Some of the more daring and 'licentious' went in to dance to the men, a gesture which was described as 'shameful' by their staider sisters, but did not seem to change their easy relations with the other women when they returned.

An enormous meal with huge quantities of meat was served around midnight, and a couple of hours later, when the company could hardly keep awake any longer (sleep was forbidden), the bride to be was brought in to be *henna*-ed.

'Henna'-ing the bride

She was placed, shrouded with a white *izar* over her head, in the centre of the room, sitting on a table on which a folded carpet had been placed. Her mother presided over the ritual. Dates, and candles burning on a bed of *henna*, were brought on a silver tray. The suitcases of *henna* were placed in front of a *sherifa* kinswoman of

167

Saleh, who took out the items one by one and placed them on a silver tray, amid *youyous*. The bride's mother called for the traditional chant praying to God, the prophet and blessing the King, while the young married 'sister' of Rashida, and Fadma – who were qualified for their role by the ostensible success of their own recent marriages – began to dress the bride in her new clothes and then tied a scarf over her face, and began to apply to her hands the viscous *henna*, like sticky spinach, which would leave a red dye. They continually referred to the older women for advice, which was given by Bedda. First the hands, then feet, then the head, she ordered. The dancing and singing began again and Rashida's mother took dates to everyone.

Entry of the bride

Saleh came in with two or three friends, and was seated with the bride between himself (on her right) and Zaid on her left. While the *sherifa* showed the clothes, some women formed a line swaying and singing behind the couple. Then the pair shared a date and the bridegroom put a gold ring on his bride's finger. Zaid was very serious and stared at the floor. One of the girls had been burning incense during this rite, and Fadma took a silver flask of perfume and sprinkled the gathering with it, each guest in turn. Saleh's mother said briskly, 'Well, what are you waiting for, hop it to your own room.' The men laughed and sheepishly made their way to the door.

The entire ceremony had a strongly casual flavour, but careful attention was paid to the sequence of events.

After this ceremony, Saleh's mother thought that Rashida might go and stay with her mother's sister in Casablanca, but Fadma thought that was scandalous, and declared that she should stay at home now and never go out. Her private opinion was that 'with a girl like that' Saleh should marry her as quickly as possible, before he got to hear the tales of her profligacy and was shamed. Afterwards he could 'control' her.

In the event, the wedding took place three months after the *henna* rather than a year later as planned. Rashida gave up college and stayed in seclusion, visiting only her mother. She was not supposed to attend ceremonies, but did occasionally, though refusing to dance. After the wedding she moved in with her husband, his mother and brother, but apparently 'contrived' to get her husband to turn out his mother and his brother. This show of uncharitableness inclined Fadma's family to say that Rashida had used witchcraft to make him marry her.

Marriage and the market

At the semi-urban wedding proper, the bride is escorted to the groom's house on the second night of the celebrations, by the *imsnayn* or the groom's male friends, in a taxi, her kin following in other taxis, going very slowly and stopping in crowded public squares. All the village gathers around the musicians and the master of ceremonies who attempts to keep the crowd back from the girls who dance with cases of *henna* balanced on their heads. At the groom's house, a ram is slaughtered on the threshold by the groom's nearest male agnate and the bride, who has neither spoken nor eaten for the previous three days, is led to a room where she is joined later by the groom and the marriage is consummated. In the morning the bridegroom's female kin come to fetch the stained *sirwal* (trousers) or sheet which attests the girl's virginity, and it is hoisted on a cane *aghnim*,[1] and carried amid wild rejoicing and ululations around the houses. The bride stays in her husband's house for at least a week, isolated from all but her husband's family. Then her mother may be allowed on a 'greeting' visit, but several weeks (generally three or four for a *ksar* bride who has married a townsman, but only one or two for the bride of a *ksar*-dweller) must pass before the bride is allowed to go to visit her former home. Men say 'She must get used to being separated from her mother.' A *ksar* bride even when she is married is in constant touch with her kin if she has married within the neighbourhood, until the demands of her children on her time and presence tie her more closely to her husband's house.

Bridewealth and bride-removal

The wife-givers are willing to consider the possibility of giving their daughter to a townsman. Through her, and indirectly her husband, a *ksar* family may gain access to such urban facilities as credit, schools, hospitals, bureaucratic amenities and jobs. But the more highly paid the spouse the more likely he is to be a government employee – a teacher or a clerk, and therefore mobile. Under these circumstances, the family lose all control over the couple's resources and over their daughter's labour. It is in the light of this risk, and the fact that rights over the girl are being definitively transferred to the stranger husband's household, that the category of dower marriages should be considered. A related factor is the lower rate of divorce for marriages

---

[1] At a boy's circumcision, silver bangles and a scarf are tied to the *aghnim* which is carried like a standard at the head of the procession in which the boy is carried to the river to 'cool his wound' (by having his leg dipped in the water).

in which the husband (pays bridewealth and thus) obtains rights of definitive removal.

Varieties of town marriage

Marriages of rich people in the town are distinguished from migrant semi-urban and rural marriages as a whole by the fact that the wife-takers (and indeed the wife-givers) have a greater pool of possible spouses to choose from, and that considerations of property transfer are always a factor in the choice. The majority of town-dwellers are employed – if they were not it would be impossible for them to live in the town, where houses must be rented and most consumption goods can only be got for cash. The goods are partially processed so that they are more expensive and the productive activity of the other members of the household (e.g. female dependants) is limited. Most urban marriages entail a dower, and some a dowry, except those of migrants whose economic means are so limited that they will tend to be attached only peripherally to the urban economy, and may return to their home villages for long intervals or eventually end up in one of the *ksour*. This category of people can be compared to the 'marginal' populations of the shanty-towns of Meknes and Casablanca, whose cultural pattern approximates to the poorer rural one, and who constitute a sub-proletariat.

Other strangers to the area are government employees, the more elevated of whom tend to be of urban origin and to make judicious marriages with a property-owning network of families based on a single region (the bourgeoisie of Fez, Sale, Tetouan, Ksar-es-Souk). Dowry is common in higher echelons of this category; teachers, on the other hand, are more often among the lower-paid civil servants, the children of peasants, and follow the petty bourgeois pattern of paying brideprice, and not receiving dowry.

Of the two battalions of soldiers, many are of humble origin and have married within their natal *ksar*; others are townsmen, who are ready to marry women from other towns. There is a category of big merchants, local administrators and landowners who tend to inter-marry. Finally there is a petty bourgeoisie, made up of traders and artisans; the more affluent are often Soussi *shurfa*, the more humble either local Ait Izdeg or immigrants from the Western areas of the Middle Atlas (Khenifra etc.), and the 'Sahara', who do not pay bridewealth. I discuss here the types of marriage contracted by members of these various groups.

Marriage and the market

The presence in Akhdar of two battalions of marriageable young soldiers tends to complicate the picture of marriage in Akhdar. Most of them are *brraniyin* (outsiders) from Agadir, Khenifra, Khemisset and the Rif, and they tend to go home to find wives. However they prey notoriously on the girls of Akhdar, especially college girls who are not secluded. Paradoxically the conditions under which they meet the marriageable category of women make them unmarriageable. A woman who would talk to a stranger-man in the street is 'shameless' and by that criterion a bad marriage risk.

In this context it is interesting to note the care which parents and brothers take to protect their marriageable female kin from the approaches which would jeopardise their marriage chances. The daughter of Baha, who was a poor woman living in Bentaleb, once went to see her brother to give him a message from her mother. He worked in a garage which was in the Larba district of Akhdar town, the quarter where most of the prostitutes lived. Some soldiers (often to be found strolling in groups down that road) started ogling her and calling out flatteries, e.g. 'come my pretty gazelle'. She began to throw stones at them, and her brother approaching at that moment saw the scene and in a fury knocked a soldier sprawling. In another context the soldier would certainly have retaliated but he recognised that he had offended the *nif* of the brother, and that his own action could not be defended, so he swore and took himself off.

Another example: one of the last tasks of the evening in the *ksar* is to empty the rubbish on a tip, which is done preferably when no one else can see. Baha and I came out of her house one evening, following just behind her daughter, who was carrying out the rubbish. A soldier and another 'stranger' who rented a house in the *ksar* did not see us, and started calling sweet nothings to the daughter. Baha flew into a rage and abused them roundly calling them jackals. They sidled off with their tails between their legs, Baha shouting imprecations after them.

In spite of the soldiers' dissolute image, the number of permanent common-law unions among them suggests that many soldiers are seeking steady partners rather than a casual sexual bargain. Such couples usually live in the Larba quarter where they are rendered innocuous. Some of the men in common-law unions had wives and children (I was told) in their home village. They did not want to risk losing their families by taking another official wife. The soldiers' reluctance to enter into formal marriages reflects their lack of local connections (especially among women) who could serve as trust-worthy intermediaries, and it reinforces their bad reputation. This in turn intensifies the disapproval expressed by a girl's parents at the prospect of her marriage to a soldier – especially if they find out that she knows him already. A further disadvantage to such a marriage is that their daughter will certainly leave the area.

For this reason many a soldier's wife is a young divorcée who is her own mistress to a certain extent. An unmarried girl who makes the same assumption gains a reputation for immorality which stigmatised all the soldier brides I knew.

The eldest daughter of a family of Aghzim married a soldier who became *commandant* and took her to the city. She herself was educated and trained as a teacher, eventually teaching in her husband's city. She had been known to 'go with men' when she was at secondary school in Akhdar. Her younger sister, Mina, also bright and beautiful, was expelled by the French head teacher from her first year at secondary school for talking to men. She continued to meet young men in the Greek bar, favoured also by 'go-ahead' administrators and teachers, and became pregnant. She had an abortion but the *fonction-naire* whom she held responsible was quickly cleared, and she was sent first to prison, then to an approved school, or its equivalent, for a year.

Mina returned then to her parents' home. She was at that time seventeen. By the next year she had entered into a liaison with an officer with whom she lived in the Larba area. She carried out the normal domestic roles, perhaps at a higher level of sophistication, dressed demurely in clothes she made herself, and tied her scarf in the 'modern' French style. She was soft-spoken but generally lived a less segregated life than other women, and her relationship with the soldier was more openly expressed, more evocative of the tenderness of Berber love-songs than of the normal cryptic conjugal relationship in Akhdar. When she was nineteen she married him, and before long bore a daughter. During the previous year she only rarely visited her parents, and they never spoke of her. (Her mother, giving the list of her children when I asked her about them, did not mention her, although she included Mina's older sister in the list.) The other women in the *ksar* called her 'bad' and did not visit her parents, unless they had close personal relations with them.

When Mina as a married woman came with her baby to the *hammam* in Aghzim, the situation was quite different. Women greeted her cheerily, scrubbed her back, and girls of her age-group talked to her quite amicably and confidentially as if her history were as respectable as their own.

Educated Government employees and 'courtship'

Government employees, among whom I include petty bureaucrats, teachers, and technical assistants, were caught between their French acculturation and their drive for high community status, with which was correlated a deep suspicion of 'free' women. They reserved their cautious attentions for serious young nurses and teachers, by whom they were generally repulsed, and for the kinswomen of their friends. It is notable that most of them tried to avoid depending on their parents for a spouse, but for many this proved unrealistic, given the scarce opportunities for meeting women. (An older man, less worried about following the companionate model, might turn to an intermediary.)

More frequently such a man, discovering that he needed someone to run his household, made enquiries among eligible families of his acquaintance and in his home village. He would then arrange two or three conversations with the most likely girl, who would perhaps be partly educated, but had to be of reputed modesty, industry and (hopefully) beauty. Before the girl met him she and her family would have made enquiries about his character and reliability. He would ask her to go for a walk with him on the road to the village where she lived so that within an hour all the village would know of the rendezvous and start discussing it. The marriage negotiations took place immediately afterwards so that the girl and future wife could not be said to 'go with men'. It was mutually understood that for him to appear to compromise her reputation was a virtual guarantee of marriage, and her readiness to meet him a virtual acceptance. The 'courtship' situation is almost as controlled as the family-sponsored marriage. However, the individuals would at least consider that their choice was their own responsibility. Depending on the coincidence of their respective scales of values and on whether they were able to judge character in a couple of half-hour talks, the interests of compatibility might be served to some degree.

The situation is complicated by the contradictions inherent in the values held by men of this class. These values really belong on two different scales. Thus such men tend to choose a girl for traditionally valued qualities such as modesty, readiness to serve, etc., supplemented by a little education, and to express frustration when what emerges from the match is not their ideal of a Western companionate marriage.

Family-sponsored marriage

Frequently, such a man (and this seems to be the norm) might direct his interest as his mother or sister suggests, a girl is even more likely than a man to accept her parents' choice and not to express a preference of her own. These parent-dominated matches occur between families who hold each other in mutual respect, by virtue of common regional origin and traditional criteria of respectability. The girl generally comes from a slightly poorer milieu than that into which the groom has moved, and often from the same one as the groom's mother. Social mobility (as a function of the labour market) and education are almost entirely male prerogatives.

This pattern of marriage is the most common among artisans and small shopkeepers – the petty bourgeoisie. It is marked by an extravagant three-day ceremony, which is however a modest version of the weddings of the 'modern' literati and rich merchant class. The bridewealth in the case of men earning up to 600 *drahem* per month does not generally top 500 *drahem* but is paid immediately, and the presents of clothes (high-heeled shoes, and a handbag as well as the more traditional clothes) may cost the groom another 400 *drahem* (£40).

Elite marriage

What I call 'the élite' in Akhdar is comprised of large merchants and landowners, the bourgeoisie of Fez, and the *Makhzen* bourgeoisie.

There are several large merchants who have immigrated from other regions such as the Ait Morghad and Soussi areas. If they have spent many years in the area, they commonly attempt to ally themselves with the *mulat-l-bled*, the owners of the region. More especially they favour marriages with large local landowners who were co-opted into administrative positions under the French and later under the *Makhzen*. By acquiring powerful local affines the merchants obtain political security.

The more opulent literati and the merchants may pay up to 2000 *drahem* in bridewealth as well as making more extravagant presents, including presents of *belghat* (leather slippers) to the bride's male and female kinsfolk. Elite weddings are signalled by processions of several cars and taxis which slowly travel through the town hooting their horns. Marvelling bystanders remark that the bride wears a white lace veil instead of an *izar* shrouding her face, and has white *gloves*.

The furnishings which the bride buys for the house, using money given as *sdaq* is forfeit by the offending party on divorce.

The 'Makhzen' bourgeoisie

The *Makhzen* bourgeoisie is the term I use to refer to the families who have been the beneficiaries of and participants in the central political organisation for several centuries. They are to be distinguished from the *ulema*[1] of the northern cities (Fez, Sale, Rabat, Tetouan) who have tended to absorb into their ranks migrants of various backgrounds. Moreover, the political influence of the *ulema* has faded with the rise of a more technocratic and capitalist élite, whose values are less compatible with their own than those of the traditional *Makhzen*. This is not to ignore the fact that the literary and diplomatic skills of the *ulema* have been frequently utilised by the central government in the past, and that *ulema* families are to be found within the administrative classes today.

This is particularly true of Fassis, who have perhaps concerned themselves with cultural professions such as education and law rather than administrative ones. In Akhdar they are intimately linked with other Fassis concerned with trade and finance. The Fassis are a conspicuous group, many of them Idrissi *shurfa*, who visit each other, attend each other's ceremonies, marry among themselves, and keep aloof from the local population. Not only do they marry Fassis but they return to Fez to do so. I have never witnessed a Fassi wedding in Akhdar.

The *Makhzen* bourgeoisie is drawn from the prosperous areas of the north and west. They, like the Fassis, speak only Arabic and have no interest in setting up local alliances, for they are geographically mobile. Moreover, their frame of reference is a national one, and their interests are common to a bourgeoisie which spans Morocco, having property in industrial and mining enterprises, finance and insurance companies, and the rich cereal lands of the north.

My discussion of élite marriage patterns, although relevant to this broad category and reminiscent of what Lahlou says of Fassi marriage,

---

[1] Scholars of Koranic law and religion, who often acted in an advisory capacity to the Sultan, and enjoyed considerable prestige and political power in their own cities.

Table 21. *Bridewealth and dowry in some Akdar marriages*

Date / Payer of bridewealth	Girl's father	Amount of *sdaq*	Henna	Dowry	First marriage	Subsequent history
RURAL						
1941 (1) Smallholder	Smallholder, Aghzim	2 old francs	Scarf Trousers *izar henna*	—	Yes	Ait Hadiddou wedding; girl ran away after 7 days
1946 (2) Smallholder	Smallholder, Aghzim	*Imtqalain*	Meal with ram Clothes	—	No	Wife bore 12 children, 9 surviving. Husband had wage but kept family in rags; squabbles. Wife ill, wouldn't get her treated. Husband threw her out because she wouldn't sleep with him
1954 (3) Peasant (soldier son)	Smallholder, Aghzim	150 d.	Clothes	—	No	Moved from city to city; wife bore 10 children, 6 survived. *Mtaʿqin*. Husband bought fields and built house in wife's village. Close relations with wife's family. Fostered wife's sister
1957 (4) Smallholder	Smallholder	—	1 pair trousers 2 cones sugar ½ sack flour Foot of sheep at betrothal Sheep at wedding	—	Yes	Girl ran away after 2 weeks
SEMI-URBAN						
1958 (5) Large landowner	Aide to *caid*	1000 d.	Clothes	—	No	Lived in Fez 2 years. No children. Divorce
1961 (6) Son, miner	Aide to *caid*	600 d.	2 gold bracelets Clothes	—	No	Lived in Akhdar. No children. Divorce after 1 year
1970 (7) Soldier	None	150 d.	Clothes	—	No	No children. Divorce
1970 (8) Miner	None	150 d. (none paid)	Clothes	—	No	Miner's children by former marriage arrived, smoked and drank. Wife left within a fortnight
1971 (9) Smallholder	None	150 d.	Clothes	—	No	No work. Wife became pregnant but still left husband after 3 months. Divorced. Remarried after 4 months

1970 (10) Teacher	Land-owner	1000 d.	Clothes 2 rams Oil 30 kilos sugar Tea *Henna* Dates Almonds	—	Yes	Wife quarrelled with husband's mother. Husband threw mother out
1970 (11) Merchant	None, brother teacher	3000 d.	Clothes Furnishings	—	Yes	Wife quarrelled with husband's mother. Husband split from father and family
1970 (12) Nurse, father landowner	Merchant	2000 d.	Clothes Refrigerator Carpets Clothes Kitchen equipment	—	Yes	Moved to Casablanca where girl had relatives, man had work
1969 (13) Timber merchant	Land-owner	5000 d.	Clothes Furnishings	—	Yes	—
1969 (14) Official	None *ksar*	Promised 1000 d.	Clothes Flour Sugar	—	Engagement broken	Presents were given as *henna sgher*. Official proposed to go to France for 3 years and marry on his return. Girl broke off engagement
1969 (15) Land-owner, son teacher	Small-holder	500 d.	Clothes worth 500 d. Sugar Animals	—	Yes	—
RURAL MIDDLE LAND-OWNERS						
1968 (16) Landowner	Wage-worker	200 d. not paid	Clothes Sugar Ram, etc.	—	Yes	—
1968 (17) Landowner trader	None	500 d.	Clothes	—	Yes	Removed to distant *bled*. Bride at home after 3 months

refers mainly to the marriage of locally integrated merchant and land-owner/administrator families who tend to model themselves after the urban *Makhzen* élite. Within this category the degree of personal choice is much greater, although the match tends to take place only with the sanction of the families of the spouses and then in conformity with their values.

During the last twenty years the élite man and woman have grown up in more similar cultural and social circumstances than their poorer counterparts. The woman's educational opportunities and social free-dom appears to be greater. It is regarded as natural that such a girl should learn to speak French and to mould herself after the French model. However, this freedom is more appearance than reality. If we examine the composition of the 'mixed gatherings' in which her behaviour and freedom to choose her own companions seems most blatant, they will be found to consist not only of her *parents'* friends and their children, but even largely of agnatic kin. Her choice is not so wide after all. Still ten years ago women in these families married men who were comparative strangers to them, because this was their *parents'* wish. The dominant consideration was that useful alliances should be created or consolidated through marriage.

Property

In an alliance of interest or property, the woman's connections are just as important as a man's and her wedding is the occasion for lavish expenditure by her parents, and their friends and kin, all of whom contribute in some measure to the dowry, the former in jewels, houses, financial assets, and gifts of clothing for the groom, the latter in cloth for *kaftans*, and other items of trousseau. Below is an account given by the educated daughter of a respected family in Akhdar with multiple kinship ties with the affluent bourgeoisie of Meknes, Rabat and Kenitra, and Fez.

The principle that the families of eligible men and women should control their conjugal choice was expressed by Jamila (a lawyer) in the dictum that it is important to know who will be the paternal and maternal uncles of the couple's children.

Once the parents of the bride and the parents of the groom have come to an agreement over the marriage of their offspring, the groom's father and other male relatives go to the bride's house to arrange what each spouse will bring to the match. The bride's contribution includes wool and furnishings (cushions, mattresses and seats) for the house, clothes such as *kaftans*, and a whole set of Western clothes down to the last cufflink for the groom as well as animals for the wedding-feast – the part of it which is held in the bride's house. The groom's contribution consists of clothes and trinkets for the bride, sometimes jewels, and a cash *sdaq*, which is placed in the keeping of the bride's father. The groom's family also provide a sumptuous feast, and the number of animals to be killed is settled beforehand. Jamila emphasised that the girl's family would come off worst in this transaction.

On the first day the contract is drawn up and witnessed. There is a celebration in the bride's house with selected guests who bring valuable gifts, guided by a 'wedding list' which has been discussed and its features passed along the grapevine for some months before the wedding. These and the girl's dowry are displayed in her house and assessed critically by the guests. It is shameful for a girl to have little to display.

On the second day more guests come to dance and sing and entertain each other. In the evening two professional 'decorators' come to dress the bride. They make delicate patterns in *henna* on her hands, and paint her face. When they have finished a bowl of milk is placed beside her, and each woman who comes to admire her takes a sip of milk and leaves some money which is used to pay the decorator (up to 100 *drahem* in all).

Dancing continues until late at night when the bridegroom and his companions come to fetch the bride in a taxi. Followed by a cavalcade of cars containing friends and kin the bride proceeds slowly to the groom's house, where celebrations continue all night, and the marriage is consummated. If it is discovered that she is not a virgin, the groom may send her home and all the marriage gifts must be returned, the bride's family forfeiting some for the shame they have brought on the family of the groom. The third morning is thus an occasion for anxiety for both families. No marriage, however opulent the family, continues for more than three days. However, when people planning a wedding are boasting about its projected magnificence they say, 'It will last for ten days, or twenty days.' The seven-day wedding typical of the more rural *ksour* is considered to be possible only because people have nothing else to do. Town-dwellers have time-tables to keep. The collective anxiety and the reciprocity of the gifts, with if anything a fatter dowry than bridewealth, reinforce the notion of bourgeois town weddings which actors as well as anthropologists hold: that they represent an alliance of interests and the consolidation of a class.

179

12

The position of the bride after marriage

The position of the bride varies according to the social milieu of her husband, and the nature of the marriage payments which have been made. A *ksar* bride may expect her relations with her established social network to be as lively as ever. She may live near enough to her family to receive and return visits every few days, if not more often, and she will be free to extend her range of connections among women by befriending her neighbours. The town bride of a salaried man has no such luck. Besides losing touch with her relatives, she may be entirely cut off from female society if her husband has no kinswomen near to replace her own. The sad effects of this situation can be seen in the case of Naima which I present in this chapter. Here the conflict between the husband's market-dominated interest and the wife's need for supportive relationships is transparent.

A lady out of luck

In order to appreciate the significance of the episode which I am presenting here, some account is needed of the participants and my own relationship with them. What 'control' of husband over wife means is well illustrated by the husband's extreme reaction to challenge.

Moulay Aomar was one of my first acquaintances in Akhdar, and he helped me to find a house near his own. He was proficient in French and worked for a Frenchman, but since his parents were dead and he had been brought up by his father's brother in another town he had not many friends in the area. He had just married his father's brother's daughter, a girl of seventeen who knew no one in her husband's town. She was jealously secluded, but by long parental conditioning she accepted this state of affairs, saying that her father used to beat her if she so much as looked out of the door.

She missed her family, and Moulay Aomar asked me to go and visit her which I did frequently, but she was never allowed to come to my house. She was a lively girl who began to feel the burden of her long isolation, for her husband was out at work from 7 a.m. until 10 p.m. and she had no other visitors, except occasionally her husband's uncle's wife who came from another town to help her sort grain. The husband would not let her visit the neighbours or go shopping but took her once a week to see his sisters. She spent her time in meticulous house-keeping, even emptying all the seats of their stuffing, washing it and sewing it in again, spinning out every task for as long as possible. Her father, hearing of her isolation, sent in turn a son and a daughter of one of his servants, but they were so bored in this truncated household, that they ran away.[1]

After I moved out of the town I saw very little of her, but I heard that she had had a miscarriage, so I went to see her, at her husband's request. She had just got up. Her house was in an unusual state of neglect, washing up undone, bed unmade, room chaotic. She said she was ill. No, she hadn't been to the hospital, because they would see that it was the kind of illness they could do nothing about. It came from being by herself with no one to talk to. She couldn't manage the housework, went hot and cold by turns, and had chopped her finger, cutting wood. She had become terrified at night, before her husband came home. She couldn't cook or eat.

I suggested that she needed to spend time with her neighbours, knowing the code, which had been expressed in my hearing more than once when she was under discussion, 'If she doesn't visit us, we won't visit her.' I recommended that she should go to the hospital. She agreed with both propositions but said that her husband did not like her to go out. I commented that he would not like her to be ill of loneliness either.

She said she missed her family, and that her mother didn't come, even now when she was ill. Her husband had promised her that she could go to see them in a month's time. She compared her present situation with that at home when the same principle of absolute seclusion had been applied. She could not go out, but her brothers and sisters were with her, and so was her mother. They had visitors all the time, and her father came back anyway at 5 p.m. She got up to help me tackle her housework, talking to herself, and to the cat, then sat down again.

Moulay Aomar came back and I decided to talk to him about Naima, hoping that my year's acquaintance with them justified this.

[1] I discussed this case in a theoretical way with men and women who did not know the couple. The husband's attitude was theoretically deprecated, even by men whom I knew to behave on occasion with equally irrational fear and arbitrary constraints on their wives' activities, especially with regard to their wives' female kin.

V.M. I think she is ill; she might get better if she could see some other people, visit her neighbours.

M.A. She is not alone. I am here. And it's not true that she is ill because she's alone.

V.M. But you are only here for a short while at night, and she has to spend all day by herself, when she has been used to having people around her, as we all need to.

M.A. I have lived by myself.

V.M. But you see people at work. She has finished her housework by noon, and must sit for the rest of the day until ten at night doing nothing. She has nothing to read and she can't knit or embroider.

M.A. If she wants to she can always find housework to do. Besides, she should know how to knit and sew before getting married. We have a saying – You can straighten a twisted tree when it is young, but not when it has grown. If she doesn't know now she will never learn.

V.M. But many girls just begin to learn at her age. If she had friends they could teach her. And it's contact with other people she needs. She has even begun to talk to herself.

M.A. Nonsense. When she was at home she was often by herself. Her father locked her in and took the key.

V.M. That was not the same. People visited her, and her family were around. If being alone makes her ill it is not good. You don't have to be like her father.

M.A. It's not people she wants – it's her mother and sisters and she's going to see them after the Aid.

V.M. Perhaps she could come with me to see *X* (of whom M.A. approved) and she might meet some of *X*'s friends who are bound to be 'upright' people.

M.A. I don't want her to know the neighbours. You don't know the Moroccan custom. A woman does not go out and shout around the streets.

V.M. But *X*, *X* and *X* do go out and visit their friends – and you must admit than Naima is not likely to shout around the streets.

M.A. I take her to my sister's.

V.M. But that is only one afternoon a week. And your sister can't come more often, she has her children to look after.

M.A. I do not want her to know anyone I have not introduced her to myself. Otherwise I would know people through my wife, and it is the man who commands in Morocco. It is the law that she should know no one without my permission.

The bride after the marriage

V.M. Why don't you introduce her to someone nice and then she could ask you if she could visit her, and you could say yes or no?

M.A. I don't know any women! I'm not one of those men who stay out at night with women and go to the cinema. I come straight home to my wife.

V.M. But can't you see that your work is very demanding, and that she needs other women to talk and laugh with, or she will go on being unhappy and ill?

M.A. If she's unhappy then she can go home to her parents for good!

He finally agreed to take her to the hospital. Naima asked: 'What did he say – you see, he won't let me go out. Men are no good.'

V.M. He said that he didn't want you to go out but if he knows the person and you ask him if you can visit her, he may say yes. It's up to you.

In the next couple of weeks, Naima's mother came to see her and to take her home for the Aid. In the summer, Naima's mother came back together with a sister who stayed for two months. She gradually recovered, and in spite of our encounter, Moulay Aomar asked me again to go and see her.

Ksar-girls who marry into the town tend to find themselves in an isolated conjugal household (this is inevitable when a girl marries a migrant) or in one which includes the husband's mother, whose failing strength is often one of the reasons for her son's marriage. 'I need someone to help me.'

Yet, under some conditions a mother may visit her town-married daughter, and the economic relationship between them becomes an exchange of services for goods, an outflow which every town husband fears and attempts to stem, pointing out that he has paid bridewealth and that this constitutes a temporary suspension of the mutuality in terms of rights over services and goods which used to exist between the bride and her kin. A *ksar*-man may also bring his wife to live with his mother, but if his parents are both alive, his marriage will enable him to set up a household of his own. This is preferred by the wife and implies a rise in community status for the husband. Only if a father owns large amounts of land will he be successful in his attempts to keep his married sons in his own household, where they and their wives will contribute to the exploitation of their common property.

The rural bride may be removed from her own kin, but she will inevitably find herself in the company of her female affines, sometimes in the same household. It is considered legitimate for her to visit her family when it is feasible.

7-2

There were only three such extended households in Aghzim and Bentaleb *ksour* put together – a total of 110 households, but in the countryside they are more common. A bride marrying into a well-to-do rural family (owning over 40 hectares) will tend to become integrated into the extended family unit headed by her father-in-law. When he dies, quarrels among the sons precipitate the setting up of new households and eventually the division of the patrimony.

Rural marriages and the couple's relationship to the husband's kin

Close communal living in the rural context appears to result as much from the small size of many rural *ksour* in the Akhdar area and the need for physical co-operation among kinsfolk, as from the larger landholdings. In the larger semi-urban *ksour* where more of the inhabitants have no land or very little, the households are pre-dominantly nuclear. The landless or small land-owning families have no incentive to stay together, and the larger landowners tend to employ workers rather than kin.

The following is an account of the marriage of Yamna's daughter from Aghzim into a large land-owning family living in a rural *ksar* in Waman area.

The head of this family, a man in his sixties, named Ali, belonged to the second generation to have lived in the *ksar*, having fled from Elkbir, after a family quarrel over land. There were two other families in the *ksar*, each with its own complex of buildings and *borj* (towers). One of these families, Ait G, was a Berber family with whom Ait Ali were on good terms and invited to all their ceremonies. The other family were *haratn*. 'We don't know them,' said Ait Ali. The total population of the *ksar* was about sixty.

Ali's daughters (four of them) had all married into *ksour* in the same area, within two hours' walk. His two married sons and three un-married ones lived in the house. One of the married ones worked at the mines as an electrician, and spoke French reasonably well. He left his wife and children in his father's compound and came home fort-nightly. The other married son worked on the land. The two un-married sons were at secondary school in Meknes, but they returned for the summer months when they would lend a hand with the harvest. Each of the married sons had a separate room for himself and his wife. The wives and their mother-in-law shared a common kitchen, and in turn took charge of the children, of cutting hay, of washing, cleaning, harvesting, weeding. All these tasks were allocated by the mother-in-law, who was the boss. As Yamna's son explained, '*da-tkomman-dan*' ('she gives the orders', derived from the French expression).

When it was decided that the second son should get married, the first area to be prospected for brides was the Akhdar area, as the commercial and administrative needs of Ait Ali took them in that direction. Moreover, they had only had kin in Elkbir but knew an old widow Ashum who lived in Aghzim (Ikm from Elkbir). They knew her because she had been born in a *ksar* in the Waman region into which one of Ali's daughters had married, and sometimes came to visit her kin there, since she had adopted the son of one of them. She was a woman of forceful personality, about fifty-five years old, who wove excellent carpets, got her fields cultivated, had many friends, and was considered not only capable but wise (a model intermediary). Since she had married a *sherif*, she was kindly considered but some people, especially men and children, were quite afraid of her. They said admiringly, 'She is like a man.' She had been known to get impatient waiting for the baker to come and do his work, and to have lighted the fire in the huge public oven and done the baking for the two *ksour*, Aghzim and Bentaleb.

Ashum was a close friend of Yamna's family, and Yamna's son was the inseparable friend of Ashum's foster-son. Yamna's husband and his brother often helped her with building and farming problems, and she was a frequent visitor to the house. She suggested that they should marry Yamna's daughter, then sixteen, to Ali's second son, and so it happened. She helped with the preparations and especially with smoothing out the ritual arrangements, since Yamna's family were not familiar with the complex six-day wedding rites of the Waman area.

Yamna's daughter remained in her new home for a month before coming to see her family, a visit she repeated at intervals of about two months until she bore a child, an event which required her mother's presence at Ait Ali's.

Within the household the women and men carried on their production and consumption activities quite separately, the companions of the women were women, the social activities of the men involved only men. Occasionally Ashum came to see Yamna's daughter and reap her share of the matrimonial success. (She went twice in a year.) The bride's brother was invited to the wedding of the daughter of the other Berber family in Ali's *ksar*, to a man who lived in the natal *ksar* of Ashum and where Ali's daughter had married. The bride's brother had a good relationship with her husband and his younger brothers, which at times approached a joking relationship, and he visited about five times during the year. The bridegroom and one of his brothers visited

185

their affines in Aghzim once alone, and they or the bride's father-in-law always escorted her when she came to visit her family. They used this opportunity to do business or go to the market in Akhdar. However, the availability of household help and of company in the husband's home formally undermined the bride's complaints to her kin that she was unhappy and overworked. She was practically 'absorbed' into her husband's kin-group.

Women in the semi-urban *ksour* often say that it is hard for women 'to marry the *khl'a* (wasteland)' because they have to work hard and have few home comforts. The implications of this attitude was illustrated in the view of his future held by the nineteen-year-old brother of the groom. He was at college and wanted to marry an educated girl, perhaps a foreigner. He was aware that if the girl was sophisticated enough for his taste, she would not be prepared to come and live in the *ksar*. He assumed that such a marriage would force him to break away from his family in a radical way. He claimed that he was ready to do this. 'Their ways are the old ways.' This marriage of well-to-do rural land-owners (who have strong links with the modern sphere through the work and education of its younger members) is clearly the apogee of the 'rural type', and typical of a restricted class. The marriage of a *khammes*, for example, could not attain such magnificence, nor be continued for six days. Even this family used the occasion of conspicuous and general consumption to circumcise two children, thus making a considerable saving without losing face.

Kin of husband and wife at family rituals

Life crises are the occasions, *par excellence*, when women's groups are mobilised. It is the variation in their composition which give some clue as to the issues with which people present are concerned. The presence or absence of the wife's female kin, especially her mother, in particular action-sets, is an eloquent comment on the type of the conjugal relationship, its structural setting, and the attitudes of the wife's kin to her marriage.

It frequently occurs that the women of the husband's family arrive in force to prepare for a feast which is to aggrandise not only its nominal giver, but the reputation of his family as a whole. This is especially evident when a boy is born, named or circumcised, above all in families where the husband is a man of means or holds a position of importance, and has paid bridewealth to his wife, whose links with her affines have become stronger at the expense of those with her kin.

The bride after the marriage

Ait Khatib. Khatib holds a responsible post in the civil service. He comes from a Berber town in the Tafilelt, and married a girl, Sadiya, from the next village. When she had a baby her mother did not come, and it was delivered by a poor woman, a kind of client to the household, but respected in the village for her strong personality, medical and craft skills. Other members of Sadiya's quasi-group came to sit with her on the day of the birth, namely the wife, sister and sister-in-law of a local notable. The next evening the mother, married sisters, and sister-in-law of the husband arrived in the company of his brother, and a week of conspicuous feasting began. The husband's kin did not contribute very much to the proceedings, the preparations being left mainly in the hands of the poor friend and her daughter.

It is possible that in such a situation the husband's kin, by expressing such an interest in the boy, make themselves his sponsors, claiming genetricial rights in the woman. Thus his membership of his agnatic kin-group is affirmed. The kin of a wealthy man, by helping him in important eventualities and generally boosting his prestige, remind him that they have a right to share in his wealth, and their descendants to share in that of his descendants. Agnation is important to the structure of some women's groups which operate over the long term. Such durability is not intrinsic to associations based on kinship among women only, because the superior power in the society is vested in men, who inhibit the functioning of women's relationships. This occurs in the case of marriages where bridewealth is paid, entitling the husband to interrupt his wife's contacts with her home.

Ait Hammou. Of the three sons of Hammou living in Akhdar, two are electricians, Nbarsh and Aziz (see case of Baha, p. 44) and the third a petty trader, Hassan. They are Berbers from the Alpha region. All of them married wives from the same home area, indeed neighbouring villages. The three wives co-operate continuously, the wife of Hassan in a slightly subservient position, more because she has no children after being married eight years than because her husband has a less prestigious job than his brothers.

At the birth of Nbarsh's sons, his wife's mother came to help, but his own mother presided over the feasts and his sister was treated with honour, her daughters helping to serve. The emphasis on the father's female relatives was similar at the birth of Aziz's son, but even more transparent, as his wife is an orphan who had been raised by her father's brother.

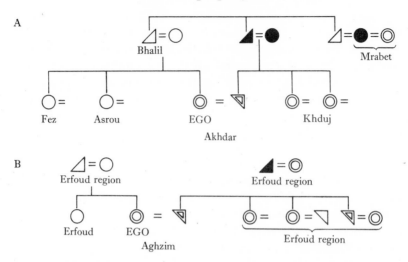

◎ ◀ indicates significant relationship with Ego of active co-operation and
material help. Labels, e.g. Aghzim, indicate place of residence in 1971.

Figure 2. The integration of the dowered wife into her husband's agnatic group.
    A. Naima: visitors and sources of domestic help
    B. Sadiya: activation of kin-ties at the birth of a son

Of all post-marital situations, that of the *ksar* bride is the most like
her pre-marital one, especially before children are born. In the other
two situations uterine kinship goes into eclipse temporarily, but the
position of divorcées in all three are surprisingly similar and involve a
'revival' of uterine ties. Most women return to their family on divorce,
but a common arrangement is for a divorcée to live with a divorced or
widowed mother until she marries again. In Aghzim and Bentaleb
there were at least four divorcées living with their mothers and
practising casual prostitution, as well as 'respectable' divorcées living
with a mother or with both parents.

Divorcées and kinship roles

The significance of a woman's kinship status as daughter or sister is
even greater in the *ksar* than in the town, because of the economic
rights which a daughter or sister holds in the patrimony of her family,
and the need for economic co-operation. This does tend to free her
from any stigma attached to her status as divorcée. Further, those
divorced women in the countryside who lead a somewhat promiscuous

life as *Huriyin*, or *azriyat* (free women), are not severely ostracised.[1] Their counterparts in the town are more obviously anomalous. Town divorcées take up roles resembling those of other unpropertied women, as clients of a wealthy patroness, dependants of a salaried brother, or more rarely, as prostitutes. Those who become prostitutes are usually women who have been rejected by their kin or who have run away from them.

When divorcées visit other women they work but generally in a less servile and self-deprecating capacity than is adopted by *hartaniyin* and widows. As marriageable young women, they have a promising future, and unlike the former two categories are considered an asset to any social gathering. It is significant, however, that as if conscious that they are a financial burden on their kin and that the job of finding themselves a spouse cannot entirely devolve on others as it does for single girls, divorcées tend to travel to kin in other towns, where they may stay for several months, always on the look-out for a new husband. For example, two divorcées frequently spend long periods with their respective sisters and their husbands, another with a brother, a fourth went on a pilgrimage, staying on the way with her father's maternal cousin for several weeks. Town divorcées seem to travel more than country ones. If they can knit or embroider they will knit for their sister's family, especially for the husband, or embroider sheets for the household. They may cook and make bread, high status tasks usually reserved for the mothers and daughters of the family, and rarely performed by *hartaniyin* or widows.

Divorcées who are not *Huriyin* take themselves seriously and will not be seen acting in a comic way, playing *tara* or ingratiating themselves with the company in ways which are quite appropriate to widows and *hartaniyin*. In this respect their behaviour resembles that of the adolescent girls who may sometimes be found helping a kinswoman with heavy routine tasks, in that both categories have the range of ascribed statuses to run. They have a right to call on their kin for help until they become definitively integrated into a group towards whom their kin have none of those obligations which widows have, because they have inherited the property of their husbands, or *hartaniyin* who have more obligations than rights with respect to other status groups. In this sense *hartaniyin* and widows are marginal

---

[1] At any one time about 4% of Moroccan women over 10 and under 40 are divorcées, this proportion rising to about 7% of women over 40. The proportion of divorced women in the female population is 2·7; that of widows is 9·3%, rising sharply after 40 years. On the other hand only 1% of men are unremarried divorcés, and 1% widowers. 'Résultats de l'enquête' (1964), 42.

members of society but divorcées have a more favoured situation. The former may be *khalti*, mother's sister, essentially outside the group, the last *ukhti*, sister, towards whom the members of the household take up a protective and sustaining role, since sisters generally have rights of usufruct with respect to their kin.

The fact that agnation is as important for women as for men is one of the factors contributing to and in its turn arising from the high divorce rate. But matrilateral kin are of greater importance to women than to men. Lewis has observed that marriage tends to be stable where the agnatic bonds are of unequal strength for women and men.[1] If a woman's husband is frequently absent or fails in other ways to perform his role satisfactorily, it is the kin who compose the primary group to which she belongs, especially her female kin, who will maintain her children if her husband does not claim them, e.g. on divorce.

[1] I. M. Lewis (1962).

13
Divorce and property

In this chapter I shall cover the relationship between capital accumulation in different social groups, and the significance of marriage and the frequency of divorce in those groups. Upon these, the nature of inheritance, i.e. whether it is in marketable property or in non-saleable land, seems to have a bearing.

Divorce rates and property accumulation

An important question to consider in the attempt to explain different divorce rates is whether the statuses held by a woman in her family of origin and her husband's family are compatible or not, and which of these offers superior rewards. We are reminded of I. M. Lewis's emphasis on unequal agnatic loyalties as a precondition for stable marriage: 'Where the wife relinquishes her premarital legal status and is incorporated in her husband's group, men and women here being subject to dissimilar agnatic loyalties, marriage is stable.'[1] If the statuses are not compatible, divorce is more likely. This is the case where a woman inherits property in land which she does not claim, or where her husband is too poor to pay bridewealth and thus acquire rights over her, which exclude those of her family. When divorce is more likely neither husband nor wife see their union as a definitive commitment but maintain an economic bond with, and emotional allegiance to, their kin.

Marriage, to 70% of the population with which I shall be dealing, means the maintenance of their economic and social *status quo*; to another 20% it means cultural assimilation to the politically dominant group. Transfer of property is the mark for a man of full Arab status and holds out the possibility of cultural and social advance to the woman. For the remaining 10%, the urban élite, the phenomenon of inheritance of movable property by women, and the independence of their kin, favours a lower divorce rate. This in turn allows for the consolidation of economic interests, which favours the rational process

[1] I. M. Lewis (1962).

191

of capital accumulation and the strengthening of bonds among a 'power élite'.

Since there is no divorce without marriage – no rose without a thorn, or no thorn without a rose, whichever way you like to look at it – it should finally appear that much of my discussion of divorce is an attempt to assess the importance of marriage as a mechanism of property accumulation among the owners of mobile capital, or as inhibiting this process in the rest of the population.

I will argue that, in the Middle Atlas at least, and probably more generally in Morocco and the Maghreb, the social importance of the relationship between husband and wife increases or decreases according to the investment which they are able to make in the new domestic unit. The transfer of movable property and, with it, primary allegiance from the couple's families of origin to the new household, is fundamental.

Put crudely, firstly marriage is less important and more unstable when men and women inherit mainly land, and more important and more stable when they inherit saleable capital. This distinction is especially significant in the case of women. Secondly, if men and women inherit land, and again the form of the women's inheritance is crucial, they are likely to retain reciprocal property rights, and therefore service obligations, with their kin, which are incompatible with a primary allegiance to the conjugal unit.

Women and the inheritance in land

A *ksar*-woman's kin attempt to forestall a definitive transfer of the woman's land outside the family, either by marrying her to someone who shares their property interests, or, because they can co-opt her husband to their working association and send her gifts, by allowing her to continue to exercise her rights of maintenance with respect to them. On the other hand, she will continue to feel herself more bound to them by obligations of an unconditional kind (especially in giving help to her female kin) than to her husband's kin, and to rely on them for contingency support. Being near it is possible for her to be in touch with them continuously and never to feel that she has passed into a new field of primary relations.

Female family relationships remain intimate throughout a woman's lifetime. They are stronger and more functional than those between a woman and her brothers or father, or those which obtain among these male relatives. Of course they assert their influence the more effectively the closer a woman's marriage household is to home. Fortes' observation is relevant here that 'Conjugal status does not replace filial status, it is added on to it; and their potentially conflicting coextension is regulated by arrangements which segregate their respective fields of operation.'[1] Neighbourhood marriages cannot achieve this degree of segregation. A woman's preferred helpers will always be the women she grew up with, until she has children of her own. The inhabitants of Aghzim realistically dub any inmarried wife in their village as an outsider (*brraniya*) until she has borne a child to secure her emotionally to their community. So it is that any married woman would prefer to be working with kin rather than affines, and the latter reciprocate the sentiment. Co-residence is notoriously difficult for them, and the more real the alternative options are, the more gloomy are the prospects for the conjugal household. In Evans-Pritchard's words, 'The real danger to the union of husband and wife is not the hostility of the wife's family, but the intimacy which frequent contact and kinship ties might bring about.'[2]

Town and country

To recapitulate, many cultural features distinguish *ksar*-dwellers from townsmen. In dress, men and women of the *ksour* conform more closely to the Berber pattern. Women do a lot of agricultural work, caring for animals and processing food, and lead an altogether freer life than townswomen. A townswoman stands to inherit movable property which can be of use to her, although the amount is negligible except among the class that I have called the town élite. Berbers, who own only land, usually manage to evade the Islamic law of inheritance for women. So the dispersal of agnates and their landholdings is slowed up.

The contrast between town and *ksar* is a striking one, because they are strongly differentiated in a cultural sense. The town–country dichotomy has been a traditional focus of discussion for historians and sociologists of North Africa but since my concern is with the relation between divorce rates and economic factors, this distinction has not proved illuminating. It would be easy to slide into the assumption that the distinction corresponded in economic terms to the sphere dominated by market forces and that not yet drawn into it. But it is misleading to concentrate on the town–country dimension under the illusion that this division corresponds to the traditional opposition

[1] M. Fortes (1962), 11.   [2] Evans-Pritchard (1964), 185.

Table 22. *Regional origin and divorce rates in the town*

Origin	Number of women	WOMEN Total number of marriages	Number of marriages per person	Divorces as a percentage of marriages
Originating in local *ksour* or Tafilalet	45	71	1·6	42
Others	32	37	1·2	28
Total	77	108	1·4	35

Origin	Number of men	MEN Total number of marriages	Number of marriages per person	Divorces as a percentage of marriages
Originating in local *ksour* or Tafilalet	19	45	2·2	53·3
Others	26	39	1·3	32·7
Total	45	84	1·75	43

Table 23. *Divorce rates in the 'ksar' Aghzim*
(*undifferentiated as to origin*)

Number of women	WOMEN Total number of marriages	Number of marriages per person	Divorces as a percentage of marriages
38	74	1·9	55

Number of men	MEN Total number of marriages	Number of marriages per person	Divorces as a percentage of marriages
24	51	2·1	49

between mobile or saleable capital created by trade and market relations, on the one hand, and land on the other, not yet treated as a commodity. Such an analysis disguises the real lines of economic cleavage which transect town and country. The tables in Chapter 4 give some indication of the economic differentiation within town and *ksar*.

When I make references to urban, *ksar*, or semi-urban, and rural categories, I do so because much of my quantitative information was collected from geographically discrete samples and not on a class basis, and because most of the members of a single category have more in common with each other in economic terms than with members of other categories. Nevertheless, the tables above show that all the members of the town, or of the *ksar*, do not by any means share the same economic fate.

Some land *is* sold, even if it is a small proportion. Most peasants and *ksar* inhabitants are related to the market, in a way which may or may not favour them, through consumption of manufactured goods, production of crops for the market and wage labour – sometimes even through bureaucratic and administrative employment in the town. Thus, even if the majority of the people in the *ksour* have less than 3 hectares of land and negligible mobile property, some are better off. Out of 110 household-heads in two *ksour*, 10 are government employees and 6 are middle or large landowners with administrative positions, or industrial and mercantile assets.

In the town, on the other hand, the entire category of small artisans, shopkeepers and labourers have little to show in the way of property though better off than the *ksar*-dwellers, who could not afford to live in the town.

I would like to stress here that I regard stability of marriage as related in a complex way to the ownership of mobile, i.e. saleable, property and not to residence in the town.

Although divorce is common everywhere the rate is higher in the *ksour* than in the town, and higher still, I believe, in the rural hinterland – say 50 kilometres away – where I am told it is common for women to marry six times, and some even fifteen.

Poverty alone may affect the rate of divorce. The six men in the urban sample whom I knew to be rarely employed had accumulated eighteen marriages and twelve divorces among them, an average of three marriages and two divorces each. However it is important to understand the mechanisms by which this is brought about.

The variable of regional origin appears to be even more telling than that of wealth, although to some extent they vary together. Thus most of the casual, unskilled and unremunerative jobs were carried out by migrants from the local *ksour* and from the Tafilalet where the population of the local *ksour* originated. The migrants retain land rights in their villages of origin and marry among themselves and with the local *ksour*. They do not pay bridewealth nor are their women so strictly secluded. Divorce especially on the part of men of this category is frequent, the rates of divorce and remarriage resembling closely those in the *ksar* sample. Women divorce less frequently than their counterparts in the *ksar* sample, being more dependent in economic and social terms on their conjugal status than on their kinship status.

Divorce and remarriage are much lower among the category of regularly employed men and their wives who come from northern and coastal towns. There is a 14% difference between the divorce rate of Tafilalet women in the towns and that of their more privileged northern sisters. The difference between the latter and women in the *ksar* sample is 27%. The difference between the divorce rate of northern men in the towns who pay bridewealth and that of their Tafilalet neighbours is 20%, and between the former and the *ksar* sample it is 16%.

Thus, although I treat the urban sample sometimes as a unit, its dual nature should be kept in mind. It seems then that the economic and social situation of women is the crucial factor in determining the rate of divorce. That is, women who move to the town are to some extent cut off from their supportive network and are no longer autonomous economically, for they cannot return easily to their kin nor ask economic help from them, and they do no agricultural work, of which half the proceeds would be theirs. Yet their status as urban and 'secluded' women is more highly esteemed than that of their *ksar* counterparts. Although women appear to divorce less frequently than men, it should be borne in mind that their marital career is fifteen to twenty years shorter. Thus in Adam's Casablanca shanty-town, Beni Msik, 6·8% of men had married more than five times, but few women. Among the migrants of my urban sample 3/19 men married four or more times, and 2/45 women.[1]

It is not illegitimate to draw parallels between Adam's Beni Msik sample, and the migrant part of my urban sample, and also that of the semi-urban *ksour*. In Beni Msik the average number of marriages was 2·4 for men, 1·7 for women, compared with the Akhdar migrants' sample, 2·2 and 1·6, and the *ksar* sample's 2·1 and 1·9. Adam observes, 'C'est dans le proletariat et le sous-proletariat que l'instabilité conjugale est la plus accusée.'[2] However he claims that the divorce rate in the town is 20% higher than that in the countryside, a statement which could not be applied to Akhdar, and which can only be attributed to the greater integration of farmers around Casablanca into the urban economy, their more fertile land, and secure income.[3]

[1] A. Adam (1967), 746.   [2] Ibid., 747.   [3] Ibid., 746.

Divorce and property

Noin gives the divorce rates in the former Spanish zone as 33% in 1956, and the same in 1962.[1] Census figures on divorce tend to be unreliable, because many divorces are not registered or admitted to, or even remembered if an individual is asked to give an account of a complicated marital history. Gaudry remarks on the paucity of reliable information for the Berber tribes of Djebel Amour in Algeria, 'Nous aurions voulu nous appuyer sur les chiffres. Impossible. En 1946, par exemple, aucun mariage, aucun divorce, aucune répudiation n'ont été transcrits sur les régistres de l'état civil.'

'Il est également impossible de connaître le nombre des unions libres dans une tribu donnée, la facilité des formalités relatives à la conclusion des mariages devant une assemblée de notables (jema'a) ou même devant un seul témoin étant si élémentaires, qu'il existe guère de différence entre l'état de droit et l'état de fait.'[2]

The figures presented in the Moroccan census of 1960 (divorces 25·8% of marriages),[3] the Tunisian census of 1965 (divorces 22·2% of marriages),[4] and in Goode's survey of family patterns in Algeria (16·2% of marriages ended in divorce in 1960)[5] should all be regarded as questionable. A journalist from Algeria discussing the 'plague' of divorce in Algeria remarked that unregistered divorces are more common than registered ones. On the other hand to register a marriage, like any other contract, gives security to both husband and wife, so that divorces are likely to appear to compose a smaller percentage of marriages than they really do.[6]

Attitudes

In attempting to explain the discrepancy between these rates, I had to take into account the discovery that people from the population with the highest divorce rates – 52% on average, against an average of 38% in the town – were quite nonchalant about it.

Peasants from the *ksar* where I lived made such philosophical statements as: 'Girls don't like marriage' (woman) or 'Women leave because they quarrel with their mother-in-law' (woman) or 'People divorce because a girl's parents welcome her home instead of making her stay with her husband' (man). The impression you get is that marriage is hard and against a girl's best interest, which is to stay

[1] D. Noin (1970), 33.
[2] M. Gaudry (1961), 190.
[3] L. Hassan-Zeghari, *Confluent*, nos. 23–4 (1962).
[4] E. de Gaudin de Lagrange, *Revue algérienne des sciences juridiques* (déc. 1968), 1112.
[5] W. Goode (1962), 93.   [6] *Révolution Africaine*, 26 déc. 1964.

with her family. Divorce is inevitable and the conjugal relationship is secondary in the eyes of the kin of both spouses.

In contrast with this resigned mood is the vehement condemnation of women by a shopkeeper who said 'Women who leave their husbands should be imprisoned,' the suspicion of the teachers who said 'Women leave when their husbands won't give them gold,' and 'Women who leave their husbands do so because they want to lead a life of licence.' Finally, note the contempt of the policeman who stated 'People divorce because women are uneducated.'

Women are portrayed as grasping, ignorant, irresponsible and in need of discipline. Yet the divorce rate in this milieu is much lower than in the *ksour*, in spite of the paranoia.

Most of these statements are by men, but women tend to agree with them that the relationship of women to society is crucial in determining the stability of marriage. In the town however there is more talk about adultery committed by men, which in the *ksar* could only be synonymous with divorce, for no self-respecting Berber women would stand for it. In the *ksar* slightly more women than men had married more than once (58% against 54%). But in the town many more men than women had done so (51% against 24%).

Divorce rates and early marriage

Women in the *ksar* initiate divorce much more often than men. A woman does this by running away to her kin, who may attempt to persuade her to return; but if she is adamant and they think she has a case they will bring pressure to bear on the husband to undertake the divorce. This a woman cannot do. Most of these divorces occur within the first year or two of marriage. Indeed, they may have something to do with the low age of marriage, which turns the marriage into something of the nature of a nubility rite, which is expected to bind the spouses for a couple of months at the most. 'L'Enquête à objectifs multiples'[1] shows that in Morocco as a whole 80% of marriages contracted by girls under fourteen ended in divorce. But in the Akhdar region, there is not a great enough difference between the marriage ages in town and in the *ksour* to account for the discrepancy in divorce rates. However, the difference of age between husband and wife was about fourteen years in the *ksour*, on average, and ten years in the town, the difference in the town being greater among the migrants than in the rest of the sample. It is difficult to

[1] 'Résultats de l'enquête' (1964), 132.

believe that this age-gap, reinforcing as it does the political inequality between husband and wife, does not contribute to the antagonism between them. The wife's extreme subordination may be as unattractive to her as the husband's 'loss of control' would be to him. However, I have no evidence for this.

Although the age-gap must be taken into account, it fades into insignificance beside the other factors which generate antagonism in the relationship, i.e. the importance of the wife's network, the failure of the husband to provide economic and social support for his wife, their different orientation to the market, and the attempts of each to subordinate the other's interests to his own primary objectives.

In the town, moreover, women seem to stick with their marriages and a much greater number of divorces are initiated by men, often after ten or more years of marriage, when there may be several children. At this stage, however, a man has clearly achieved the cultural and political transition from his Berber or rural origins to Arab citizenship. Divorce in the town is generally seen as a major disaster by women because it is especially harmful to the wife and children.

Legal causes and consequences of divorce

The precipitating causes of divorce which are generally used as pretexts[1] in the law-courts are the failure of a husband to provide his wife with adequate food, clothes and shelter; failure of a wife to perform domestic services; impotence, barrenness, adultery, madness, physical ill-treatment, absence of the husband over a year. If the *caid* adjudges the husband at fault, he must pay a settlement which is part of the bridal payment or *sdaq* and forfeits the furnishings of the house which the wife bought with the other part of the bridal pay-

[1] It is significant that in Tunisia, where the laws affecting the status of women and divorce procedures are more favourable to women than those in any other North African country, for women can demand divorce, over half the divorces registered between 1962 and 1964 were by mutual consent, and another quarter were requested by the husband '*sans motif*'. It may be that these reflect precisely that incompatibility of the interests of husband and wife which is under discussion.

I cite below the relative importance of the various reasons given for divorce in the 13,188 divorces which were registered in 1962-4 in Tunisia: 55 for non-payment of maintenance (requested by wife); 198 for husband's abandonment of the household (ditto); 3540 requested by husband, '*sans motif*'; 6 requested by wife '*sans motif*'; 19 for moral reasons (requested by husband); 1986 requested by either of spouses for maltreatment; 7193 by mutual consent.

The same is true in Algeria: 'Les chiffres peuvent affrayer mais il est incontestable que la plus grande partie des divorces sont prononcées après accord mutuel des époux. Viennent ensuite les divorces prononcés par défaut d'entretien ou pour cause de longue absence etc. Les cas de répudiation par le mari ne constituent qu'un nombre relativement faible.' Cheikh Mekri Aoussi, *Revue algérienne des sciences juridiques* (déc. 1968), 1099.

Table 24. *Divorce and remarriage as a function of age:*
town quarter

	MEN				
	Number of wives ever married				
Age	1	2	3	Over 4	Total
15–20	—	—	—	—	—
21–35	10	4	2	—	16
36–50	9	6	2	2	19
Over 50	2	4	1	2	9
Totals	21	14	5	4	44
	WOMEN				
	Number of husbands ever married				
Age	1	2	3	4 or more	Total
15–20	4	—	—	—	4
21–35	35	4	2	—	41
36–50	13	3	3	1	20
Over 50	6	4	—	2	12
Totals	58	11	5	3	77

Table 25. *Residence of women after termination of marriage: town quarter*

Residence with...	Both parents	Mother	Daughter	Son	Other	Alone	Total
Age							
15–20	—	—	—	—	1 (div) (brother)	—	1
21–35	1 (div)	1 (div)	1 (wid)	—	1 (wid) (foster parents) 1 (div) (brother)	1 (wid) 1 (wid)	7
36–50	—	1 (wid)	1 (wid)	—	1 (div) ZS	2 (wid) (1 with children) 1 (div)	6
Over 50	—	—	3 (wid)	2 (wid)	1 (wid) Z	4 (wid) 2 (div)	12
	1	2	5	2	5	11	26

div=divorcée; wid=widow.

200

Divorce and property

Table 26. *Divorce and remarriage as a function of age: Aghzim*

	MEN Number of wives ever married				
Age	1	2	3	Over 4	Total
15–20	1	—	—	—	1
21–35	7	1	—	—	8
36–50	2	3	3	1	9
Over 50	1	2	1	2	6
Totals	11	6	4	3	24

	WOMEN Number of husbands ever married				
Age	1	2	3	Over 4	Total
15–20	4	2	—	—	6
21–35	6	7	3	2	18
36–50	4	3	3	—	10
Over 50	2	1	1	—	4
Totals	16	13	7	2	38

Table 27. *Residence of women after termination of marriage: Aghzim*

Residence with...	Both parents	Mother	Daughter	Son	Other	Alone	Total
Age							
15–20	—	2 (div)	—	—	—	—	2
21–35	1 (div)	1 (div)	—	—	—	—	2
36–50	—	—	1 (div)	—	—	—	1
Over 50	—	—	2 (wid)	1 (wid)	1 (wid)	3 (wid) 2 (wid) near sons	9
Total	1	3	3	1	1	5	14

div=divorcée; wid=widow.

house which the wife bought with the other part of the bridal payment. He must pay her three months' maintenance which he is also bound to do if the wife is at fault. In the latter case, she forfeits the *sdaq* and the furnishings.

Male children over two go with the husband, or with the wife until the husband remarries. Female children and infants under two

201

go with the wife, who will leave them with her parents when she remarries.

If there is property to distribute, the marriage must have been of the bridewealth or dowry type, and the litigants townspeople. I have heard women alleging that men always win such divorce suits, because the women do not understand what is going on, and do not have the material resources to sweeten the judges or to hold out as long as a salaried man can. This is another factor contributing to the relative rarity with which women in the town initiate divorce, compared with their rural sisters, particularly if they live far from male kin who can take their part, or if they come from poor families.

Of all the inhabitants of the town quarter who had ever been married, and had been divorced or widowed, three men and twenty-four women had not remarried at the time of the survey. Of the men, one (aged 28) lived alone after his divorce, one (aged 40) lived in his sister's household, a third divorcé (aged 35) lived with his mother. The tables above show the distribution of the women by age. It could be said that all these women return to uterine kin.

Of all the inhabitants of Aghzim who had ever married and been divorced or widowed, one man and twelve women had not remarried. The tables above show their distribution by age.

The only unremarried man was divorced (aged 30) and lived with his mother.

Comparison of divorce and remarriage for men and women in town and country

Men marry later and apparently more often than women. Men are always eligible for marriage, in their qualities of bread-winner and progenitor. The transient nature of the qualities for which wives are especially valued, those of sexual object and genetrix, tends to give limits to their marital career. The structure of authority within the conjugal unit means that men, who are masters, are likely to enjoy marriage more than women, who are servants.

The other discrepancy between the figures for men and women concerns the fact that men rarely live alone, or, if they have been once married, return to kin, but a large number of women do both these things. This fact can be attributed, not only to their differential eligibility for remarriage, but to the availability of approved and practicable alternative statuses for women. Since a woman is in the position of minor in her husband's house, returning to kin is not an

Divorce and property

indignity. Moreover women usually have good emotional relations with their children, especially daughters. But for a man, celibacy means dependence and ridicule, or a life of tension with a son whom he suspects of designs on his possessions. Given the sexual division of labour it is impossible for a man to live alone, performing his own household tasks without feeling this to be a humiliation.

Town/country. In the town sample, a larger proportion of men than women had married more than once (51% against 24·5%) and more men than women had married more than three times (20% against 10·4%). However in Aghzim the figures for remarriage of women are virtually the same as for men. (54·1% of men married more than once as against 52·6% of women. 29·1% of men married more than three times as against 23·7% of women.)

The greater remarriage rate for women in Aghzim is probably due to the more rapid divorce rate in the early years of marriage (half of the women who claimed to have married more than three times were under thirty-six). However it is clear that in an economy where women do much of the agricultural work, a wife will still be an important asset to a man, long after she has ceased to bear children and her charms have faded. But in the town where she is chiefly childminder, and status symbol, she is regarded in middle age as a parasite, and it is at this stage that town divorces generally occur, initiated by the husband.

By age, and residence after the termination of marriage. There is a marked tendency, especially in the *ksour,* for young women to live with their mothers if they are divorced or widowed, and for older ones to live with their daughters. Because of long and intimate co-operation, the mother–daughter tie is deeper and more relaxed than the father–daughter one, and even than that between mother and son, although this is romanticised by women, whose status in the community is enhanced by bearing sons. The mother–daughter bond is at any rate more functional and durable, to judge from these samples. Foster daughters will often return to their foster-mother, if they have marital difficulty, especially if the relationship is long-standing.

In Aghzim, unremarried women either live alone, or with children, but in the town many such women are living with other relatives, particularly siblings. This is a further reflection of the importance of a wider range of kin, especially collaterals, in the town than in the country, which has already been discussed in the analysis of household composition. It is probably important that a woman's chances of marriage are greater in the town, that men who live in the town are generally in employment and more able to support an unmarried sister than their parents, and that their domestic help is valued by celibate men, especially of the professional type. Such a man tends to have grave misgivings about marriage, and the prospect of being tied to an illiterate person for whom he feels contempt. Yet he is not prepared to marry an educated girl, because of her independent ways. The presence of a sister is an aid to procrastination.

Life-cycle of men and women and tendency to divorce. A woman's marital career tends to span her child-bearing and child-rearing years, and then to come brusquely to an end. Women consider that marriage after this age is an unnecessary burden – 'Why should I work again?' A man on the other hand always has a wife, and is always interested in finding a new one. The marital career of women, unlike that of men who generally remarry within weeks of divorce, is intermittent. Not only does a woman visit her kin regularly during marriage, but she spends the periods between divorce and remarriage at their home. This period is rarely less than six months (the legal minimum being three months) and may extend up to four years. As she grows older, her focus of attention shifts on to her children, and rather than move to live with her brother and compete with his wife for resources, she will prefer to stay with her sons and daughters who have a legal and moral obligation to support her. She will often stay in the house of her deceased husband, if she is widowed, since it is there that all her children can reassemble, while she retains her position of authority. Sometimes she may live by herself.

Age of women who initiate divorce. It appears that there is a strong tendency for *ksar*-women to divorce when they have good chances of remarriage. The phenomenon of 'terminal separations', in which women past the menopause voluntarily leave their husbands, does not seem important in Morocco (see E. N. Goody, *Marriage in Tribal Societies*). The marriages of all Aghzim women in this age group who were not currently married had ended in death, not divorce. The divorcées were much younger, and could be expected to remarry.

This pattern is typical of the town as well. Although it is probable that women divorced on their husband's initiative around the menopause will not remarry, there does not seem to be a large-scale voluntary drifting away at this stage. So older unmarried women tend to have the status of widows, rather than divorcées. It is rare too that men will initiate divorce, for two reasons.

If a man has lived with a woman for several years, he will usually have several children by her. He himself is much older than she is, and if he wishes to attract a new wife, he must rely on the old one continuing to take care of the children, who would otherwise count in his disfavour in the wife-hunt. He will generally continue to support the first as his wife, paying an allowance for his children, and go himself to live with the new wife. This is the solution of the rich man in the prime of life. But as a man grows older, remembering always that he may be anything from ten to thirty or forty years older than his wife, his dependence on her strength increases. A man would not willingly be rid of such an asset, particularly as few men get on well enough with their children to enjoy living with them.

Sometimes a man may leave his widow with wealth enough to attract a new husband, but these cases are rare.

One woman, a *sherifa*, was left at the age of forty-five with huge estates and flocks of sheep to manage. Having no sons or male kin, she offered to leave this property to a young labourer who had worked for her husband, on the condition that he marry her. The couple had no children but fostered a boy. The husband's amours were not few, but he managed the estate efficiently, protected the widow's honour, made her last years comfortable, and became very rich.

Extra-marital relations and initiation of divorce by men. I have remarked above that the slight chances of remarriage of older women discourage them from provoking divorce. More important is the function of children in deciding a woman's economic and emotional dependence on the marriage. A man remarries at almost any age, earns his own living, and will probably not live to be supported by his children. His emotional as well as economic ties with his children are more tenuous than a woman's. In fact men seem to become more liable to initiate divorce as the number of dependent children increases. There seem to be a number of reasons, chief among them being acute rivalry with his older sons, and his frustration at the limitations placed on his transactions in the public sphere.

So the middle-aged husband, living in a house full of demanding children, who obviously receive prior attention from his wife – herself growing care-worn, and increasingly immersed in a cultural sub-world which is remote from his own – is expected to look for new excitement – in a word, release. Sometimes the wife, in an attempt to keep the situation under control, may herself suggest that her husband re-marry. I have known several cases where she has even chosen the wife, thus acquiring a maid for herself.

More often the husband becomes an absentee householder, spending his evenings drinking and gambling in the cafés frequented by *Huriyin*. These women may either be professional prostitutes or dallying divorcées. The former are more respected; they are seen as constrained by circumstances to earn their living in this way. The latter are merely 'women without shame'. Sometimes a man forms a relationship with a divorcée which is regularised by marriage, but people say 'It will only last a few months.' *Huriyin* are regarded as having rejected the authority of men, and are therefore unfitted for a long liaison. They are clearly distinguished from 'honourable' divorcées whose base is sometimes their father's house, and whose object is marriage and children. The *Huriyin* are believed to be versed in the arts of love, and if a woman's husband leaves her to live with one, she will claim that he has been bewitched.

The following case illustrates the dependence of a woman with children, the strong sexual jealousy which survives marriage, and the relative strength of the relationships of mother and father with their children. The spouses' common commitment to children ensures the continuity, in some respects, of a conjugal relationship which has been formally ended.

The witch. Sadiya, an orphan from Ceima, was first married at eleven by her grandfather and step-grandmother, and ran away after a few days. Then at sixteen she was married to a man from the Tafilalet twenty years her senior, who became a well-to-do garage owner in Akhdar. Sadiya bore him six children, four of them sons, and they lived in a big house, well supplied with furniture and clothes. When Sadiya was twenty-eight and the eldest of her sons twelve years old, her husband (now forty-eight) deserted her. He went to live with a divorcée aged about thirty-eight, with three children of her own. Sadiya spoke of him with bitterness as a *rul* (a man-eating ogre) and claimed that the *Morghadiya* was a woman of low morals whom he had met in a bar. The *Morghadiya* was old and ugly, whereas she herself was still young and attractive, so that it was clear that she had practised *s'Hur* (witchcraft).

After a year Sadiya went to the *cadi* to claim that she had been deserted and that she wanted to claim an allowance for herself and her children. The *cadi* gave her a certificate obliging her husband to pay her 350 *drahem* a month, and awarding her occupancy of the house. Since they had been living well, and the husband had taken away carpets and record-player, Sadiya felt that hers was a hard lot. When I met her, her husband had been living with the other woman for five years, and she had had a child by him. Sadiya claimed that he had not married her, but since the penalty for adultery is one to two years' imprisonment, and there are few disadvantages in marrying since polygamy is legal for men, it is probable that he drew up a marriage certificate but did not pay bridewealth.

Sadiya seemed to experience violent sexual jealousy, pointing out the house of 'that woman'. Once when I stopped to talk to a friend of mine, Sadiya was shocked to the core, because she had thought for a moment that it was her rival.

She was ambitious for her sons, urging the eldest not to leave school to take up some limited salesman's job for a foreign firm (most Akhdari families would have been delighted with this prospect) which a friend of her husband offered him. She was probably aware that her husband would divorce her when the children were grown up, and she would have to rely on them for help. She wanted their future to be out of his control. Yet she encouraged them to take advantage of his obligations to support them while they were being educated, in order to pursue their education as far as possible.

Her eldest son helped his father during the holidays in order to earn money and gain experience, but his attitude was ambivalent. He said he would cut all ties when he had a job of his own. The other children would ask their father for clothes, but would make their relationship with him conditional on his bounty to them. One small son refused to go and see his father who called him in the street, because the parent had changed his mind about giving him a sweater. The father never saw his daughters at all (aged five and six).

Resilience

Rural and *ksar* marriages seem to be much less resistant than town marriages to the pressures which I have mentioned as 'precipitating causes' of divorce, as well as to the more general stress resulting from incompatibility, quarrels with kin or harsh treatment by a husband. In the town I repeatedly found instances where husband, but more frequently wife, tolerated events which would have proved quickly fatal for a *ksar* union. Since the majority of *ksar* divorces occur during the first few years of marriage, I quote, for comparison, only town marriages of less than three years' standing. They showed resilience in the face of quarrels between the wife and the husband's mother and sisters (5 cases), quarrels between the husband and the wife's kin (3 cases), illness (3 cases), childlessness (3 cases – all dowried marriages in the Fez style), infidelity by the husband (6 cases – 3 of them dowried marriages), financial deprivation and neglect (2 cases), physical violence (2 cases), mental breakdown (2 cases).

The following two cases are intended to bring out the contrast between the reactions of the urban bourgeoisie and those of *ksar*-people to stress within marriage and the respective attitudes of the couples and the kin to divorce. The stakes to be played in marriage are considered high in the former category and low in the latter – where neither partner stands to lose social or cultural status by divorce.

The marriages of Itto

The main points which I wish to remark upon in this case are the scant rewards and therefore motives for marriage in a rural context for women, the much greater rewards for men and the variation of their views on divorce.

The husband retains his status as a member of a mutually supportive kin-group and in many cases continues to exercise the property rights which this entails. The wife is forced to give all this up but the implication is that she does so conditionally and temporarily. This creates an atmosphere of norms which are ambiguous, seen from the perspective of a renegade wife. It is probable that those of her kin to whom she is most nearly attached – her mother and sisters – will sympathise with her disillusion and will have few strongly felt counter-arguments to those she presents in justification of her flight. To behave otherwise would be to disallow her right to claim maintenance in her capacity as a member of the property-holding group.

Itto was the youngest of the five daughters and one son of Bedda, a widow whose husband died in 1956. Since he had served and was twice decorated in the French army, Bedda received a quarterly pension from France: £14 for herself and £8 for each of her children until they reached eighteen years of age. Bedda lived in her husband's house in Aghzim together with her blind mother and such of her daughters as returned between divorces, or during their husband's periods of absence or bad temper, or to spend holidays in the summer, or to celebrate feast days.

When Itto was sixteen, living in the house with her mother,

grandmother, one divorced sister and one betrothed sister, a man came to ask for her in marriage. He was a shopkeeper/peasant from a remote village 80 kilometres away in the coldest part of the Middle Atlas. He had come to pay the *henna* of another girl but had changed his mind and someone had told him to make enquiries about Itto. The match was agreed upon. As frequently happens with marriages involving the removal of the bride from her parents' neighbourhood, this one was splendid: the bridewealth reached enormous proportions for a *ksar* family (1000 *drahem* or £100), not to speak of the clothes presented to the bride and the provisions for the wedding feast.

Itto stayed only three months in her new home. When her mother and sister came to visit her she swore to kill herself if she had to stay any longer. It was cold and bleak. There was no electricity. The work was heavy. She didn't like the 'foreign women', and was frightened of the guard dogs. It is significant that neither she nor anyone else mentioned the nature of her relationship with her husband as a factor in the situation. He refused to divorce her and her family reasoned with her because he was 'a good man'. She was adamant and finally a soldier living in Rabat persuaded her husband to divorce her. All the bridewealth was returned, to the chagrin of the bride's family.

After less than a year, Itto married again, this time to a forty-year-old miner who lived about 30 kilometres away. He came with his brother, who knew Bedda slightly, to ask for her hand. He swore that he had no vices, and that the four children of his late first wife lived with their grandmother and would be no trouble.

His offer came at a time of financial stress for Bedda, who was depressed because her small wheat crop had just been ruined by hail. She saw her daughter's marriage as a relief to her resources since she would no longer have to provide her with clothes (cf. the comment of Itto's sister on the remarriage of a third sister: 'She must have a husband to buy her shoes and food. My mother hasn't anything to give her'). Bedda and her family made only the most superficial enquiries, not even making the gesture of going to inspect the miner's house. After a quiet family feast, Itto went away with him.

Within a week she was back again, announcing that she had left her erstwhile husband for good, because his house was dirty and shabby and she had only a grass mat for furnishings. Two days after she had moved in, the mother of his previous wife had put his children on a bus and sent them to be looked after by the new housekeeper. Itto found this exasperating. She complained, too, that he earned little money which he spent anyway on drink and cigarettes. She weighed heavily on the atmosphere of deceit, as if to point out that she would be forswearing the family honour by living with such a person. Besides, he was old.

The next day Bedda and Itto heard that the miner was looking for his wife. He was drunk and threatening to kill her. They went to ask advice from the *sheikh* who told them that they should lie low and wait for him to go to the cadi and pronounce divorce, thus forfeiting the clothes and becoming liable to pay *sdaq*. If he delayed they should go themselves. (Although *ksar*-people tend not to have recourse to *Shari'a* justice until they have reached deadlock in their attempts to sort things out by meditation and discussion, they express confidence in its efficacy. When I asked Bedda how she expected the cadi to view the case she said '*ad-itish-i ku-yuwun lhaq-ns*' ('he will give to each person his right').

After a week, during which the husband sent repeated messages to Itto to return, which she ignored, his brother arrived to break the match. He sympathised with Bedda, saying that his brother was a bad type. The four of them arranged to go to the court and the clothes were returned. Bedda said they didn't want anything of his.

Itto got her divorce from the miner in June. The following January she accepted another marriage proposal, this time from a 28-year-old man, Haddou, who had never been married before. Haddou and his two elder sisters had been orphaned when they were still small, and he had been brought up by their father's brother and his wife. When their father's brother died they stayed on in the house of his son, gradually coming into their inheritance of fields and houses in Ceima, 2 kilometres from Itto's village. The younger sister married a friend of her brother's from the same *ksar* and it was she and her husband who set about finding a wife for Haddou.

He had little to offer, for he was unemployed and had been living for years off his inheritance, gradually selling off the harvests and fields to supply himself with the wherewithal to survive. Bedda, however, liked the family and put no obstacles in the way of the marriage negotiations, which Itto seemed very willing to undertake. As a twice-married woman she was given full responsibility for the choice. Haddou, his sister and brother-in-law, and the eldest sister, bought the clothes for Itto and *wrqtu* ('made the ticket', i.e. settled the *sdaq* of 150 *drahem* to be paid on divorce, and registered the marriage at the court).

Two weeks later Itto came home, not for good, but already the cracks were beginning to show. Haddou was still unemployed. House-painting, in which he was trained, was not a steady occupation. Itto said he wasn't looking for work. Her mother took her complaints lightly and told her she wasn't a child to keep running home and that Haddou was a good man. Bedda visited Itto frequently and Haddou's sister and brother-in-law helped them generously with supplies of grain. Nearly two months later Itto came home again, this time with her suitcase, insisting that she had left Haddou for good, since he brought nothing home and was not looking for work.

By this time she was pregnant. There was no sense of drama. Itto's mother and sisters teased her, Bedda querying how *she* could support both Itto and her baby. Of course she must return to her husband. Itto insisted that she would not live with someone so irresponsible. 'At eleven he gets up, goes for a stroll, comes back for lunch, goes to sleep, wakes up for afternoon coffee, then spends the rest of the day drinking and gambling in the café.' Bedda was clearly shocked that her daughter had no firewood in the depth of severe winter. The entire regiment of female kin was aghast that Haddou had sold his wardrobe, Itto's most treasured status symbol. Her own respect for him was shattered.

Three days after Itto left Haddou, Bedda received a message to the effect that his sisters and brother-in-law were coming to ask her to go back. Bedda said '*Bi-ssif* you go back' (by the sword, it is absolutely imperative). Itto swore she would not. The delegation arrived from their *ksar*, 2 kilometres away. First they went to the house of Mohand, an old man who had once or twice been *amghrar* in Bedda's *ksar* and who knew the father of Haddou's brother-in-law. He came with them as mediator.

After at least an hour had passed in banalities in Bedda's house, the subject of the marriage was broached. Each person appeared to speak his mind firmly. The brother-in-law was most vocal: 'They are both young; they should stay and build something together, sometimes fasting, sometimes feasting.' His wife said that they should have patience, '*ad-sbrr*', and wait a while until better times came. Surprisingly Bedda took her daughter's part vehemently, saying that no woman could be expected to stay with someone who never worked, or sit without firewood in winter. The women tended to take a political stand, each defending their relative, whatever their private doubts. That this was a defence of *en-nif* (nose, or honour) became clear when the elder of Haddou's sisters burst out after everyone had spoken, saying that she was shamed and dishonoured that people should talk of her brother-in-law, of her own father and mother in this way. The girl was his wife. She should stay and do her work, sweep and fetch water until better times came. Later this speech was criticised as haughty and affected.

Mohand said little, occasionally agreeing or making aphoristic noises when he was appealed to. Itto herself listened behind the curtain which screened the door, occasionally announcing: 'I won't be married to him!' Haddou's brother-in-law invited her to sit down calmly and take a full part in the discussion. Finally she gave in to their pressure and went crying to the house of Haddou's sister and brother-in-law where she stayed for the next two weeks. During this time Bedda was invited to their house for a meal. Haddou also came but Itto refused to have anything to do with him and escaped laughing when he tried to catch her to take her home with him. Later, to demonstrate that he still could make conjugal claims he called to her to bring him some water. 'No,' she shouted in a tone which scandalised the other women. She insisted that she would not go back, even if he were to find work, because he drank and gambled – an argument her mother called weak because she had been warned of this by Haddou's relatives before she married him.

The relations between Bedda and Itto's affines grew yet more amicable and soon Itto was persuaded to go back to Haddou's house. Her return was celebrated with a meat-feast. Haddou's brother-in-law continued to supply the couple with grain but in spite of all these efforts Itto ran home after a week. It was clear that she was set on divorce. Bedda asked Mohand to coax Haddou and his kin into agreement and ran rejoicing to thank him when she heard of his success.

Itto and Bedda arranged to meet Haddou on an appointed day to get a divorce from the cadi. Haddou was very distraught and went into a café to get drunk. Itto said gaily: 'Two divorce certificates a year will just about do me.' The cadi awarded rights to Itto who kept her clothes and ruled that her ex-husband should pay her the 150 *drahem sdaq* and three months alimony (a full nine months if he wished to claim the child). So anxious were Itto and Bedda to get the divorce that, knowing he had no money, they *smehu*, relinquished their rights with respect to him, thus losing both *sdaq* and alimony. They also paid for the divorce certificate which should have been Haddou's liability.

Itto's reactions to stress in any of her marriages are to be contrasted with those of the parties to a 'bourgeois marriage', such as that I shall describe below. The economic circumstances of Itto's marriages were not generally favourable but nor are they in the case I have chosen to illustrate 'resilience' in marriage. However, the economic *expectations* of the latter are higher – the sources of aid more numerous, and connections more powerful. People whose marriages are 'resilient' often enjoy a much higher degree of economic and political security than the majority of *ksar* inhabitants.

Love and war – the case of Zineb

The couple with whom I am concerned in the case of Zineb had some acquaintance with each other before marriage. Their families were of equal social and political status. Difficulties were more likely to be resolved by discussion on a more or less equal basis. When the wife discovered her husband's penchant for another woman she either ignored it or fiercely defended her *conjugal* status against the woman outsider. In a *ksar* marriage, a wife would tend to regard her family honour as blemished by the man outsider, her husband. She would return home putting her husband in the position of external threat; the significant relationship to be defended is that with her family. I heard several *ksar*-women comment with amazement on the case of Zineb: 'I would leave him at once if he beat me.'

Zineb was a 21-year-old girl from a fatherless but well-to-do family in Rabat. One of her brothers held a remunerative government post; another was a plumber. Her sister, who was separated from her husband, lived with her family. Zineb met her husband, Mohammed, a skilled Rabati technician, through the husband of another sister. During the betrothal period which lasted a year, after a sumptuous *henna sgher* (betrothal ceremony) she used to slip out to meet her fiancé without her brothers' knowledge.

Soon after they married Mohammed was transferred to Akhdar. She became pregnant. Her husband was going through some financial difficulty. Their isolation in the area, partly a function of their contempt for their Berber neighbours in the *ksar* where they lived, combined with Mohammed's volatile, taut personality and habits of hard drinking, contributed to the high level of tension within the household. Winter came and Mohammed did not provide any kind of heating for his wife, although the snow was at times 1 metre deep and the wind always bitterly cold. Finally, Zineb had a bad attack of pneumonia.

Often during this period, Mohammed would come home in the small hours drunk and quarrel with his wife, sometimes beating her.

213

She would fight back with energy and the shouts and screams carried to all the houses nearby. Sometimes this would happen during the daytime and crowds of childen on their way from school would gather to hurl pebbles into the courtyard of the couple's house. None of the neighbours would intervene saying that strangers from the town could sort out their own troubles. They would have nothing to do with them.

Meanwhile, Mohammed, who was a dashing young man, was paying attention to a college girl and sent her a dress. Zineb came to hear of it and went in a fury to demand that the girl return the dress. Mohammed denied that anything was going on and blamed a local woman for sowing dissension between himself and Zineb in order to marry him off to her own daughter.

Zineb had only a couple of acquaintances in the *ksar* and never complained about her husband to them. A month before she gave birth she and Mohammed had a violent argument and he struck her violently so that she screamed for help. Mohammed's sister's son, aged five, who was living with him, began to yell too. When Mohammed had left the house a woman from the *ksar* went in to make sure that Zineb was safe. Zineb told her that nothing was wrong. She had merely fallen over and the boy was frightened and began to cry.

The atmosphere between them was not always as turbulent. Sometimes Mohammed and Zineb would chatter and laugh as if each could not wish for better company than the other. When 'her month' was due, Zineb's mother and (separated) sister came to stay. The latter lent money and a radio to Mohammed. However, he quarrelled fiercely with them and several days before the birth he disappeared so that a *ksar*-woman had to find a taxi to take Zineb to the hospital to have her baby.

Mohammed did not come back for three weeks, to the scandal of everyone, since he thereby deprived his son of the naming ceremony, *sebueh*, on the seventh day after his birth. The women were left without supplies or money. Since they were townswomen, used to living in seclusion, they were helpless and of too high a status to provide for themselves. A *ksar*-woman had to make bread for them and draw water, exercising her tongue on the absurdities of *ait-l-medina* (townspeople). Mohammed finally came back, in the company of several soldiers and as many bottles of whisky to celebrate the birth. The difficulties with his affines persisted until one day he literally threw them out with their belongings – his debts to them unpaid.

Divorce and property

The new baby became ill. The couple used every resource, including the medical skills of the *ksar*-woman who had helped them, and she was reputed to know how to cure children. She asked Zineb why she didn't leave her husband. She smiled and said, 'I'm afraid he'll try to take the child. I'll wait till I go to stay with my family and then not come back.' When the child died she was beside herself with grief. The *ksar*-woman rebuked her for such a show of sentimentality, saying that he was Satan come to plague her and was she the only woman to lose a child. Mohammed, however, acted kindly, arranging the burial. He even designed an inscription to the child's memory, romantically incorporating the parents' photographs in a heart. Mohammed's sister and her family came to stay, in an effort to help Zineb over the loss.

Soon Mohammed was given sick-leave, since he was judged to be suffering from 'tension'. When he returned, relations between himself and Zineb were more peaceable but there was one episode when Zineb began to climb out of the window screaming that Mohammed was about to murder her and another when Mohammed emerged from the house limping after a quarrel.

Zineb became pregnant again and her mother and her eldest brother came to stay, the former helping to prepare for a *sebueh*, but acting circumspectly towards her son-in-law. Mohammed boasted of the great feast in the offing, and harmony prevailed. Divorce was far from the scene.

The dissensions within this marriage are extreme by any standard. But the elements of infidelity, neglect, financial hardship, isolation of the wife, quarrels with affines (especially during the first few years of marriage before the wife has established her position by child-bearing) occurred singly or in combination in most of the 'bourgeois' marriages with which I was familiar, without leading to divorce. In rural marriages any of these factors was enough to provoke desertion by the wife, until she had borne children enough to bind her emotionally and economically to her conjugal household.

What is at stake

It seems then that some women have less to gain by marriage and less to lose by divorce than others. The other side of the picture is that the roles open to *ksar*-women outside marriage are more satisfactory to them than to their bourgeois counterparts in that they are socially endorsed, even that of '*Huria*' or free woman ('*Huryin*' are generally

215

divorced women who engage in affairs and temporary casual prostitution but may get married later).

What kind of commitment to marriage, in terms of transfer of commitment from the families of origin of the spouses, is made by men and women from different economic environments? Compare first of all the obligation to perform labour and the right to reciprocal services. The wife who marries a salaried townsman goes into seclusion. She has no agricultural work to do and does not generally contribute to the financial needs of the household. (A poorer woman might sell the cloth and carpets she weaves at home.) The townswoman is a high consumer of finery and furniture. The corollary of her freedom from responsibility is economic dependence, subjection to the authority of her husband and isolation from kin and community.

This kind of marriage, giving rights of 'bride-removal', in traditional anthropological parlance, is generally brought about by a payment of bridewealth from husband to wife. It usually consists of first *lhenna* (Arabic) or *tamendilt* (Berber) which comprises clothes for the bride and provisions for the wedding feast; second, the *sdaq*, a cash payment of 200–5000 *drahem* with which the wife buys furnishings, a further amount to be paid on divorce. It constitutes an indirect dowry or dower, in that it acquits the woman's kin of some of their economic obligations towards her, at least for the time being. But it establishes the husband's cultural and political status on a level with that of town Arabs. Levy quotes Shaybani, Jami-el-Saghir, who discusses the relationship of 'true' Arabs to converted tribesmen in the countries settled by Arabs: 'Among non-Arab Muslims, a man was by birth the equal of an Arab if both his father and his grandfather had been Muslims before him; but only then if he were sufficiently wealthy to provide an adequate *mahr*, or marriage endowment.'[1] The payment of dower is also a statement referring to the wife's status: 'The *mahr* is paid to the bride only if she is a free woman.'[2]

Dowry and inheritance

The cash *sdaq* rises in amount according to the value of the property which the bourgeois bride brings to the marriage. Among the urban bourgeois of Fez, for example, this corresponds to a veritable dowry.

Under these circumstances, the marriage becomes a business alli-

[1] R. Levy (1957), 63.
[2] Ibid., 127.

ance – the arranged marriage *par excellence*, of the type especially favoured by the big merchant and financier families of Fez, Meknes and Sale, who express a strong preference, according to Lahlou, for parallel cousin marriages.

Moroccans are explicit about the fact that the dowry of jewellery, furniture, houses and financial assets taken into marriages corresponds to the inheritance of the outmarrying daughter – half the share of a son. On divorce this property remains hers. If she is repudiated the *sdaq* also comes to her but she forfeits it if she leaves. On the surface it might seem that with such economic autonomy a woman would tend to divorce easily. But most townswomen are psychologically ill-equipped to live alone, and a dowried woman's family has made a serious gesture of disengagement from her in handing over her inheritance and putting it under the management of her husband. They would not welcome her back. The low divorce rate among such people can be attributed to: (1) the care with which such marriages are contracted – compatibility seems to be a major consideration; (2) the interest of the property-owning network to which both spouses belong, since the husband has become a business partner, in sustaining this alliance; (3) the wife's economic status within the marriage.

Inheritance in land: no bridewealth, or 'a little bit of bread and no cheese'

The crucial difference between the townswoman's and *ksar*-woman's relation to marriage is that the latter inherit property in land. Since land is not convertible, a woman, by all accounts, cannot and does not realise her inheritance in movable property. I myself have only come across one case where a woman claimed her fields, selling them to her brother who had managed them up to that point. She did this only under the most extreme pressure, when her husband's fields had been ruined by a flood and the couple and their four children were forced to migrate to Akhdar in search of a living. An Akhdar lawyer told me that in his experience over 75% of women leave their fields to be worked by their kin who send them a token share of the harvest. After a woman's death it is shameful for her children to claim her fields, although their rights to maintenance are recognised.

A woman thus maintains a strong interest in her home community. This is reinforced when she marries into another peasant family, for the use of labour – intensive techniques in domestic and agricultural activities – means that she and her female kin will tend to call continuously on each other's services.

The continuous contact between the wife and her female kin, mutual visiting and interdependence, tend to corrode the marriage relationship. Its fragility is reflected in the limited liability of the husband for his wife's needs, above the bare minimum. Thus a woman in need of medical treatment, extra funds for clothing or jewellery, relies on her kin, not her husband, to supply them.

Moreover, the bridewealth which is transferred by the husband is negligible or non-existent. The norm among *ksar* and rural people is for the husband to undertake to pay a *sdaq* around 500 *drahem*, half to be spent on clothes during the marriage, half to be paid on divorce. The latter sum never materialises because the majority of those who make this kind of marriage just haven't the cash, nor do they pay the maintenance to which a woman is entitled on divorce. I was told in the *ksar* where I lived, many of whose inhabitants were descended from Ait Haddidou, that among the people of this tribe, the handing over of the *sdaq* at marriage is itself a test of the durability of the union. The groom gives 30 *drahem* to his bride when they make the marriage contract in the *biru*. As soon as the couple get outside, he says to her 'Hand over!' If she refuses, he knows that she will not make a submissive wife and divorces her on the spot.

The frequency of divorce and the importance for a woman and her kin of their mutual bond means that not only will the divorcées be welcomed home but that the status of divorced daughter or sister is a common and not undignified one.

Hypergamy

The woman who marries a *ksar*-dweller has considerable bargaining powers because of her economic role. There is a powerful tendency for *ksar*-people to marry within the same or immediately neighbouring villages. Affines pool their agricultural working resources (labour and equipment). Husband and wife do not pool their capital as in dowry marriages. Sometimes in the *ksar*, the marriage may be arranged to consolidate a working association between the kin of the spouses, but since one working association can easily be exchanged for another, divorce does not bring economic catastrophe.

To marry within the neighbourhood does not bring immunity to divorce. In a *ksar* sample 50% of marriages were contracted between people living within 2 kilometres of each other, but it should also be noted that 58% of divorces were between people whose home villages were within 2 kilometres of each other.

Divorce and property

The propertyless woman who marries a man who pays bridewealth, however (and he is usually a townsman), moves up the social ladder. In contrast to the woman who marries a peasant, her role as wife has greater attractions than her role as daughter–sister. Moreover, her family will tend to encourage her to stay married and the kinship contact which threatens *ksar* unions is prevented by the girl's seclusion. Evans-Pritchard's generalisation is relevant here (although the case of extra-*ksar* marriage has nothing to do with rules of exogamy): 'When marriage relations are established outside the kindred the number of possible mates is increased and new social relations are established which are of a type independent of kinship structure and which tend, indeed, to break down its exclusive control. New social relations, especially political relations, become possible. Bridewealth and rules of exogamy are therefore functions of one another and form an interdependent system.'[1]

The secluded wife whose contact with her kin is restricted becomes dependent on her husband. She is considered a greedy parasite, continuously asking for gold. During the early years of marriage her husband is suspicious of her, especially if he is of a peasant family but has made good in the town. He regards her demands as illegitimate, an encroachment on his patrimony. He suspects her of attempting to amass enough gold to enable her to leave him. Because of this possibility, gifts of gold from husband to wife are considered in society at large (especially that of other women) to be a mark of the husband's esteem, and the healthy state of the marriage. It is an index of *tifqa*, mutual trust or good faith between husband and wife. It is one of the rewards of marriage for a woman who marries a man with a salary or capital. Her family does not provide her with such security and marks of status. A woman who marries a peasant and keeps up the links with her kin can expect no luxuries from her husband.

It seems then that the circumstance of property rights consisting of marketable capital rather than land has a great deal to do with the following:

1. The greater significance attaching to the husband's economic roles and status than to those of the wife.

2. That the dowried wife is generally secluded, does no agricultural work, and does not need to co-operate closely with kin. Husband and wife are more closely related to each other, economically and socially, than to kin. This leads to a high degree of 'conjugal

[1] Evans-Pritchard (1964), 186.

isolation' and the claims of kin do not pose a threat to the marriage; in their role as affines, they may reinforce it.

3. The tendency to regard marriage as an alliance with long-term economic or integrative significance and not as an arrangement of temporary convenience.

4. That divorce is therefore seen as a disaster, especially from the economic point of view, not as a fact of life.

Marriage stability and capital accumulation

The factors enumerated above all tend to promote the relative stability of marriage (which is yet highly unstable, by any standards) at least over a longer period than in the *ksour*. These conditions enable the payers of bridewealth and dowry to treat affinal ties as long-term relationships with an important economic dimension.

This is not possible for small-holders, whose only stable economic relationships are with the co-heirs to a property constant in form and value – whose value, indeed, is reckoned in social not economic terms. Since each person has a unique configuration of affinal connections, these tend to exercise individualising influences. When these relationships have an economic dimension, individualism too takes on an economic aspect. There is room for entrepreneurship and speculation. Economic behaviour is determined more by market forces than by social obligations.

Among those groups holding considerable marketable capital (e.g. the urban bourgeois of the northern cities), marriage with dowry and dower provides opportunities for more fruitful use of those resources, through economic co-operation with affines. Divorce is rarer than in other groups for it implies the reduction or withdrawal of capital resources, disrupting the productive process. The rarity of divorce in turn inclines people to regard marriage ties as the cement of economic alliances.

Affinal relations are more significant than kinship relations but do not necessarily disrupt them (N.B. the preference for patrilateral parallel cousin marriage in Fez, Sale, Tetouan).

Among the groups more modestly supplied with convertible capital rather than, or as well as, land (salaried parvenus and traders) marriage, generally hypogamous for men, means that a husband risks claims on his resources by poorer affines. He can reduce these claims to a minimum by reducing the wife's contact with her kin. If he pays dower, with the right of bride-removal, he secures a monopoly over the woman's services. Divorce is inconvenient in the early years of marriage, while he is establishing himself economically and before his family is large and hungry enough to be a serious burden. He will need to make one financial settlement on divorce, another on marrying again. If his children are still young there will be trouble between them and their stepmother – a notorious problem in Morocco. Divorce at this stage is inconvenient for a woman too, as it will mean separating from her children. Moreover, she will have nowhere to go, since her contacts with kin have grown tenuous over the years. Her status will fall with her standard of living, unless she has adult children who can support her. Divorce in this group generally occurs less often than in the *ksour* and at a later stage in the developmental cycle.

The largest category of people in the Middle Atlas are rural peasants and *ksar*-dwellers. For them divorce entails neither the withdrawal of capital and a severe loss in services for men, nor a loss of security and status for women. These values are continuously supplied by kin, and do not cease on marriage. Changes in social relationships are a function of kinship not of entrepreneurship or conjugality. Marriage establishes new relations of reproduction rather than of production. Even these are conditional on the success of the marriage, not a guarantee that it will continue. Many are the daughters of divorced couples who grow up with their maternal grandparents, even adopting their grandfather's name. Given the frequency of divorce, no rights are definitively transferred on marriage, which cannot serve therefore to cement economic alliance.

The replication of traditional relations of production in the countryside tends to lead to a deterioration of their situation vis-à-vis the more wealthy groups who are engaged in a more purposeful manipulation of market forces. Not least among their assets is the possibility of using marriage to effect and reinforce economic alliances.

Conclusions

In the course of this study I have attempted to illuminate two interrelated sets of problems. The first has to do with the historical process which has distributed political and economic power unevenly throughout the population of Akhdar, and with the social structures, chiefly the multi-dimensional system of social stratification, which provides the framework for this process to continue, resulting in the chronic impoverishment of the mass of the population and the enrichment of a few. The second set of problems concerns the way in which this process affects the roles and social circumstances of women in different milieux, and is in turn affected by them.

Two major categories of people are excluded from the exercise of formal political and economic power. These are women, who have never controlled offices or property, and the rural and urban proletariat, who cannot produce enough for their needs, as farmers or artisans, nor sell their labour for wages. The exclusion of women has important repercussions. Even if those men who can get a living within the market economy can resist the demands of their less fortunate male kin by acting according to the tenets of the market and of class, it is more difficult for them to act in the same way towards women, who control the means of reproduction. As sisters, women get men wives. As wives, women get men children. Economically, women are ultimately dependent on men, but socially the situation is reversed. It is this relationship which is reflected in the inheritance rights held by women.

My first set of problems includes also the informal economic roles performed by women. Having no economic prospects within the market economy and no security through their conjugal relation to men, for marriage is very unstable, women come to depend on their female associates. Thus uterine kinship ties and patron–client relations become extra-market channels of economic and social help, linking women who live in different economic circumstances. Those men who are frustrated in their attempts to get a living by selling their labour tend also to depend on these links.

Conclusions

But those men who are relatively well situated economically regard these ties among women as a threat both to their hard-won incomes and to the principle of male authority and agnation. They attempt to stem the two-way flow of resources along these channels. The élite on the other hand utilise social links with and through women to reinforce their political and economic supremacy. One of the results of this first set of investigations is to establish a relationship between the differing significance of relationships with and among women and the existence of classes with different economic and political power.

The second set of problems concerns the situation of women married into different social milieux. As long as women are forbidden to work on their own account, or to enter the 'public sphere' they must participate in relationships as dependants. The nature of marriage and of the marriage payments is important in determining whether and to what degree emotional and economic reliance on kin will be transferred to affines. In the proletariat this process gets under way, if at all, at a late stage in the marriage, for divorce is frequent. The non-conjugal roles performed by women in this milieu are so vital to the survival of the population that there are substantial rewards to both men and women if they continue to carry them out. Referring back to the first set of problems we may note that it is this factor which inhibits the penetration of the 'market mentality', for economic relationships are disguised by kinship terms and modified by the loyalty and sense of honour proper to kinship.

In the salaried and small merchant class, on the other hand, there are advantages to the husband in tearing the wife away from her kinship and patronage networks in order to restrict the outgoings of the household. Although the wife is generally kept in style and idleness, her position is perhaps worse than any since she is deprived of economic and social roles outside those devoted strictly to her husband's domestic well-being. The rate of polygamy in Anne-Marie Baron's Casablanca sample was 21% in this class compared with less than 2% in the other two classes with which we are dealing here.[1] A study on the rate of mental disturbance in this milieu compared with the others would also be valuable.

Elite women are only better off in as far as they retain non-domestic roles, including those of kinship. Some gain a certain economic autonomy by working, but unless they occupy prestigious positions, they cannot prevent their husbands from appropriating their earnings. The political control of the husband is a bone of contention, even if

[1] A. Adam (1967), 735.

the common orientation of the spouses towards the public sphere works in favour of the marriage.

Yet the segregation of roles according to sex obtains throughout the society, and this, combined with the woman's experience of subordination to her husband, makes links with other women all the more desirable. Further, the experience of dependence results in a continual search for security. Women are conservative not only of their kinship status which they tend to retain in a latent form, but in an economic sense. They convert what they gain as wives into gold against the day of their divorce or widowhood. They borrow readily, taking risks with the property of others rather than their own, for dependence breeds irresponsibility.

In the Akhdar region, élite women too meet with those assumptions of dependence and subordination which surround the existence of the entire female population – and the female population of societies other than that of Morocco. The study raises many questions of more general interest. It is remarkable, for example, that the pattern of female education and employment in Morocco replicates precisely that of Western European societies. Most working women are nurses, teachers, secretaries or unskilled manual operatives. How far has this pattern been imposed by the industrial countries under whose aegis Moroccan industry has developed, and how far does it imply shared social assumptions in Morocco and Western Europe concerning women's roles? If the latter is true, it might be worth while considering the relevance to Western societies of some of the propositions developed in this study, bearing always in mind that Akhdari society is characterised by high unemployment, segregation of sex roles, marital instability, strong social links among women, and multiple systems of social stratification, and that this combination, while unlikely to be unique, will be found more probably in underdeveloped countries of similar economic structure to Morocco's than in Western Europe.

Nevertheless it may be true that women's participation in the public sphere is everywhere partial. Does the limitation of women's occupations in Western societies reflect the permeation of women's economic relationships by considerations peculiar to their domestic and ascriptive roles? Further, to what extent is the restriction of women's activity within the public sphere (in Italy for example) a function of the superior social and economic rewards for everyone of women's 'extra-market' activity when there is high unemployment? Does the notorious 'conservatism' of women derive from economic dependence and does it extend to the conservation of kinship status?

Conclusions

Finally, where the dominant principle of social organisation is class, where do women stand? Is there a tendency here, too, for women to derive their social identity from ascribed status and to form networks, which although probably situated within classes, may be internally governed by the status-principle and do not therefore preclude cross-class linkage? How far do élite or career-oriented women share the general perspectives of their sex, and how do the perspectives of working women differ from those of their male counterparts? Finally, to what extent do different systems of social stratification co-exist in Western societies, and what determines whether a man or a woman tends or not to regard the market economy as the arena of individual or collective struggle? If my study of a Moroccan society has thrown some light on these problems, and if it has exposed new areas of ignorance about our own and other societies, I am content to conclude with a question-mark.

Glossary

a'ajr: (Ar.) grace, religious merit.

'abid (pl. *-in*): (Ar.) slave.

aghjdim: (Ber.) sitting, squatting.

ahrir: (Ber.) wheat gruel, often served on feast-days and at *rites de passage.*

Ait: (Ber.) people of − , brothers of – ; indicates membership of a group, a household, a territory or a political segment.

amghar (pl. *imgharn*): (Ber.) old man; elder; the elected holder of a *ksar*-office usually for one year only.

ar: (Ber.) a conditional curse which a man places on another (of another clan) whose help he needs. He sacrifices a sheep on the latter's threshold, thereby creating a kinship relation, whose terms of mutual obligation cannot be broken without incurring divine punishment.

asmun (pl. *ismun*): (Ber.) one who accompanies, friend.

atumlilt: (Ber.) the white one, generally a euphemism for the black griddle – black being inauspicious.

baraka: (Ar. & Ber.) blessing, increase, charisma.

bedawi (pl. *-yin*): (Ar. & Ber.) tent dweller, an Arabic-speaking nomadic pastoralist from the Eastern plains.

belgha (pl. *blaghi*): (Ar.) pointed leather slipper.

biru: (Ar. & Ber.) 'bureau', meaning the administrative office-complex in the town.

Bi- smi-allah: (Ar.) in the name of God, pronounced at the beginning of any activity of uncertain outcome.

bled (pl. *beldan*): (Ar.) country; the country as opposed to the town; home region.

brra: (Ar. & Ber.) outside.   *brrani* (pl. *-yin*): outsider.

cadi: (Ar.) legal official.

caid: (Ar.) official in charge of the administration of part of a *cercle* or district.

couscous: (Ar.) a festive dish prepared by steaming for three or four hours a kind of semolina, over which a meat or vegetable stew is poured.

dahir: (Ar.) a royal edict.

darija: (Ar.) colloquial Moroccan Arabic.

dif-l-llah: (Ar.) guest of God, label given to a stranger who presents himself at the house of someone, asking for a favour.

djellaba: (Ar.) long hooded garment, worn by men over their clothes. The winter version is of wool, the summer one of cotton, the women's of fine cotton embroidered at the seams.

drahem: (Ar.) the currency of Morocco, until recently tied to the French franc, but worth slightly more since the franc was devalued. Subdivided into 100 francs, and roughly equivalent to 10p.

eud: (Ar.) an Arabic lute.

Fassi: (Ar.) native of Fez.

fdela: (Ar.) pious action performed to gain grace, also name given to the day spent fasting or in vigil before a religious feast-day.

fellah (pl. *-in*): (Ar.) cultivator, land-owning peasant.

Glossary

fqih (pl. *fuqaha*): (Ar.) Muslim teacher and prayer-leader.

ghitar (pl. *ghiyat*): an Arabic oboe, played at *rites de passage*.

gish: (Ar.) certain tribes of the areas surrounding the royal capitals, who submitted to the temporal and spiritual rule of the Sultan, Moulay Ismail, and in return for supplying military and administrative cadres were relieved of taxes and rewarded with land.

hajab (pl. *hjuba*): (Ar.) amulets containing verses of the Koran, worn to ward off and exorcise evil spirits.

hammam: (Ar.) Turkish baths, with hot and warm rooms, visited weekly or fortnightly by town-dwellers and whenever possible by *ksar*-dwellers.

hartani, hartaniya (pl. *haratn, hartaniyin*): (Ar.) black descendants of slaves, lit. ploughmen. They still occupy inferior status.

hashuma: (Ar. & Ber.) shame, modesty.

hedra: (Ar. & Ber.) ecstatic dancing with special music and rhythms, practised in religious brotherhoods and among *ksar*-women.

henna: (Ar.) red dye applied for protection at *rites de passage*, and to restore to a peaceful and healthy state. It is used by women for decoration on hands, feet and hair.

henna sgher: (Ar.) betrothal ceremony, when bride is *henna*-ed.

hizb: (Ar.) superfluous religious practices.

Huria (pl. *Huriyin*): (Ar.) 'free woman'. Often divorced or unmarried, she conforms not at all to the norms of female behaviour.

Huriyin: often form groups of dancers hired to entertain, e.g. wedding guests.

Imam: (Ar.) prayer-leader, in charge of chief mosque.

imgharn: pl. of *amghar*.

imsnayn: (Ber. dual of *asmun*) two friends of groom who help him ask for bride, escort her to his house and act as best-man.

imtqalain: (Ber.) two tikkal – a form of money, each coin worth about 10p – used in bridal payments in 1930–40.

inurar: (Ber.) threshing-grounds.

ishiwal: (Ber.) seasonal workers from Tafilalet, who harvest the wheat in exchange for money.

izar (pl. *izarat*): (Ar.) cotton sheet, used by women as a 'cover-all' and veil.

jema'a (pl. *-iya*): (Ar.) traditional Berber assembly, composed of house-holders of the village. It was generally called ad hoc to discuss specific issues, and elected office-holders every year.

jnun (pl. of *djinn*): (Ar.) capricious spirits living under the earth, and haunting the upper world.

juj: (Ar.) the area which can be ploughed by two animals in a day.

kaftan: (Ar.) Arab woman's dress, often elaborate.

kerr: (Ber.) get up.

khadam (pl. *khadam*): (Ar.) worker, servant.

khalifa: (Ar.) the administrative official who is second-in-command to the *caid*. He has special responsibility for a series of *communes*, and is often of local origin.

khammes: (Ar.) share-cropper, receiving one-fifth up to a half of the harvest.

khl'a: (Ar.) the wilderness.

kissaria: (Ar.) area of the town where cloth is sold and made up.

ksar (pl. *ksour*): (Ar.) hamlet, community.

kskas: (Ar.) pot for making *couscous*.

lwiza (pl. *-at*): (Ar. & Ber.) 'louis d'or', gold coin used by women as a jewel, and to ward off the evil eye.

Glossary

madrassa (pl. *-at*): (Ar.) Koranic school, sometimes primary school.

Makhzen: (Ar.) the government, administration, authority.

malak (pl. *mala'ika*): (Ar.) angel.

medina (pl. *-at*): (Ar.) town.

merhaba bi kum: (Ar.) welcome to you.

mesakin: (Ar.) the poor.

meskin (s.): poor man, good-hearted man.

mokhazni (pl. *-ya*): (Ar.) policeman, guard attached to the administrative complex.

moud: (Ar. & Ber.) unit of weight.

mrabt (pl. *-en*): (Ar.) saint, holy man (Fr. *marabout*).

mtafqin: (Ar.) agreed, in mutual trust.

muezzin: (Fr.) call to prayer.

mul (pl. *-at*): (Ar.) owner of –, he of the –.

mul-l-bled: (Ar.) native, owner of the land.

mul-l-daf: (Ar.) office holder, salary-earner.

mussem: (Ar.) religious gathering and celebration.

nif: face (as in losing face), honour (lit. nose).

nikwa: (Ar.) family, tribal segment.

nud: (Ar.) get up.

qim: (Ber.) stay, rest, sit.

Ramadan: (Ar.) period of thirty days' fast (during the month of Ramadan).

sadaqa (pl. *sdaq*): (Ar.) alms, gift.

saleh (pl. *-in*): (Ar.) holy site.

sebueh: (Ar. & Ber.) the celebration of the seventh day after an event, e.g. a child's birth.

shari'a: (Ar.) Koranic law.

sheikh: (Ar.) the elder whom the government has invested with authority over a *commune* (two or three hamlets).

sherif, sherifa (pl. *shurfa*): (Ar.) descendants of the Prophet.

s'Hur: (Ar. & Ber.) witchcraft.

siba: (Ar. & Ber.) ungoverned.

sirwal: (Ar.) trousers, women's pantaloons.

suq (pl. *swaq*): (Ar.) market.

surat (pl. *swar*): (Ar.) verses of the Koran.

tajma'at: (Ber.) *jema'a* (Ar.); traditional village assembly.

tamdint: (Ber.) town.

tamghra (pl. *timghriwin*): (Ber.) first marriage, marriage ceremony often of several days' duration.

taqbilt: (Ber.) tribe.

tariqa: (Ar.) way, religious sect.

tfina (pl. *-at*): (Ber. & Ar.) over-dress worn by Berber women.

tolba (pl. of *taleb*): (Ar.) religious scholar, student.

tshamir (pl. *-at*): (Ber. & Ar.) dress worn by Berber women.

ulema: (Ar.) religious scholars in Fez, Tetouan and Salé who often acted as counsellors to the Sultans, and installed a new one.

umma: (Ar.) Community of Islam.

youyou: (Fr.) ululation; trilling noise made by women to draw attention to an event, e.g. to express joy at a *rite de passage* or alarm at a disaster. Berber – *da-turutnt:* they (f.) ululate.

zawia (pl. *-at*): (Ar.) community of religious scholars originally attached to a village which supported them. Sometimes the *zawia* cultivates land of its own.

Select bibliography

BOOKS

Adam, A., *Casablanca*, Vols. I & II, Paris, 1968.
Une enquête auprès de la jeunesse musulmane du Maroc, Aix-en-Provence, 1967.
Amin, S., *The Maghreb in the modern world*, London, 1970.
Amine, A. *et al.*, *Histoire du Maroc*, Paris, 1967.
Ashford, D. E., *1964, Perspectives of a Moroccan Nationalist Totowa*, Bedminster Press, 1964.
Barth, F. (ed.), *Ethnic Groups and Boundaries*, London, 1969.
Basset, A., *La Langue Berbère*, O.U.P., 1952.
Ben Bachir, S., *L'administration locale du Maroc*, Casablanca, 1969.
Bensimon Donath, D., *Evolution du Judaïsme marocain sous le Protectorat français (1912–56)*, Paris, 1968.
Berque, J., *Structures sociales du Haut Atlas*, Paris, 1955.
French North Africa, the Maghreb between two World Wars, London, 1967.
Bonjean, F., *Confidences d'une fille de la nuit*, Paris, 1939.
Bonsal, S., Jr., *Morocco as it is*, London, 1893.
Boserup, E., *Woman's role in economic development*, London, 1968.
Bourgeois, P., *L'univers de l'écolier marocain*, Min. of Education, Rabat, 1959.
Bovill, E. W., *The Golden Trade of the Moors*, O.U.P., 1970.
Brémond General, *Berbères et Arabes*, Paris, 1950.
Chombart de Lauwe, P. H., *Images de la femme dans la société*, Paris, 1964. Especially Forget, N., 'Femmes et Professions au Maroc', 137–83; and Nouacer, K., 'Evolution et travail professionnel de la femme au Maroc', 184–92.
Chouraqui, A., *La condition juridique de l'Isréalite marocain*, Paris, 1960.
Cohen, M. and Hahn, L., *Morocco: Old Land, New Nation*, London, 1966.
Coon, C. S., *Tribes of the Rif*, Harvard African Series, Vol. IX, Cambridge Mass., 1931.
Couleau, P., *La paysannerie marocaine*, C.N.R.S., Paris, 1968.
Denat, Capt., *Étude du droit coutumier berbère des Aït Hadiddou*, Paris, 1936.
Drague, G., *Esquisse d'histoire religieuse du Maroc*, Paris, 1951.
d'Etienne, J., *L'Evolution sociale du Maroc*, Paris, 1948.
Fanon, F., *L'An V de la revolution algérienne*, Paris, 1959.
Fortes, M. (ed.), *Marriage in Tribal Societies*, C.U.P., 1962.
Gaudry, M., *La femme chaouia de l'Aurès: étude de sociologie berbère*, Paris, 1929.
La société feminine au Djebel Amour et au Ksel, Alger, 1961.
Geertz, C., *Islam observed: religious development in Indonesia and Morocco*, New Haven, 1968.
Gellner, E., 'Sanctity, Puritanism, Secularisation and Nationalism in North Africa', in Peristiany, J., *Contributions to Mediterranean Sociology: Mediterranean Rural Communities and Social Change*, Acts of the Mediterranean Sociological Conference, Athens, July 1963; Paris, 1968.
Saints of the Atlas, London, 1969.

Bibliography

Goichon, M., *La vie feminine au Mzab*, Paris, 1927.

Goode, W., *World Revolution and Family Patterns*, Free Press of Glencoe, U.S.A., 1963.

Goody, E. N., 'Conjugal Separation and Divorce among the Gonja of Northern Ghana', in Fortes, M. (ed.), *Marriage in Tribal Societies*, C.U.P., 1962.

'Kinship fostering in Gonja', in A.S.A. VIII, *Socialisation, the Approach from Social Anthropology*, ed. M. Banton, London, 1970.

Goody, J. (ed.), *The Developmental Cycle in Domestic Groups*, C.U.P., 1966.

Gordon, D. C., *Women of Algeria, an essay on change*, Harvard, 1968.

Hoffherr, Rene & Morris, R., *Revenus et niveaux de vie indigènes au Maroc*, Sevey, 1934.

Hoffman, *The structure of traditional Moroccan rural society*, Paris, 1967.

Ibn Khaldun, trans. Rosenthal, F., *The Muqaddima*, London, 1958.

trans. Le baron de Slane, *Histoire des Berbères*, Paris, 1969.

Jacques-Meunié, D., *Le Prix du Sang chez les Berbères de l'Atlas*, Paris, 1964.

Lacoste, Yves (ed.), *Le Fèodalisme*, C.E.R.M., Paris, 1970.

Lahbabi, M., *Les années 80 de notre jeunesse*, Casablanca, 1970.

Laoust, E., *Cours de Berbère marocain*, Paris, 1939.

Le Tourneau, R., *Position Sociale et Culturelle de l'Elite Dirigeante d'Afrique du Nord*, Princeton University Conference, 5 mai 1967.

Levy, R., *The social structure of Islam*, C.U.P., 1957.

Lewis, B., *The Arabs in History*, London, 1966.

Marx, K., *Pre-capitalist economic formations*, London, 1964.

Mauchamp, E., *La Sorcellerie au Maroc*, Paris 194?.

Meakin, B., *The land of the Moors*, London, 1899.

The Moorish Empire, London, 1899.

The Moors, London, 1902.

Mercier, H., *Vocabulaire et textes dans le dialecte des Ait Izdeg*, Rabat, 1937.

Montagne, R., *Les Berbères et le Makhzen dans le Sud du Maroc*, Paris, 1930.

La naissance du prolétariat marocain, Paris, 1951.

Montety, H. de, *Les femmes de Tunisie*, Paris, 1958.

Mrabet, F., *La femme algérienne, les Algériennes*, Paris, 1969.

Noin, D., *La population rurale du Maroc*, Vols. I and II, Paris, 1970.

Ossowski, S., *Class Structure in the Social Consciousness*, London, 1963.

Peristiany, J. (ed.), *Honour and Shame*, London, 1967.

Pesle, O., *La femme musulmane, dans le droit, la religion et les moeurs*, Rabat, 1946.

Peters, E. L., 'Aspects of rank and status among Muslims in a Lebanese village' in *Mediterranean Countrymen*, ed. Pitt–Rivers, J., Paris, 1963.

Stephens, W. N., *The Oedipus Complex, a cross cultural study*, London, 1962.

Stewart, C. F., *The Economy of Morocco, 1912–1962*, Cambridge Mass., 1961.

Sullerot, E., *Women, Society and Change*, London, 1971.

Terrasse, H., *History of Morocco*, London, 1950.

Tillion, G., *Le harem et les cousins*, Paris, 1966.

Villeneuve, M., *La situation de l'agriculture et son avenir dans l'économie marocaine*, Paris, 1971.

Weber, M., *The Sociology of Religion*, London, 1966.

Westermarck, E., *Marriage ceremonies in Morocco*, London, 1914.

Ritual and Belief in Morocco, Vols. I and II, London, 1926.

Zartman, I. W., *Morocco: Problems of New Power*, Atherton Press, New York, 1964.

Bibliography

PERIODICALS

Amin, A., 'L'évolution de la femme et le problème du mariage au Maroc', *Présence Africaine* 68 (4e trim. 1968), 32–51.

Barth, F., 'Father's brother's daughter marriage in Kurdistan', *South Western Journal of Anthropology* 10 (Summer 1954).

Berque, J., 'Qu'est-ce qu'une tribu nord-africaine', *L'Eventail de l'Histoire* (1953).

'Droit des terres et integration sociale au Maghreb', *Cahiers Internationaux de Sociologie*, Vol. xxv (1958).

Coatalen, P., 'Réflexions sur la société chleuh', *Annales Marocaines de Sociologie*, Rabat (1969).

Coliac, J., 'Usury in Sefrou', *Bulletin Economique et Social du Maroc* (July, 1936).

Crawford, R. W., 'Cultural Change and Communication in Morocco', *Human Organisation* I (Spring 1965).

'Enquête d'Opinion sur la Planification Familiale au Maroc, 1966', *Bulletin Economique et Social du Maroc* xxix, 104–5 (jan–juin 1967), 95–149.

Gellner, E., 'Patterns of Rural Rebellion in Morocco: Tribes as Minorities', *The European Journal of Sociology*, Vol. iii, no. 2 (1962).

'A Pendulum Swing Theory of Islam', *Moroccan Annals of Sociology* (1968), 5–14.

Goody, J., 'Feudalism in Africa?' *Journal of African History*, Vol. iv, no. 1 (1963).

and Goody, E. N., 'The Circulation of Women and Children in Northern Ghana', *Man* (n.s.) 2(2), 226–48.

'Marriage Prestations, Inheritance and Descent in Pre-industrial Societies', *Journal of Comparative Family Studies* (1970).

Gravier, L., 'La limitation des naissances se heurte aux traditions religieuses et populaires', *Le Monde*, 14 août 1966, 4.

'Un séminaire nationale a fait ressortir les progrès de la notion de planning familial au Maroc', *Le Monde*, 15 août 1966, 5.

Guepin, J., 'La vie traditionelle au Maroc et ses problèmes humains', *Confluent* nos. 45–6 (1964), 909–20.

Hart, D. M., 'Segmentary Systems and the role of the "five-fifths" in Tribal Morocco', *Revue de l'Occident Musulman et de la Mediterranée* no. 3, Ier trimestre, 65–95.

'Clan, lignage et communauté locale dans une tribu rifaine', *Revue de Géographie du Maroc* 8 (1965), 50–62.

Hassan-Zeghari, L., 'La femme marocaine et sa préparation à la vie familiale et professionnelle', *Confluent* nos. 23–4 (1962).

Jamous, R., 'Réflexions sur la segmentarité et le mariage arabe', *Annales Marocaines de Sociologie*, Rabat (1969).

Lahlou, A., 'La bourgeoisie, symbole et reflet direct de l'occidentalisation de la société marocaine', *Civilisations* xiv, 1–2 (1964), 62–80.

'Etude sur la famille traditionelle de Fes', *Revue de l'Institut de Sociologie* 3 (1968).

Leveugle, 'Sept années d'education populaire au Maroc, 1955–62', *Confluent* (mars, avr., mai 1963), 367–90.

Madani, H. 'Le contrôle des naissances et Islam', *Confluent* (avr., mai, juin 1965), 323–7.

Marais, O., 'La classe dirigeante au Maroc', *Revue Française de Science Politique* xiv, 4, (août 1964), 709–37.

Martensson, M., 'Attitudes vis-à-vis du travail professionel de la femme marocaine', *Bulletin Economique et Social du Maroc* xxviii (jan–mars 1966), 100.

231

Bibliography

Menneson, E., 'Ksour du Tafilalt', Revue de Géographie du Maroc, 8 (1965), 85–92.

Radi, A., 'Processus de socialisation de l'enfant marocain', Annales Marocaines de Sociologie (1969).

Souriau, C., 'La Société Féminine en Libye', Revue de l'Occident Musulman et de la Mediteranée no. 6, 1er and 2e semestres (1969).

Waterbury, J., 'Marginal Politics and Elite Manipulation in Morocco', European Journal of Sociology v, 8, no. 1, 94–111.

Zartman, I. W., 'Farming and Land Ownership in Morocco', Land Economics, Vol. 39, no. 2 (1963), 187–98.

Zeghari, M., 'Evolution des structures familiales dans les pays en voie de transformation sociale, économique, politique et institutionelle', Famille dans le Monde, Vol. xv, nos. 3–4 (1962), 132–49.

Zghal, A., 'Les reflets de la modernisation de l'agriculture sur la stratification sociale dans les campagnes tunisiennes', Cahiers Internationaux de Sociologie xxxviii (janv.–juin 1965), 201–6.

'Révolution Africaine', published Algiers
'L'Algérien au travail', 17 oct. 1964.
'Le divorce (i) L'esprit et la lettre', 26 déc. 1964, '(ii) Les faits', 2 jan. 1965.
'Pour une politique de l'enfance deshéritée', 20 mars 1967.
'La tribu des cols blancs', 25 sept. 1967.
'Les divorces: un fléau', 24 jan. 1968.
'La famille maghrébine et le droit', mai 1968.

'Revue algérienne des sciences juridiques, économiques et politiques' Vol. v, no. 4, déc. 1968
Issad M., 'La rôle du juge et la volonté des parties dans la rupture du lien conjugal', 1065–90.

Aoussi, Cheikh M., 'Les causes classiques de l'instabilité du mariage', 1091–100.

Foudil, A., 'De quelques causes modernes d'instabilité du mariage. De la procédure en matière de divorce et du rôle du juge', 1101–8.

Gaudin de Lagrange, E. de, 'Causes de divorce en Tunisie', 1109–16.

El Jazouli, N., 'Les causes de l'instabilité du mariage. Les modes de dissolution du mariage en droit marocain', 1117–26.

Haroun, M. A., 'Les causes modernes d'instabilité du mariage', 1127–38.

Faidi, A., 'L'adoption', 1139–42.

Gaudin de Lagrange, E. de, 'L'adoption ou une ancienne pratique tunisienne devenue loi', 1143–8.

Becheur, A., 'La notion de garde dans le droit tunisien de la famille', 1149–60.

Hadj Ali, M. M., 'L'entretien de l'enfant de parents divorcés', 1161–8.

Benhalima, S., 'Les problèmes de l'enfant naturel', 1169–72.

OFFICIAL PUBLICATIONS

Gouvernement Cherifien, Service Central da Statistiques
'Aspects de démographie marocaine', Rabat, 1950.
'Population rurale du Maroc', recensement demographique (juin 1960), Rabat, 1962.
'La situation économique du Maroc en 1966', Min. du Développement, chargé de la promotion nationale et du Plan, Rabat, 1967.
'Population du Maroc', Vols. i and ii, Recensement Officiel 1962, Rabat, 1963.

Bibliography

'Résultants de l'enquête à objectifs multiples', Rabat, 1964.
'Education in Morocco', Annual Report, Ministry of Education, Rabat, 1960.
U.N.E.S.C.O. 'Access of girls and women to education outside the school', Paris, 14 Jan. 1960.

UNPUBLISHED SOURCES

Bidwell, R., 'French Administration of the Tribal Areas of Morocco', unpublished Ph.D. thesis, Cambridge, 1969.
Joseph, R., Jr, 'Rituals and Relatives – a Study of the Social Uses of Wealth in Morocco', unpublished Ph.D. thesis, Univ. of California, 1967.
Peters, E. L., 'Sex-differentiation in two Arab communities', unpublished paper, 1970.
Strathearn, A. M., 'Women's status in the Mount Hagen area of New Guinea', Ph.D. thesis, Cambridge, 1968.
Tapper, N. S. S., 'The role of women in selected pastoral Islamic societies', unpublished M.A. thesis, London, 1968.

Centre de Hautes Etudes d'Administration Musulmane (now *sur l'Afrique et l'Asie modernes*)
Balby de Vernon, Lieut. de, 'Les jema'as et l'expérience faite en pays Ait Hadiddou', Memoire for A.I. course, C.H.E.A.M., 1950.
Boula de Mareuil, M., 'Notes sur la condition des femmes en Assoul', Memoire for A.I. course, C.H.E.A.M., Paris, 1948.
Clément, Capt. J., 'La population berbère et l'usure dans l'ancien commandement territorial de Sefrou', Memoir for A.I. course, C.H.E.A.M., Paris, 1938.
Coudino, 'Coutumes Berbères: Le Serment en Ait Mguild d'Azrou', Memoire for A.I. course, C.H.E.A.M., 1937.
Feaugas, 'L'enseignement dans le Moyen Atlas', Memoire for A.I. course, C.H.E.A.M., 1948.
'Les transhumants Marmoucha', Memoire for A.I. course, C.H.E.A.M., n.d.
Fievet, 'Deux ans chez les Ait Ouirra, Berbères du Moyen Atlas', C.H.E.A.M., 1952.
Guillaume, 'L'action politique et l'action militaire dans la pacification de l'Atlas Central', C.H.E.A.M. (publié dans le Bulletin de l'Enseignement Public au Maroc), 1944.
Le Tourneau, 'L'enseignement des filles musulmanes au Maroc', C.H.E.A.M., 1939.
Molinari, 'Les Juifs dans le Maroc indépendant', C.H.E.A.M., Paris, 1957.
'L'évolution de la femme marocaine', C.H.E.A.M., Paris, 1958.
Ougrour, J., 'Le fait Berbère', C.H.E.A.M., 1958.
Ruet, C., 'La transhumance dans le Moyen Atlas et le Haute Moulouya', Memoire for A.I. course, C.H.E.A.M., 1952.

233

Index

235

Index

land: colonial appropriation of, 17, 20, 31, 35; and definition of community, 28, 37; rare sales of, 32, 36, 40; migration from, 32; women's rights in, 42, 158–9, 192

land tenure: in Aghzim, 54–5, 195; by migrants, 37, 42, 58, 160; in Morocco, 33–7; title to land, 35–6

language: Arabic, 27, 74, 79–81; Berber, 27; French, 79, 80–1; men bilingual, 28; wife's idiom, 27

Levy, R., 216

lineage, 12, 29, 30; property focus of, 40, 42; threshing ground of, 59; undermining of, 72 (*see also* agnatic kinship, *and* Berber tribes, segmentary organisation of)

mahakma (law courts), 21, 36 (see also *Shari a*)

Maher, C., 33

Makhzen (Moroccan government), attitudes to, 74–5; bourgeoisie, 175–7; cultural aspects of, 16; institutions of, 4, 6, 53; and tribes, 6, 9, 10 (*see also* government)

Mareuil, G. de, 15

market economy, 1, 4, 6, 222, 225; and Arabs and Berbers, 28; and capital accumulation, 3, 5, 220–1; and cash, 1, 22; and consumer goods, 2, 18, 22, 31–2, 40; as distributive mechanism, 1, 4; labour market, 1, 37, 38, 42, 174; pre-Protectorate, 15, 18; relationships created by, 2, 23, 24, 41, 53, 222; religion, 89

market-place (*suq*), 15, 18, 64, 111; women and, 111–12

marriage, 149–80; age of, 150–2; as alliance, 3, 158–62, 174–8, 220–1; arranging of, 46–8, 61, 158, 164–5, 173–5; attitudes to, 88, 153–4, 173–5; ceremonies, 153, 165–9; choice of spouse, 157–62; conditions of, 149; conflict in, 2–3, 89, 102, 151, 154–7, 208–15; conjugal relationship, 117–18, 149, 151–2, 154–7, 180–3, 205–6, 213–15; contract, 164–5; courtship, 173; instability of, 2, 3, 180, 192, 218; intra-neighbourhood, 61, 157; of migrants, 44–6; patrilateral cousins, 153, 158, 162; payments, *see* bridewealth *and* dowry; preferential, 61, 157–62; resilience in town, 207–8, 213–15; as rite of passage, 153, 163; uxorilocal, 51, 129; Western ideas of, 173–4

Meknes, 76

men, family roles of, 107–14

menstruation, 101, 102

mental illness, 52, 117, 154, 180–3

migrants: age at migration, 22; marriages of, 44–6, 160; patron–client relations among, 42

migration, 22, 32, 160; implications for women, 22; without land-sales, 37, 42, 58, 160

mines, lead and zinc, 20, 31, 174

Mohammed, 144, 213–15

mokhazni (soldiers attached to administration): high status of, 64; as mediators, 21

Moulay Ali (saint), 24

mrabt (*marabout* or saint), 53, 94–8; women's, 98

Naima, 102, 180–3

nif, *see* honour

nikwa (named clan), 12, 159

Noin, D., 197

oath, see *Ait Ashra'a*

occupational structure, 23, 54, 64–6

Officier des Affaires Indigènes, 8, 19, 20

Ossowski, S., 37, 39

outsider, see *brrani*

patron–client relations, 1, 4–5, 40–53, 89, 189, 222; among women, 42–4

polygamy, 206, 223

poste (French outpost), 19

poverty, 32, 33, 35, 40, 158, 209, 222

prostitutes, 156, 171, 188–9, 206–7 (see also *huriyin*)

Rashida, 165–9

religion (Islam), 62, 89, 90; brotherhoods, 94–6, mosque, 59, 61, 62, 63; and social stratification, 89–103; and spirits, 92–3; and witchcraft, 103; and women, 62, 90–1, 96–100

rites of passage, 33, 42, 46–7, 51–2; celebration in *ksour*, 60; guests at, 166; kin at, 186–8; water in, 57

Rosenfeld, H., 68, 70

Ruet, C., 8, 9, 18

sadaqa (alms), 98–100

Sadiya, 206–7

Safiya, 155–6

saints, see *mrabt*

Saleh, 165–9

sebueh (naming feast), 52

seclusion, of women, 83–5, 101, 104, 117, 120, 180–3, 216–17, 219

sex: before marriage, 91, 150, 163, 171–2; segregation of roles by, 49, 104, 110–17, 224; and witchcraft, 102–3, 104–5, 168, 206–7

sexual: anxiety, 90–1, 93, 101, 169, 179; intercourse, 101, 165; interest, 101; jealousy 101, 206–7

237

Index

Shari'a (Koranic law), 21, 32, 210 (see also *mahakma*)

shurfa (sing. *sherif*), 10, 13, 14, 37; arbitration by, 10, 11, 14; marriage of, 25, 149; rites of passage, 166–8; seclusion of women, 25

siba, 9, 10, 92, 160 (see also tribes)

social mobility, 37–9, 70, 77–8, 90, 160; women's lack of, 174, 224

social stratification, 2, 4, 24, 223, 224; and divorce, 191–2; and education, 32, 73–89; and marriage, 170; and religion, 89–104

soldiers, 77; and marriage, 163–71

status, relationships based on, 2, 3, 6, 30, 41, 53, 151

stock-raising, 7, 8, 33; reduction of, 18, 29

Sufism, 10, 25, 30

Sultan, and tribes, 9, 10

Tafilalet, 8, 24, 194–6

taxation: exemption of *shurfa*, 13; under French, 20; pre-Protectorate, 10

transhumance, 8, 9; elimination of, 17, 18, 20

tribe, 12, 101 (see also Berber tribes)

Tunisia, 197, 199

ulema (religious officials of national importance), 175

umma (Islamic community), 14, 15, 16; women in, 102

unemployment, 1, 22, 37, 38, 224

uterine kinship, 104, 188–90, 222; and fostering, 143, 146–8; and marriage, 159, 183, 188–90; mother–daughter, 107–8, 124–7; mother–son, 61, 108; among women, 42, 158, 192–3, 208, 222

Villeneuve, M., 33–5

virginity, 149, 155, 169, 179 (*see* sex, before marriage)

war: European, 22, 77; tribal, 8, 9, 10, 11

Weber, M., 92

widows, 49, 50, 97, 188–90; managing fields, 57, 114; as match-makers, 48

witchcraft (and sorcery), 93, 102–3, 206

women: attitudes to, 63, 72, 84–5, 93, 99–103; childless, 103, 134, 141, 187; education of, 77, 83–8; élite, 88, 178; impurity of, 101–3; inheritance by, 43, 58, 192–3, 216–18; in *ksar* and town, 47, 150–1, 193, 196, 214; limited linguistic skills of, 27–8; effects of male migration on, 22–3; and market economy, 31, 38, 42, 112, 117; and marriage arranging, 44–7, 48, 61, 72, 158, 164–5; patron–client relationships among, 4–6, 49, 50; relationships among, 3, 5, 49, 117, 121–31; religious practices of, 61, 63, 96–102; and rites of passage, 42, 46–7, 51–2; roles of, 1, 2, 42–3, 81–2, 110–11, 225; socialisation of, 107, 111, 121–4; social mobility of, 29; and uterine kinship, 124–31, 218; witchcraft by, 102–3, 206; work of, *see* work, women's

work: men's, 55, 63–4, 109, 111–15, 161–3; women's, 49, 50, 53, 87–8, 110–12, 115–18, 184–5, 216, 217, 218

Yamna, 128–9, 152, 185–6

Zaid, 153

238